WITH STAFF AND PEN

John Lawrence May
ARCHBISHOP OF ST. LOUIS

One Liguori Drive
Liguori, MO 63057-9999
(314) 464-2500

ISBN 0-89243-460-0
Library of Congress Catalog Card Number: 92-72597

Excerpts are taken from *The Teachings of the Second Vatican Council,* Introduction by Gregory Baum, copyright © 1967, Catholic Publishers, Nashville, Tennessee.

Excerpts from the English translation of *The Roman Missal,* copyright © 1973, International Committee on English in the Liturgy (ICEL); excerpts from the English translation of the *Rite of Baptism for Children,* copyright © 1969, (ICEL); excerpts from the English translation of the *Rite of Confirmation,* Second Edition, copyright © 1975, (ICEL); excerpts from the *Rite of Marriage,* copyright © 1969, (ICEL), are used with permission. All rights reserved.

Diligent effort has been made to locate and secure permission for the inclusion of all copyrighted material in this book. If any such acknowledgments have been inadvertently omitted, the author and publisher would appreciate receiving full information so that proper credit may be given in future editions.

Cover design by Denis Thien
Interior design by Pam Hummelsheim

Table of Contents

Editor's Foreword

With his appointment in 1959 as vice president and general secretary of the Catholic Church Extension Society, John L. May became editor of the *Extension Magazine.* For a decade, May wrote a regular column for the magazine and occasional articles.

When he became Bishop of Mobile in December 1969, May started to write a weekly column for the diocesan newspaper, *The Catholic Week.* He continued this practice following his translation to St. Louis, where his columns have appeared weekly in the *St. Louis Review.* Additionally, May has sent lengthier private communications to the St. Louis clergy about five times a year on pastoral, liturgical, theological, and administrative matters. Entitled *Notanda* ("To be noted") and printed on blue paper, they quickly became known among the clergy as The Blue Notes.

This literary production comprises close to fourteen hundred articles. The Archbishop explains the thinking behind his writings as follows:

> It has been my conviction that the traditional episcopal pastoral letter, a rather extended treatment of a specific theological or pastoral issue, is not read very widely and often is not a great help to the vast majority of the faithful. I have always felt that a regular column by the local Bishop speaking to his priests and his people can achieve a much more steady and wider readership and accomplish much more in communication between the Ordinary and his people. Accordingly, I have tried to follow that practice through the years.

The selections in this volume, published to commemorate twenty-five years of pastoral service to God's people as a bishop, are mostly taken from these articles. Those designated "Mobile" are from *The Catholic Week.* The "St. Louis" excerpts are from the *St. Louis Review.* Since this is not a publication for scholarly or archival purposes, abridgements in the original text are mostly not indicated.

If the selections have a common theme, it is the Archbishop's desire to explain and implement the teachings of the Second Vatican Council. This was a central concern even before May's appointment as a bishop. The January 1965 issue of *Extension Magazine,* mostly devoted to explaining the Council and starting with a lengthy "Primer on the Council" by Monsignor John L. May, received a unanimous first-place award from the Catholic Press Association for "good writing, originality, knowledge, and attractive presentation."

The Archbishop's manifest desire to be, above all, "a Vatican II bishop," dictated the decision to introduce the chapters, wherever possible, with citations from the Council documents.

John Jay Hughes

- 1 -
DOCTRINE

Teaching...is one of the principal duties of bishops.
(Decree on the Pastoral Office of Bishops, #12)

"Why do we have to go to Protestant churches to learn about the Rapture?" This question from my mailbag is typical of many I receive. There are all kinds of exotic theories abroad these days about the "end time."

Catholic teaching about the end of the world and Christ's Second Coming is firmly based upon holy Scripture. The Bible's statements about these matters, however, are full of symbols and images. They are not prose, but poetry, which is never intended to be taken literally.

The word *rapture* is a good place to start. You cannot find it in the Bible. It is used by some modern fundamentalists to refer to Paul's teaching in 1 Thessalonians 4:17. There he writes that when Jesus returns at the end of time, "we who are left alive shall be caught up in clouds to meet the Lord in the air." To understand such a passage properly, we have to know Paul's world-view. All the biblical books reflect the ideas then prevailing, not our ideas today. Like everyone in his day, Paul assumed a three-story universe: a flat earth on top of a dark underworld, topped by a heaven beyond the sky. Paul naturally assumed that at his return, Christ would descend from his dwelling place above the sky. Christians then alive could go to meet him only by rising into the air. If Paul were describing these things today, he would use quite different concepts based on our scientific world-view. The important point is not Paul's astronomy or ours, but the spiritual message he brought us.

The "clouds" Paul mentions in this passage are symbolic. Throughout the Bible, clouds symbolize the presence of God. God appeared to Moses in a cloud atop Mount Sinai to give him the Ten Commandments (Deuteronomy 5:22). God spoke from the same cloud at Jesus' transfiguration (Mark 9:7). Jesus disappeared into a cloud at his ascension (Acts of the Apostles 1:9). He said he would come again "on the clouds of heaven" (Mark 14:62).

In Luke 21, Jesus speaks of the coming destruction of the Jerusalem Temple. Asked "When will this occur?" Jesus declines to say. Instead he talks about wars, earthquakes, plagues, and famines: "...and in the sky fearful omens and great signs." It would be a complete misunderstanding to search for these portents with a telescope. Jesus was using symbolical and poetic language to describe *a time of troubles.*

The gospel for the First Sunday of Advent this year is another example of language used in a nonliteral way. Jesus warns us that at his return "two men will be out in the field; one will be taken and one will be left. Two women will be grinding meal; one will be taken and one will be left" (Matthew 24:40). Speaking to people in an agricultural society, Jesus used the only language they could understand. Today he would use quite different language, drawn from our modern world of automobiles, electric lights, and supersonic flight. But the message would be the same: be prepared for the Lord's coming.

Nowhere does the Bible give us a *timetable* for predicting the end of the world. The Bible tells us simply that we live in the "last age." How much longer this age will last we cannot know. What we do know is that history is not aimless. It is moving toward an end predetermined by God. At the end, the power of evil, already crippled by Jesus' victory on Calvary, will be swept away, and God will reign unhindered.

The Bible tells us that we prepare for this great final event not by speculation about the date, but by living here and now in the light of Christ's return and God's final triumph. This means living not for ourselves but for God and for others. It means pursuing justice instead of exploitation: practicing love, not hate; striving for self-giving, not self-seeking. For those who try to live in this way, Christ's coming will be the return of a familiar and dearly loved friend. Those who live heedless of the "Last Things," on the other hand, will be taken unaware. They will be like the Palestinian homeowner who slept while thieves dug through a mud-brick wall of his house. Too late, he discovers that everything he has is gone (Matthew 24:43).

The Bible's statements about Christ's return in glory at the end of the world are not so much for our information, it has been said, as for our transformation. The choices we make every day and every hour have eternal consequences. One day we shall discover that God has *ratified* these choices. This is judgment. Whether the "Last Things" will be joyful for us, or fearful, depends on the fundamental direction of our life here and now. God does not demand perfection, or even success. He does demand our best effort. If we are constantly trying to choose *him,* then no matter how often we may fail and fall, we need not fear. When the "last things" come for us, we shall be able to say the words of the responsorial psalm for this First Sunday in Advent: "I rejoiced because they said to me, 'We will go up to the house of the Lord.' "

(St. Louis, November 21, 1980)

– ♦ –

Bible Christians

You know, Catholics are rarely put into the category of "Bible Christians" in public discussion. Sometimes that is just as well because the term is often used disparagingly to describe folks who spout one text after another after they have buttonholed you with that endearing question, "Are you saved?"

But it really is sad that we are not generally known as Bible Christians. And it is sad that occasionally on a talk show someone will still call to ask, "Are Catholics allowed to read the Bible?" We should be known as Bible Christians.

Congratulations to more than fifty thousand Catholics in this archdiocese who have been meeting weekly in our RENEW program to ponder and pray over the holy Word of God. You are doing exactly what the Church asks of you.

The Constitution on Sacred Revelation of the Second Vatican Council states that "the Church has always venerated the divine Scriptures as she venerates the body of the Lord," and especially in the twentieth century, the popes have called upon all members of the Church to learn the Scriptures, teach the Scriptures, and live the Scriptures.

The Second Vatican Council also tells us that the Catholic Church should learn from other churches and enrich itself through the work of the Spirit wherever it is found. The familiarity of our Protestant friends with the Scriptures should urge us to similar zeal for knowing the Word of the Lord.

Protestants and Catholics have had in the past, and to a degree still do have, different approaches to the Scriptures. For many of the Protestant traditions, the Scriptures are the sole rule of faith; they have a power of their own that illuminates and inspires the individual reader. Through the book, God speaks to the individual.

Catholics agree with this approach to the Scriptures, but in a sense go beyond it. For us, the Bible is not only the book of the individual, it is a book given by God to the whole community. The Church as a whole studies the Bible, meditates upon its meaning, and shapes its beliefs and practice according to God's revelation, which is found in a major way (although not an exclusive way) in the Scriptures.

One practical consequence of the difference in approach is that for the Protestant, the literal meaning of every individual word and verse of the Bible is fundamentally important, and so memorizing verses and recognizing passages is the way the Scriptures are taught. For Catholics, the Bible speaks not so much in terms of isolated lines or verses but in the totality of its meaning. Themes and ideas are more important than isolated passages, and so understanding biblical concepts like incarnation, grace, salvation, and the like have had more prominence in the Catholic tradition and religious education than literal passages from the Scriptures.

So don't be hesitant about Bible study; go at it. Get more deeply into the Scriptures. Share with others the help and consolation that you have received from God's Word, and let them share theirs with you. Realize that we base our theology on the totality of the Scriptures and the tradition given us by God. I hope that Catholics can learn from Protestants more respect for the literal Word of God in the Scriptures. I hope that Protestants can learn from Catholics more about the community formed by Scripture and the themes and concepts taught by the Bible. (And I ask the indulgence of my Scripture-scholar friends for oversimplifying somewhat the Catholic and Protestant views of the Bible.)

The liturgy of the Mass and all the sacraments almost always devote most of the time to readings and preaching from the Bible. So every Catholic, every Sunday, hears much of the Bible. "Faith comes by hearing," but we also need the personal, private reading of God's holy Word. Priests and religious do that each day in the breviary. It should be part of every Catholic family's life. Why not read a passage each night around the table as you begin supper? You'd be surprised how many interesting discussions it would lead to. It would definitely brighten up your supper hour. Supper should be a time to feed our minds, not just our stomachs. Good appetite!

(St. Louis, January 10, 1983)

– ◆ –

Confirmation Refresher
"Be Sealed With the Gift of the Holy Spirit"

In the past months, thousands of our Catholic girls and boys and many hundreds more adults and young people who have entered the Catholic Church by baptism or profession of faith have heard these solemn words. They are what theologians call the "essential form" of the sacrament of confirmation. It might be helpful for us all to refresh our knowledge of this sacrament.

The ordinary minister of confirmation is the bishop. Under certain circumstances, a priest may also confirm. In all cases, however, the person being confirmed is anointed with "chrism," one of the three kinds of oil that is blessed by the bishop in the chrism Mass on Holy Thursday. Even when the bishop is not personally present, therefore, those being confirmed are linked to him by this anointing.

Unity: This link is important. The bishop is the chief pastor of each local church or diocese. He in turn links his local Church with the universal or worldwide Church. The bishop does this by his communion (which means his fellowship and solidarity) with the pope.

The pope is himself a bishop, the chief pastor of the local Church of Rome. He is also universal pastor of the whole Church as successor of Saint Peter who preached and died in Rome. This means, for instance, that the pope can confirm or ordain anywhere in the world. I celebrate these sacraments outside our local church of St. Louis only when invited to do so by the bishop of the diocese concerned.

Confirmation, then, is in a special way the sacrament of unity with the bishop — who links us with our Holy Father in Rome and through him with all our sisters and brothers in this great family of God that we call the Catholic Church. Being a Catholic Christian is never a private God-and-I affair. In addition to our "vertical" relationship with the Lord, we have vital "horizontal" relationships with the other family members.

Spirit Sealed: Confirmation is also in a special way the sacrament of the Holy Spirit. Here is where things begin to get a little complicated. Baptism is *also* the sacrament of the Holy Spirit. Following the baptismal act, the celebrant says:

> God the Father of our Lord Jesus Christ has freed you from sin, given you a new birth by water and the Holy Spirit, and welcomed you into his holy people....

People sometimes ask why they have to receive the Holy Spirit "all over again," so to speak, in confirmation, when they have received him already in baptism. God doesn't ration his gifts, giving only a little at a time. When God gives, he gives totally. What is limited is our capacity to receive. That is why, to take another example, we come repeatedly to holy Communion. There we receive the Lord himself — all his goodness, all his love, purity, and power. We come again and again because our ability to benefit from the Lord's total self-giving is limited.

Confirmation celebrates the same reality as baptism: that we are people sealed forever with the Holy Spirit of the living God, empowered to live by his standards and not those of our self-centered humanity. He told his apostles and us, "You shall receive the Holy Spirit and then you shall be witnesses for me in Judea and Samaria and even to the ends of the earth" — even to St. Louis in Missouri. Originally, baptism and confirmation were given together, given only to people who had made a personal decision for Jesus Christ and had been instructed in the meaning of that decision for daily life. Today adult converts still receive baptism and confirmation in one celebration.

Those baptized as infants are, of course, too young to be instructed in the meaning of their Christian discipleship. What was originally the "second half" of baptism (confirmation) is postponed until they are old enough to receive the instruction still given before baptism to people who make their decision for Jesus Christ in adolescence or later.

(St. Louis, May 30, 1986)

– ♦ –

Just recently, a beautiful blond in the last pew interrupted my homily with applause several times at a confirmation Mass. At the reception following, I told her how rarely my sermons received such a response and how grateful I was for her appreciation. She smiled sweetly and gave me her name: Shannon. She also said she was three years old.

(St. Louis, November 21, 1980)

– ♦ –

Postponing Baptism?

Q We were always taught that babies should be baptized as soon as possible after birth. Now the priest has told my daughter he can't baptize her son because she and her husband are married outside the Church and don't attend Mass. Why should my grandson be punished for the faults of his parents? What if something should happen to him? We were always taught that unbaptized babies went to limbo. Has the Church's teaching changed? I'm confused.

A Many people share your confusion. Your questions are important. Let me try to help you.

Limbo?

Perhaps you have heard of Cardinal Joseph Ratzinger. He is the prefect (head) of an important office in Rome called the Congregation for the Doctrine of the Faith. Here is what Cardinal Ratzinger has said about limbo:

> Limbo was never a defined truth of faith. Personally — and here I am speaking more as a theologian and not as prefect of the Congregation — I would abandon it since it was only a theological hypothesis. It formed part of a secondary thesis in support of a truth which is absolutely of first significance for faith, namely, the importance of baptism....One should not hesitate to give up the idea of "limbo" if need be (and it is worth noting

that the very theologians who proposed "limbo" also said that parents
could spare the child limbo by desiring its baptism and through prayer),
but the concern behind it must not be surrendered. Baptism has never been
a side issue for faith; it is not now, nor will it ever be.

(The Ratzinger Report, pages 147-148;
Ignatius Press, San Francisco)

Catholic teaching about baptism is based on Jesus' word to Nicodemus:
"I solemnly assure you, no one can enter into God's kingdom without being
born of water and Spirit" (John 3:5).

That teaching is reflected in the Church law, valid for the whole world,
which says, "Parents are obliged to see to it that infants are baptized within
the first weeks after birth…" (Canon 867, §1).

Your daughter has run into difficulty, however, because of a provision
in the next law. This says that baptism may not be administered unless there
is "a founded hope that the infant will be brought up in the Catholic religion;
if such a hope is altogether lacking, the baptism is to be put off according
to the prescriptions of particular law and the parents are to be informed of
the reason" (Canon 868, §1).

You write that your daughter has married outside the Church and does
not attend Mass. I also receive letters about cases of parents who are not
married at all, even civilly. In none of these cases are the parents practicing
the Catholic faith. Yet in the baptismal ceremony, they must promise to
bring up their child in the faith.

How much "founded hope" is there that this promise will be kept when
the parents' example — which for years will be the primary formative
influence on their child — is so clearly *against* the practice of the faith?
Permitting parents to make a promise to educate their child in a faith they
do not practice themselves is not honest. More, it fails to take the parents
seriously. That is treating people like children who are not responsible for
their actions.

Punishing the Child?

The sacraments are necessary for us. They are not necessary for God. He
is a God of love, not a stern judge who punishes us for failing to find our
way through a maze of rules. God's hands are not tied by what we do or fail
to do. God can call one of his little ones home to himself with or without
baptism.

Recognizing that, theologians have always spoken about substitutes for baptism. Rare, but possible, is "baptism in blood": an unbaptized person who dies a martyr's death for Jesus Christ is assured of salvation.

Equally important, and far more common, is the "baptism of desire" mentioned by Cardinal Ratzinger. People who desire baptism, but who through no fault of their own die without receiving it, are treated by God as if their desire had been fulfilled. In the case of those too young to have this desire themselves, cannot God accept the desire of someone else on their behalf — especially when this desire is supported by prayer?

So pray for your grandchild — and for his parents. Believe me, you are not the first parent to experience heartache because of a son's or a daughter's decision about faith. Saint Monica grieved for years over her brilliant son's rejection of Christianity. One day, distraught because all her prayers for him seemed to remain unanswered, she laid her grief before a bishop. After hearing Monica's story, he told her, "Go in peace. It is impossible that the son of so many prayers and tears should be lost."

In time the prophecy was fulfilled. Monica's son abandoned his wayward life, received baptism — and later ordination as priest and bishop. He is Saint Augustine, Bishop of Hippo in North Africa from 395 to 430, and one of the Church's greatest theologians.

You might want to take Monica and her son Augustine as your heavenly patrons in your daily prayer for your daughter and her husband — and for the child God has given them.

(For more reading on this matter, see *U.S. Catholic* magazine, February 1987, and its lead article: "The New Baptism: You Can't Get the Water and Run.")

(St. Louis, February 13, 1987)

– ◆ –

Theologians and a Climate of Fear

(Address to Catholic Theological Society of America, June 7, 1989)

Usually on an occasion like this, the bishop of the local church speaks of the importance of theology, the work of your society, or the proud story written by the Church in his city. Because of the present situation in the Church in this country, however, I should like to depart from that format.

There is one issue I want to address, one which I think demands to be addressed.

Very bluntly: I think the Church in the United States suffers from too many anxious, warning voices that would divide the bishops against theologians. There are too many sweeping accusations leveled at the theological soundness and creedal fidelity of the theologians. There are too many vague but insistent attacks telling bishops that the theologians will supplant them in their teaching office or ignore their pastoral guidance or lead the people of God into antagonism, division, and virtual schism.

Usually these charges are as sweeping as they are indistinct. It is breathtaking to read, for example, that sundry modern theologians undermine the authentic demands of Catholic orthodoxy by their disbelief in the resurrection or that modernist theologians are winning the day. The theologians are not named, their works are not cited, the offending passages are not quoted. Nothing makes concrete the accusations dropped so casually about this denial of Catholic faith by those dedicated to reflect upon it. To assess these warnings and general threats is like attempting to pin down allegations that flourished and destroyed so many during the McCarthy period.

Even more intimidating are the warnings that theologians as a group either directly or indirectly are assuming the position of the magisterium. Bishops are urged to take care lest their own teaching function be undermined or subsumed by theologians who would remove from the episcopal office its teaching authority and reduce it to coordinating pastoral activities.

I want to say very clearly that this has not been our experience in the United States. Whatever one may say about this or that theologian or this or that bishop, our experience in this country in general has not been one either of heterodoxy or of effective schism. On the contrary, theologians have given great emphasis to cooperation with bishops in the doctrinal and in the more obviously pastoral ministries of the Church.

Repeatedly, the Catholic Theological Society of America has invited the bishops to explore with theologians ways in which "episcopal responsibility and academic competence can best work in harmony for the enrichment of both theological inquiry, teaching and publication, and effective pastoral leadership."[1] Bishop after bishop could tell of the collaboration he has

---

1 So said a resolution in your 1988 convention in Toronto regarding cooperation between bishops and theologians, *CTSA Proceedings* 43 (June 15-18, 1988) 196.

received from men and women theologians as members of diocesan theological boards, faculty for his seminary, conciliar and curial experts, instructors in continuing education of the clergy and religious and those involved in adult education, advisers and even vicars for theological affairs, and as dogmatic, scriptural, or moral consultants — to say nothing of their work in the theological instruction and research that goes on in his diocese, the work of mediating between the gospel and national culture to which the Second Vatican Council invited theologians *(Gaudium et Spes,* #44, 62).

To speak of the American episcopate in general, the National Conference of Catholic Bishops numbers consulting theologians on almost all of its staff, distinguished men and women who have given long hours freely and willingly to enhance the effectiveness of the pastoral leadership of the bishops of the United States. The Committee on Doctrine alone counts some fifteen theologians assisting the major committee and its various subcommittees. The recent and influential pastoral letters on peace and the American economy would have been impossible without the dedicated and exacting work of the many theologians associated with the committees responsible for drafting these documents.

Undoubtedly, there are moments of tension between a bishop and a theologian, sometimes healthy, sometimes detrimental. But this has always been true of the Church. History, even recent history, demonstrates that similar tensions can exist together with great mutual goodwill even between bishop and bishop — as the recent public controversy about the AIDS document proved once more. Such tensions are part of life and often make for growth. In any event, tensions, and even serious problems on occasion, constitute an inevitable dimension of the human element in the Church.

But it is one thing to experience and recognize inevitable tensions and problems. It is quite another thing to stigmatize theologians as a group who menace the episcopal office or sound belief.

The effect of such wanton accusations upon theologians has been a growing fear. These attacks themselves come out of fear, and they engender an atmosphere of greater fear. A climate of suspicion so harmful to the Church as a whole is fed by casual remarks about the fidelity of others, by ungrounded accusations, and by warnings whose urgency is sometimes, perhaps often, in inverse proportion to their authors' command of hard facts. Singular problems are exaggerated into symptoms of the pathological state of theology in general. All of this threatens to form a cloud of fear that would poison the air in which we do our work.

In retrospect, perhaps there was something of this communicated by the recent meeting between the American Archbishops and the Holy See. A recent article in *Commonweal* noted the warnings about theologians during that meeting and commented that "no one came to the defense of theologians in general." The article continued, "In the mind of theologians, the Rome meeting can only be the latest Vatican and episcopal vote of no confidence in the scholarship."[2]

This impression, if given, is false. The fact is that the discussion of last March became quickly focused on general problems of culture, the theme of the meeting. I suspect that the reason no one pursued this issue in defense of the theologians in the United States is that the soundness of our relationship with you seemed so obvious, so taken for granted, so unquestionable among us.

I stress this fact because I think there is too much fear in the Church today. Nameless accusations and ungrounded suspicions threaten to divide bishops from theologians and theologians from bishops, debilitating our attempts to support one another in our specific ministries for the good of the Church. This climate of fear could come to stifle our collaborative initiatives under a pall of anxiety that will not dissipate — unless we determine that we have had enough of it. I believe we have. American Bishops in general further recognize the truth of your society's statement of last year concerning the growing urgency of "the problems confronting theologians as they seek to pursue appropriate Catholic theological inquiry."[3]

And so this evening I stress how imperative it is for you to realize that you have the strong and grateful support of us bishops for your work in dealing with problems of enormous complexity and difficulty — problems that bear crucially upon the belief and the practice of the Church. You have assisted us so continually and in so many ways over the years. You must be able to count on our understanding, support, and encouragement for your own inquiry, debates, research, and explorations. Pope John Paul II has taught that theologians "perform an inestimable service to the Church," and during his 1987 visit to this country he explicitly expressed his "support for the humble, generous, and patient work of theological research and education."[4] I am sure I speak with my brother bishops in offering you support,

---

2 Joseph McNeal, "Audition for Tragedy," *Commonweal* 116/8 (April 21, 1989) 229-30.
3 *CTSA Proceedings* 43, 186.
4 John Paul II to the leadership of Catholic higher education, Xavier University, September 12, 1987, as in *Unity in the Work of Service* (Washington D.C.: U.S. Catholic Conference, 1987) 73-74.

conscious as we are of the debt in which the whole Church stands for your labors — and also keenly aware of the attacks to which you are exposed and the efforts being made to divide theologians from bishops and bishops from theologians.

We must not let these attacks destroy the *communio* in which we live nor allow ungrounded and ungovernable suspicions to descend like a fog over the Church in the United States. In spite of all this negativity and prophecies of gloom, we together must "make every effort to preserve the unity which has the Spirit as its origin and peace as its binding force" (Ephesians 4:3). In this way, and only in this way, can we build up the Church together in love and theological wisdom for the glory of God.

(Origins 19 [1989] 87-89)

- 2 -
LITURGY

Bishops enjoy the fullness of the sacrament of orders
...Therefore bishops are the principal dispensers of
the mysteries of God, as well as being the governors,
promoters, and guardians of the entire liturgical life
in the church committed to them.

(Decree on the Pastoral Office of Bishops, #15)

A s general secretary of the Extension Society of Chicago, the then
*Monsignor John L. May showed his interest in the liturgy in a long
article in* Extension Magazine *for September 1964 entitled:
"Where will it all end? The future shape of the liturgy."*

*"No one really knows" where liturgical change will end, May wrote.
Change itself, however, is necessary. "The liturgy must be a living thing,
and some adaptation to changing times and various national cultures will
be forever necessary in the changeable parts of the Mass liturgy."*

*Heading the article was a picture taken at the National Liturgical Week
in St. Louis in late August 1964, when, for the first time in the United States,
Mass was celebrated in the vernacular. Standing at the altar, facing the
people, was the celebrant, the famed liturgical pioneer Monsignor Martin
B. Hellriegel. Seventeen years later, presiding at Hellriegel's funeral Mass
in the St. Louis Cathedral on April 14, 1981 (Tuesday in Holy Week), May
remarked: "Monsignor Hellriegel arranged to celebrate the Liturgy of Holy*

Week in heaven. And, of course, he would never have interfered with the Triduum. "

Concern for the reverent and joyful celebration of the liturgy remained a prominent concern during May's episcopate in Mobile and St. Louis. The following typical excerpts also explain the clerical jest that good liturgy, in May's view, must include "wine, women, and song. "

The introduction of Communion in the hand as an option on November 20, 1971, was the subject of four columns in the Mobile Catholic Week *for October 14 through November 7, 1971.*

The Cross: Take a look at the cross, the symbol of our faith. It is made up of a vertical bar and a horizontal bar. Both can remind us of the two great truths we believe about Jesus Christ — he is true God; he is true man.

The vertical bar reminds us that Jesus is "God from God, Light from Light, true God from true God" (Creed).

The horizontal bar reminds us that "by the power of the Holy Spirit he was born of the Virgin Mary, and became man."

The Holy Eucharist: We believe in the Real Presence of Jesus Christ under the species of bread and wine in the holy Eucharist. So Jesus is present as he lives today, the risen Jesus Christ at the right hand of God the Father. Jesus is present in the holy Eucharist as true God and true man.

How, then, are we to approach Jesus in the Eucharist? In one sense we should fall to our knees or even flat on our face before him because we are sinners in the presence of the all-holy God. As Peter said, "Depart from me, O Lord for I am a sinful man." In another sense we should feel free to approach Jesus easily, as he invited Peter and all sinners to do, "Come to me all you who labor and are heavily burdened, and I will give you rest." He gave us the holy Eucharist not to be a sign of majesty dominating us but to be our daily bread when he said, "Take this, all of you, and eat it: this is my body....Take this, all of you, and drink from it: this is the cup of my blood....Do this in memory of me."

Balance: In the history of the Catholic Church, there has been a different emphasis in the approach of people to the Real Presence of Jesus in the holy Eucharist in different periods.

In the first nine centuries of the Church, Catholics approached Jesus in the Eucharist much as his disciples approached him here on earth. We read in the Acts of the Apostles, the letters of Saint Paul, and in the writings of the early Church Fathers that it was the regular practice to receive holy Communion at every Sunday liturgy. The people generally received the Eucharist in their hands as the apostles did at the Last Supper. There are many ancient writings and works of art attesting to this fact.

Then a change set in. More and more, the clergy took over all aspects of the liturgy, which became more elaborate, and the people watched from a distance. The laity felt less and less worthy to approach the Eucharist because Jesus was more and more proclaimed as God in the face of heretics who denied this fact. Finally, people felt so unworthy that they had to be obliged to come to Communion at least once a year (the Easter duty), and they could no longer touch the Eucharist. Only the priest could dare do so. The Church emphasized this awesome reverence until early in our own century when Pope Pius X began pleading for frequent holy Communion for all Catholics once again. He also gave the holy Eucharist to children for the first time in many centuries.

So here we are trying as a result of Vatican Council II to renew and reform our Catholic liturgy. For roughly the first thousand years of the Church's history, Catholics received holy Communion frequently, and they received in their hands. For the next thousand years, they received only rarely and then only on their tongues from the hand of the priest. What should we do in the years ahead?

It is the plea of the Church in Vatican Council II that we keep the best of our rich Catholic tradition. We must keep a careful reverence in receiving Jesus in the Eucharist, because he is always our Lord and our God. At the same time we must not fear to approach him as the people in the gospels did "because he is meek and humble of heart, a man who was also tempted as we are but never sinned" (Saint Paul).

In summary, the Church asks us to keep our balance — not to over-emphasize either the divine or the human nature of Jesus Christ in the holy Eucharist. It is simply the intention of the liturgy to bring us to know and love Jesus, true God and true man.

What Is Changeless: Just consider a beautiful diamond engagement ring that a young man slips on the finger of the love of his life. She will wear it proudly, the symbol of their love, along with the wedding band soon added to it.

The years go on and the setting of that diamond wears thin and tarnishes, and then one day, thanks to a thoughtful husband, that exquisite diamond is polished, surrounded by a new setting, and, lo and behold, it is more beautiful than ever. The diamond is changeless, but the setting is changed as the years pass.

So it is with the Eucharist, the central jewel in Catholic liturgical devotion. The eucharistic liturgy is basically changeless as it has always been — the offertory, consecration, and Communion (we used to call them the "principal parts of the Mass"). But the setting has been restored and developed in the liturgical renewal introduced since Vatican Council II — the so-called "changes in the liturgy."

What Has Changed: While I know that abler writers than I have tried to explain the reasons behind some of the liturgical changes these past years, I will have a go at it once again.

- *Congregational Singing:* We read in the gospels that Jesus and the apostles sang a hymn at the Last Supper, and Saint Paul urged the early Christians to "sing gratefully to God from your hearts in psalms, hymns, and inspired songs." This early Church practice gradually faded through the centuries as clergy and choirs took over almost all the singing at Mass and the people became more and more silent. Now all our people are asked to sing the Mass once again, to take their rightful role in the liturgy, but there are also to be periods of silent devotion.
- *Communion Under Both Kinds:* Jesus said "take and eat; take and drink" when he gave Communion at the Last Supper and so did the early Catholic Church for about twelve hundred years. Then gradually the distribution of the host only became the norm. Vatican Council II restored the original practice of Jesus, and this will be increasingly the usual form of holy Communion in the years ahead.
- *Extraordinary Ministers of the Eucharist:* In the first nine centuries of the Church, lay Catholics received holy Communion in their hands as the apostles did at the Last Supper. Certain members of the congregation were also permitted to carry the Eucharist to the sick and to keep it for distribution at times during

the week when no priest was present. Then there came a period of over a thousand years when finally only ordained clergy were allowed to distribute holy Communion, and we learned that "only the anointed hands of the priest are allowed to touch the host." Pope Paul VI has decided to reintroduce the original discipline with proper preparation and safeguards. He has done so, insisting on continued reverence for the holy Eucharist but mindful of modern needs of God's people. Because there are just not enough priests, religious, and lay Catholics, men and women may be appointed by the bishop to give holy Communion when there is a large congregation and when shut-ins would not otherwise be able to receive holy Communion often. This is not just a return to ancient customs but a gracious response of the Holy Father to the needs of his children in this day and age.

Accordingly, in our diocese we have gratefully accepted this favor of the pope; and in many of our parishes, we have extraordinary ministers of the Eucharist at crowded Masses. Increasingly, we shall also see them bringing holy Communion from the parish Mass to the members of the congregation who are sick at home or in hospitals or nursing homes.

In Summary: These changes and many more, like the use of English in place of Latin, the altar facing the people, receiving holy Communion standing as the priest does — all these developments have been introduced since Vatican Council II. They have shaken up many people and made them wonder. Such a reaction is natural, since change of old ways is always difficult.

But we must always remember that these changes are only the renewal of the setting of our Eucharist liturgy. In the center, as changeless as ever, is the diamond — the holy Eucharist. It is really the same Mass that we and our ancestors have loved through all the centuries from the Last Supper. Let us never forget what is changeless and what has changed.

– ♦ –

Q Why are we being offered the option of communion in the hand?

A fter about fifty other nations around the world petitioned Pope Paul for permission to restore Communion in the hand, the American Bishops did so for these reasons:

- It seems good to return in this regard, as in much other liturgical renewal, to the practice of the early Church — a return to our roots.
- No change in belief is involved; in fact, no change in practice is involved either for those who prefer to continue receiving on the tongue.
- Communion in the hand should remind us that all our bodies are temples of the Holy Spirit, anointed in baptism and confirmation for the holy Eucharist. Surely our hands are not less worthy than our tongues.
- This restored tradition should emphasize what every Catholic should be, laypeople as well as clergy, "a chosen race, a royal priesthood, a holy nation," in the words of Saint Peter.
- Receiving holy Communion in this way calls for reaching out and communicating ourselves, a more active response of the people to the words of Jesus, "Take and eat."
- Communion in the hand seems more adult and dignified, since only infants and helpless invalids are normally fed by mouth.
- It seems more relaxed and hygienic to receive the host in one's hand, since often the priest's fingers touch lips and tongues as communicants stream by.
- Finally, this option does permit people who wish to receive in the hand to do so while it also permits people who wish to receive on the tongue to continue doing so. There are considerations on both sides, and the bishops wish to recognize that fact.

How? When this option of Communion in the hand is introduced on November 20, it will be carried out in practice in this way:

- The communicants approach as now. They extend their tongue or their hand to indicate their preference as the priest holds the host before them. The communicant makes the decision, not the priest. Neither method may be forced on a communicant by a priest or an extraordinary minister.
- No matter which method is chosen, the greatest care must be taken as now that fragments of the host not be lost.
- In receiving Communion in the hand, approach the priest with one hand resting on the other, palms up. The priest places the host

in your hand, saying, "The Body of Christ," and your reply is as usual, "Amen." Then you step immediately to the side and place the host on your tongue. You may then receive the precious blood from the chalice if it is offered, and only then return to your place. *It is never permitted for any communicant to walk away with the host in his or her hand.* Nor is any communicant to reach out and snatch the host from the priest. Rather, it is always to be *received* reverently into one's open and outstretched palm.

- Children should be given the same option and obviously they should be well instructed. They need further reminders to approach only with clean hands, and so forth. The emphasis must always be on careful reverence.

Here is what Saint Cyril of Jerusalem said to his people in the fourth century, and I would like to say the same to all of you today:

> When you approach [Communion], do not come with your hands outstretched or with your fingers open, but make your left hand a throne for the right one, which is to receive the King. With your hand hollowed, receive the body of Christ and answer *Amen*...consume it, making sure that not a particle is wasted, for that would be like losing one of your own limbs. Tell me, if you were given some gold dust, would you not hold it very carefully for fear of letting any of it fall and losing it? How much more careful, then, you should be not to let fall even a crumb of something more precious than gold or jewels! After receiving the body of Christ, approach the chalice of his blood. Do not stretch out your hands, but bow in an attitude of adoration and reverence, and say *Amen.*
>
> *(Mystagogic Catechesis V, 21, 1-22, 4)*

"Be filled with the Spirit, addressing one another in psalms and hymns and inspired songs. Sing praise to the Lord with all your hearts." One of the first bishops of the Church, the apostle Paul, wrote those words in his letter to the Church of Ephesus.

As I go around from church to church, I am happy to see so many parishes following the words of Saint Paul and the example of those early Christians. I have seen a marked improvement in liturgical participation these past two years, and I am grateful for your efforts.

I call upon all of you to pick up those missalettes and open your mouths and hearts. In some parishes it is still a puzzle to me to see certain stalwart souls with compressed lips and empty hands proclaiming their refusal to join in the final song as I walk down the aisle after Mass. They just will not take part. But these silent souls are, gratefully, in the minority everywhere.

Sometimes people complain that there is too much noise in church. They have a point. There should be periods of silence at Mass — before a prayer, after the general intercessions, after holy Communion, and so forth.

And outside of Mass, there should be reverent silence in church in the presence of the Blessed Sacrament. I have been concerned about carelessness in this traditional Catholic reverence at times, before a wedding, for instance.

There are times for private, silent prayer. There is a time in church to "make a joyful noise to the Lord." And there is a time "to be still and know that I am God." Every Catholic should know which is which.

Hopefully, we will have the very best liturgy according to the new rite without losing the reverence we all treasured in the old rite. Why can't we all blend the best of both?

(Mobile, February 11, 1972)

A 1974 question about "extraordinary ministers of holy Communion" was answered as follows:

From the earliest years of the Church, permission was given to laypeople to bring holy Communion to their fellow Christians in cases of real need when no priest or deacon was available to do so. This was especially true in mission areas and in time of war or persecution. People were also often appointed to bring holy Communion to the aged and to "shut-ins."

In March 1971, Pope Paul authorized the local bishops to grant this ancient permission once again whenever there was a genuine need because of a shortage of priests. Since then, this permission has been granted rather widely in many places in our country.

In making his request, the local pastor must outline the need, submit the names of the persons nominated, give them adequate preparation, explain this special permission to all the parish, and install these extraordinary ministers in their new role in a solemn ceremony at Mass after they have been appointed by the bishop.

Please note that these people are then authorized to assist the priest whenever the number of communicants is too great for him to serve alone. They are not to replace him or free him to do something else at the time.

This special permission is granted not for the convenience of priests but for the better service of our people. Extraordinary ministers are directed to use the greatest reverence in distributing holy Communion and always to do so in proper, dignified garb.

Despite this careful instruction of our Holy Father and its implementation, some people find it difficult to receive holy Communion from a layman or laywoman. This is understandable from an emotional standpoint, but we must remember in Faith that what we receive is what matters. We receive the same Lord Jesus in the holy Eucharist whether from the hand of the priest or the hand of a specially appointed layperson. This ancient practice in the Church that has now been revived should never be an occasion for less reverence for the Real Presence of Jesus in the holy Eucharist. In her desire to serve all her people more fully, the Church is trying to form us more and more into a truly eucharistic people, priestly people, God's holy people.

(Mobile, March 8, 1974)

Q Are girls permitted to serve in place of altar boys?

A The traditional discipline of the Church specifies that girls are not to serve at the altar. Just recently, requests have been sent to Rome for a revision of this law so that girls may serve on an equal basis with boys, not in place of them. Thus far, there has been no response.

As you know, women are now permitted to read the Scriptures at Mass and even to serve as extraordinary ministers of the Eucharist under certain circumstances. To many, it seems inconsistent that they be barred from serving at the altar. Hopefully, all this will be clarified before long (before all our grade-school girls grow up!).

(Mobile, March 28, 1975)

The American Bishops were still awaiting a response in 1992.

– ♦ –

"Take This, All of You and Drink From It..."

These words are part of the consecration of the precious blood in every Mass. Recently, the American Bishops have given us the opportunity of receiving holy Communion from the cup much more frequently.

Since 1970, the sharing of the cup at Mass has become familiar on a number of occasions: for the bride and groom at their wedding, for all the faithful on Holy Thursday and at the Easter Vigil, as well as at weekday Masses year-round.

In November 1978, the bishops of the United States granted permission for the use of Communion under both kinds to the faithful at all Masses on Sundays and holy days of obligation. Careful planning and preparation can enable Communion under both kinds to become part of normal parish liturgy.

1. Background: As we know from the Bible, Jesus gave his apostles holy Communion under the forms of bread and wine at the Last Supper. We also know from the Bible and other ancient writers that in the early Church all present at the celebration of the Eucharist shared the bread and drank from the cup. Yet these Christians had no hesitancy in allowing Communion under the form of bread alone or from the cup alone in extraordinary circumstances.

Eventually, this emphasis shifted. Still, it was twelve centuries before Communion from the cup was limited to the priest.

Throughout all this, the common practice of the Eastern Churches has remained Communion under both kinds.

A single phrase in Vatican II's *Constitution on the Liturgy* has allowed the restoration of the earlier practice: "...communion under both kinds may be granted when the bishops think fit..." (#35).

2. How the Cup Is To Be Shared:

- The people should always be aware that the decision to take Communion from the cup belongs to the individual. *It is the communicant's option.*
- When the altar table is prepared, the wine should be brought forward in one large chalice or in one chalice with one or more flagons rather than in many chalices or cups. This, along with the one plate of bread and the book, is all that belongs on the altar during the eucharistic prayer.
- At the "Lamb of God," while the bread is being broken, the ministers of Communion bring the other Communion cups to the altar to be filled from the one container. The cups should be filled

in a manner that is reverent and yet does not delay Communion of the faithful.

- A sufficient number of ministers of the cup should be provided so that the Communion rite is done with proper dignity and without undue haste or prolongation of the liturgy. *Normally, this will mean two ministers of the cup for each minister of the bread.* When possible, the ministers should stand some distance apart so that those who choose not to receive from the cup may return to their places without complication or embarrassment. In this way, there is time for the others to take and eat the body of Christ before they are offered the cup.

- The cup is to be offered to the communicant. *It is never left on the altar or in another place for the communicants to take themselves, nor is it to be passed from one communicant to another. Those who receive the host are not to dip it into the cup: such a practice weakens the symbol of eating and drinking.*

- The minister should address the communicant, saying: "The blood of Christ." The communicants respond: "Amen." Then the minister gives the cup to the communicant. Except for good reason (a parent holding a child, a person who does not have full use of hands), the minister should not attempt to guide the cup but should place it entirely into the hands of the communicant.

- After the communicant has received the precious blood, the minister takes the cup, wipes the rim with a cloth, turns the cup slightly, and addresses the next communicant. Medical studies have shown that the alcoholic content plus this practice of wiping the rim and turning the cup assure that there is no danger of communicating germs. Of course, those with colds or similar illness will wish to refrain from drinking from the cup at such times.

- In pouring from the large flagon into the cups, in going to their Communion stations, in their posture and gestures, the ministers of Communion should move and speak with careful reverence.

- After Communion, the ministers consume the remaining consecrated wine. This should be done at the side table, not at the altar.

3. How to Begin. In our parishes I would hope that Communion from the cup will become normal practice, not something for great feasts only.

Catechetical instruction should be provided very carefully beforehand. This instruction should touch on the history of Communion under both kinds, but even more, it should stress how this is a stronger expression of our Catholic piety. Ministers of Communion will also need special instructions before their appointment by me and their installation in this ministry.

4. Conclusion. The Second Vatican Council's General Instruction is quite clear: "The sign of Communion is more complete when given under both kinds, since in that form the sign of the Last Supper appears more clearly. The intention of Christ that the new and eternal covenant be ratified in His blood is better expressed" (#240). It is what we hear at Mass: "Take this, all of you, and drink from it...." In this simple way, taking bread and cup, we experience who we are — a holy, priestly people.

(St. Louis, April 11, 1980)

– ◆ –

Q How and why did the practice of the kiss of peace or shaking hands at Mass originate? How can this practice be avoided by those who find it obnoxious?

A The kiss of peace is among the oldest rites connected with the Mass. At least five times, the New Testament speaks of Christians greeting one another with a "holy kiss" or a "kiss of love." We know for sure that around the year 150, the kiss, as an expression of unity and peace among Christians, constituted a regular part of the eucharistic liturgy.

For centuries the pax (peace) was exchanged by everyone at Mass. Toward the late Middle Ages, the practice began to be observed only by the attending clergy. This was the situation until recently, when the Church's official new Order of Mass stated that just before the breaking of the bread in anticipation of Communion, "all exchange the sign of peace and love, according to local custom."

Thus, in spite of your misgivings, the sign of peace has deep roots as a fitting external expression of the meaning of the Mass and holy Communion. In the beginning, the rite took place early in the Mass but soon found its way to the time around Communion, the sacrament which we still call "the sign of unity and the bond of love."

If we really believe that in receiving the Eucharist, we share the supper that Jesus provided to feed our family unity as his brothers and sisters (and therefore as brothers and sisters to one another), doesn't it seem just natural that we Catholics would reach out to one another in a gesture of charity and unity just before going up the aisle together to receive the body of the Lord?

I hope before holy Communion we all will offer a gesture or a word of peace to those near us. If you find that obnoxious, just bow your head and pray about it. I am sure that no one will bother you.

(St. Louis, May 9, 1980)

– ♦ –

Here is a letter recently received which I print with the hope that the situation described is a rare exception here.

> I am a Catholic and I have practiced the Catholic religion for forty-eight years. I am writing this letter to express my concern regarding certain practices in my parish within the St. Louis Archdiocese.
>
> My first concern is that my pastor refuses to allow women to distribute the holy Eucharist or to hold the chalice in order that parishioners may receive the consecrated wine. While he is willing to use men as extraordinaries to perform these services, he refuses to use women, even our nuns who teach at the parish school. My pastor expressed at Mass today his concern that we will not get enough men to volunteer to act as extraordinaries and that we really do need more volunteers if we hope to receive Communion under both species. Some women have asked to distribute Communion, but he will not hear of it. I cannot understand his reasoning. He depends on the women of the parish greatly for other tasks, such as baking, cleaning, and raising money, so why would he deny women the wonderful privilege to serve God by allowing them to distribute Communion and hold the chalice? I do not feel angry or mad about his attitude, but I do feel sad that so many women of God cannot also join in this privilege. I am not asking for myself, because I would feel awkward performing such a wonderful task, but I am asking for women who have expressed themselves to me that they would want so much to do this.
>
> – Mater Ignota

(Notanda, January 10, 1981)

– ♦ –

"I believe that I shall receive the sacred body of Jesus Christ to eat and his precious blood to drink. I believe this with all my heart." These words, or some such similar expression, formed part of the setting within which many of us received first Communion and began a whole new dimension in our love life with the Lord.

Manners: It is about this gift — the Real Presence of Jesus the Lord in the sacrament of the Eucharist — that I would like to talk with you today. My words, I'm afraid, will not challenge you to deep theological insights or profound mystical experiences. They concern matters far more simple and a lot closer to home. I almost entitled this column "Good Manners." They are the habits we have learned to show respect and regard for others (and for ourselves) when we are in their presence. There is definitely such a thing as "good manners" in the presence of the Lord in the Blessed Sacrament.

It is this eucharistic presence in our churches that makes them something more than mere places for the assembly of the faithful. They are that, of course, and a church is never more alive than when filled with believers actively engaged in worshiping the Father in spirit and truth. There, if anywhere, is the promise of Christ fulfilled: "For where two or three are gathered together in my name, there am I in the midst of them" (Matthew 18:20). But it is also the abiding presence of Jesus in the Eucharist that makes our churches more than a hall or auditorium. He is there before and after the liturgy is celebrated, before and after we come to Mass.

Reverence: That is why we genuflect in churches where the Blessed Sacrament is reserved. I know there are other signs of reverence and respect, but this gesture of acknowledgment and adoration on entering or leaving church is a venerable tradition in the Catholic Church of the Latin or western rite. It is a witness where actions speak louder than words. I hope we never lose it. As with all things that become more or less habitual, we need a reminder from time to time to do them well. I wish to emphasize that in our archdiocese, clergy and laity are all expected to genuflect to the Blessed Sacrament when entering and leaving church (unless there is a separate chapel for the reserved Sacrament that is not visible in the body of the church — as in our cathedral). This act of our faith and reverence is needed more than ever today.

Similarly, many who used to sense something special, something awesome in the atmosphere and attitude of Catholics before, during and after worship, might wonder what has happened in some churches in recent years. Now I know all about the horizontal outreach of love of neighbor as a necessary complement to the vertical love of God. But the way in which we manifest such an outreach in church, in the presence of the eucharistic Lord reserved, should differ from our approach (and tone of voice) in the shopping center or at a cocktail party. And then there is the charity that respects with a little quiet those who are still engaged in prayer and thanksgiving. It is all a question of "good manners" and my conviction that we should mind them. I ask that we observe silence and reverence in our churches before and after Mass in the presence of the Blessed Sacrament.

Perhaps you didn't need any of this little review or perhaps you did. Sometimes we slip into bad manners without noticing or intending it, and an occasional checkup is never out of place. I don't know if it has ever happened to you, but in my life I have come across a number of people who asked in all sincerity whether Catholics really believe that Christ is present in the Eucharist. I have often invited such a seeker to Mass to see for himself or herself. I hope that in all our churches, our reverence will shout forth our faith more clearly than any words from me.

(St. Louis, September 27, 1985)

− ♦ −

Q Now that we are offered holy Communion from the chalice along with the host, isn't there a health problem in receiving from a common cup?

A Many people fear germs indiscriminately and unreasonably. We coexist with many germs as part of our environment. Some microorganism, or "pathogens," bearers of disease, are the subject of our concern more than germs in general.

The most significant factors that inhibit the transmission of disease in sharing a common cup are (1) the relatively small number of diseases that infect through mouth-saliva-mouth contact, (2) the resistance of the healthy human body to small doses of pathogens, and (3) the observance of proper procedure in handling the cup. Other factors that may offer further security are the disinfectant properties of both wine and the surface of a silver cup.

Under no circumstances should the Eucharist ever become a source of anxiety or contention or controversy. In the Church's long history, however, there have been times when anxiety and worry and even fear have attended upon the reception of the Lord's eucharistic body and blood. There are times when sickness prevented a communicant from receiving one or both species. There have been times when epidemics have prevented large numbers of Christians from approaching the Lord's table for fear of becoming infected with disease. In the last several months, a similar concern has come into being among some Catholics with regard to the transmission of acquired immune deficiency syndrome (AIDS) and other communicable diseases when receiving the sacred blood of Christ from a common chalice.

Great Benefit: As a liturgical practice, Communion under both kinds was recently restored among Catholics in the United States with full approval from Rome. It has been and continues to be a gift of great spiritual benefit. When first implemented according to the norms of *This Holy and Living Sacrifice: Directory for the Celebration and Reception of Communion Under Both Kinds,* the bishops of the United States affirmed the Church's traditional preference for reception of the blood of Christ directly from a chalice: "Because of its ancient sign value from the institution of Christ, Communion from the cup or chalice is always to be preferred to any other form of ministering the precious blood."

At the same time, however, the *Directory* also cautioned ministers of the chalice to take ordinary precautions for hygiene: "After each communicant has received the blood of Christ, the minister shall carefully wipe both sides of the rim of the cup with a purificator. This action is both a matter of courtesy and hygiene. It is also customary for the minister to move the chalice a quarter turn after each communicant for the same reasons."

AIDS? There has been a recent report (September 4, 1985) on this subject from the acting director of the Center for Disease Control of the U.S. Department of Health and Human Services in Atlanta. It says specifically, "If any diseases are transmitted by this practice, they most likely would be common viral illnesses such as the common cold....During the past four years since AIDS has been studied, there has been no suggestion of transmission of the virus that causes AIDS by sharing utensils, including the common Communion cup, or through any other means involving saliva...."

Obviously, there can be no assurance of complete safety in receiving holy Communion from the cup, but the same is true as the priest gives the host to many communicants and inevitably touches some lips, tongues, and hands. Some people can become almost hysterically finicky about germs in this matter.

Accordingly, in view of the entire governmental medical statement mentioned above, the Bishops' Committee on the Liturgy does not believe that parishes need to suspend Communion under both kinds. The Committee, however, encourages those who may feel compelled to change their practice in this regard to minister the blood of the Lord by the method of intinction until further medical evidence warrants a return to their former practice. At the same time, pastors should advise those who are fearful that they have the option of receiving Christ under the species of bread alone. "For Christ, whole and entire, exists under the species of bread and under any part of that species, and similarly the whole Christ exists under the species of wine and under its parts" (Council of Trent).

Pastors should exhibit common sense and pastoral solicitude both for the concerns of their people and for the liturgical practice that enables the faithful to experience the fullness of the Lord's presence in both the signs of bread and wine. Pastors should also advise communicants who have communicable illnesses to refrain from drinking from the chalice and to receive by intinction or receive the consecrated bread only.

It should also be noted that persons with AIDS are more at risk from infections than those who do not suffer from suppression of the immune system. The Church must demonstrate great pastoral care and solicitude for those who suffer from this affliction through prayer and works of charity.

As the "sacrament of love" and the "bond of charity," the Eucharist must always be the source of our unity in the saving death and resurrection of the Lord Jesus, who cared for the sick and afflicted. It is all too easy in our concern for our own well-being to forget or ignore the needs of those in our midst who suffer from illness or even to attempt to exclude the sick from our midst out of fear. But the love of God and the eucharistic food of heaven, Christ's body and blood, compel us to ever greater acts of love for our fellow human beings.

(St. Louis, January 31, 1986)

– ◆ –

Do you discuss with every bereaved family whether they wish to have a sung Mass at the funeral of their loved one?

I just presumed we had music at all our funerals. Recently I have had complaints from families who experienced a recited funeral liturgy. If a family is agreeable to such an impoverished liturgy, that is tolerable. Otherwise, I just presume we follow the *Sacramentary,* which also presumes music at funerals.

(*Notanda,* December 15, 1983)

Reverence Again

At the Extraordinary Synod in Rome last fall, great concern was expressed for true reverence in the liturgy. Recently, a Protestant minister told me of visiting one of our major parishes for a first Communion and a wedding. He said he was appalled both times at the lack of dignity and reverence compared to what he remembered through the years from visits to our churches. So once again I plead for decent dignity in our churches.

A recent incident in one of our parishes illustrates what I mean. At the sign of peace at Sunday Mass, the celebrant announced that it was the birthday of the priest who was standing nearby to help with Communion. By prearrangement, the organ played and the congregation sang "Happy Birthday to You." The "birthday boy" was mortified and refused to appear at the next Mass, lest this disedifying scene be repeated. Despite the good intention (showing priestly solidarity), it is a grave abuse to use the liturgy for personal purposes, especially its most sacred moment when we should be concentrating on the Lord, present in his body and blood. The sign of peace should be restrained and reverent. When it becomes an occasion for boisterous socializing and effusive embraces, the liturgy is being abused and our good Catholic people are offended. They sense that "something is wrong," even if they cannot always say what it is. I ask that we do everything possible to foster reverence, not undermine it. Young people especially need to learn the meaning of "awe." We teach this best by our own example. Perhaps we need to ponder God's words to Moses: "Take off your shoes, for the place on which you stand is holy ground" (Exodus 3:5). (Talking about doffing shoes, I have heard that Holy Week ceremonies were beautiful around the archdiocese. Congratulations!)

(Notanda, April 10, 1986)

Spruce Up: Once upon a time we had pastors who used to upbraid parishioners who came to church without suit coats, and women with "hankies" or tissues on their heads were regularly denounced. That was a bit extreme.

But have we hit the other extreme in the casual clothing we see at Mass in some churches today? I know this is better left to the individual pastors, but as the pastor of all the flock, I am often embarrassed by the appearance of some folks in church — especially during these summer Sundays.

Jesus was very insistent about proper reverence in God's house. Are we?

(St. Louis, July 15, 1988)

– ◆ –

Last Sunday I mentioned my dismay, and that of many pastors, in seeing that many children are not being brought to Sunday Mass every week. I added that attendance in a Catholic school can be canceled out to a great extent by parents' carelessness about Sunday Mass. The child is given a contradictory message in school and at home. Today I just want to follow up with a bit more on this point.

I appeal to the parents of our children. Demonstrate your love for the liturgy by your own example, teaching them the prayers and responses. When your children hear you singing and see you standing and kneeling, they will follow your example.

I recognize and sympathize with the great responsibility you have as parents and I do not want to add to your burdens. But I would be failing in my role as bishop, as well as doing you a disservice, if I did not point out forcefully that one of your weightiest duties is to worship with your family on Sunday. Many of you, at no small cost, sacrifice to pay tuition; then why waste the investment in education by not bringing your children to Sunday Mass?

I appeal to the Catholic teachers of our children: instill in our children a love for the liturgy. Help them participate according to their ability. If you are a member of the parish in which you teach, your example does not end when class is over. The part you take in the worship and prayer of the parish liturgy on Sunday is as vital as your teaching in the classroom.

I appeal to the clergy who preside at Sunday Eucharist. Prepare well during the week for this sacred duty. Be bold in expressing your love for the liturgy by the tone of your voice, the beauty of your gestures, and the reverence of your demeanor. Your respect and your warmth at the liturgy will encourage people to return the following Sunday. Work hard to preach a good homily! Do not allow any room in your liturgical style for minimalism. Rather, overflow with hospitality and let your liturgical style be penetrated with a sense of awe.

I appeal to those Catholics who work with our youth as coaches of sports and directors of dramatic productions. Your example of service by what you do — and many of you are generous volunteers — is a powerful lesson to our youth. So is your example at Sunday worship. Our young people look up to you for leadership and example; do not fail them! If you are not in church on Sunday, you should not be on the field or court or stage. Your Sunday absence negates your example during the week.

The aim of liturgical renewal has been to enrich the Church's life of prayer and worship. Ceremony was not at the heart of the liturgical movement's concern. Rather, it looked to a renewal of the Church's life and spirituality and sought to return to the depths of our heritage in Scripture and tradition. Liturgical renewal is not simply a matter of pushing furniture around or changing language or dropping and adding rituals.

It is the Resurrection of our Lord that we gather to celebrate every Sunday of the year. Sunday is our day to celebrate our incorporation into Christ's death and resurrection, and so we gather in spirit and act of eucharist, of thanksgiving, to make our return to the Lord. Therefore, the quality of our parish Sunday liturgy should be commensurate with what we are and what we have been given.

The first responsibility of every parish priest is the celebration of the liturgy. He does not do this in a vacuum. He does this with and for the people charged to his pastoral care.

Over the past years as your bishop and chief liturgist, I have been heartened by the efforts that many priests and parish liturgy committees have made in enhancing the quality of public worship, especially the Sunday liturgy. But liturgical renewal is not over; it is barely started!

(St. Louis, May 26, 1989)

Some time back I read the following reasons for not going to the World Series (or was it to Sunday Mass?):

1. My parents took me to too many games when I was growing up.
2. The games are on my day off…the only day I can sleep.
3. Every time I go to a game, somebody asks me for money.
4. Whenever I've been to a game, no one is friendly enough to speak to me.
5. The seats are hard and uncomfortable. Sometimes I have to sit down front.

6. I often suspect there are hypocrites there. They just want to be seen at a game.
7. There is this guy in a black suit who makes decisions I don't agree with.
8. Most games last too long.
9. The organ often plays songs I've never heard before.
10. I have a good book on baseball, I'll just read that.

(St. Louis, October 17, 1980)

- 3 -
PRAYER AND SPIRITUALITY

Rejoice in hope, be patient under trial, persevere in prayer.

(Romans 12:12)

Rejoice always, never cease praying, render constant thanks.

(1 Thessalonians 5:16f)

There is so much we take for granted — so many people behind the scenes who serve us quietly and efficiently with no fanfare. Just think of the telephone operators; men and women in the water, sanitation, and health departments of large cities; the garbage men; and so forth.

Then, too, there are the contemplatives — men and women who live totally cut off from the noise and confusion of today's world so they can spend all their time praying and doing penance for the rest of us. Theirs is a life many people just cannot understand. But to those who are called to the contemplative life by God, it is the only life worth living — the only thing necessary.

Just recently, I heard of a salesman who stopped at one of these convents, hoping to make a sale. About to ring the doorbell, he heard the Sisters chanting the Divine Office. He listened and said he stood there a long time. It was a new experience for him, since he was not a Catholic. Finally, he said he just left, unwilling to call any Sister away from such an important duty. He came back the next day to make his sale.

It is a wholesome experience to visit one of these convents and join the Sisters in prayer. And it is reassuring to know when you leave they will stay and pray day in and day out for us all.

(Mobile, July 31, 1970)

– ◆ –

Q Why does the Church say we must go to confession? My sins are a private affair between God and me. If God forgives me, why do I have to go to a priest?

A The Church has never obliged us to confess *every* sin in the sacrament of penance, only the so-called *mortal* sins. *All* sins are serious because every sin offends against God's infinite love for us. But Jesus himself taught that there are degrees of sinfulness — for instance, when he warned against criticizing small faults in others while overlooking major ones in ourselves (Matthew 7:3-5). It is the Church's constant teaching, based on Scripture, that there is an essential difference between sins that kill the divine love or grace given us in baptism, which are called deadly or *mortal* sins; and sins that, while they *offend* against God's love, do not *exclude* us from his grace and love. These are *venial* sins. Saint Augustine (d. 430) tells us that God sometimes leaves the exact boundary between mortal and venial sins in a given case unclear, lest we take venial sins too lightly.

The Church teaches that *venial* sins can be forgiven in many ways. These include, in addition to the sacrament of penance, devout attendance at Mass and reception of Communion, reading or hearing the Word of God and trying to put it into practice in daily life, praying for forgiveness privately or publicly (for instance, as we begin Mass), patient acceptance of hardship and suffering, almsgiving and other acts of practical love for God and neighbor, forgiving those who wrong us.

Even *mortal* sins, the Church teaches, can be forgiven by an act of *perfect contrition:* when, out of love for God and not merely from fear of punishment, we tell God we are sincerely sorry for the sin and wish to amend. This will to amend necessarily includes acceptance of the Church's discipline. Part of this discipline is the requirement to make a full confession of all

46

mortal sins in the sacrament of penance. Let me explain the reason for this requirement.

Our sins are never a purely private affair between us and God (as the question above maintains). At baptism we become members of God's great family, the Catholic Church. Sin not only impairs our personal relationship with God. It violates the fundamental law of God's family, which is love. When we *consciously* and *deliberately* break God's law in a *serious* matter (the three conditions for mortal sin), we are choosing to live not in light but in darkness. This is a refusal of Jesus' call to every one of us to be "the light of the world, a city set on a hill" (cf. Matthew 5:14). This remains true even when the refusal is known only to God.

The Church requires us to seek reconciliation with the Lord and his basic law of love we have violated. We do so by confessing all mortal sins to the representatives Jesus has appointed. These are his priests, who receive at ordination the commission given by the risen Lord to his apostles: "Receive the Holy Spirit. If you forgive people's sins, they are forgiven; if you do hold them bound, they are held bound" (John 20:22f). When a priest pronounces absolution in the sacrament of penance, however, he acts not in his own name but in that of Jesus Christ. He is the one to whom we confess our sins, not his human representative. And Jesus Christ is the one who bestows on us, in this sacrament, the forgiveness he won for us on the cross. "All this is done by God, who through Christ changed us from enemies into his friends and gave us the task of making others his friends also....Here we are then speaking for Christ....We plead on Christ's behalf; let God change you from enemies into friends" (Paul — 2 Corinthians 5:18, 20).

"Going to confession" is not like going to the dentist or something we don't particularly like but which we know is good for us. This sacrament, like all the sacraments, is a *personal encounter with someone who loves us beyond all imagining.* Many people complain today about the anonymity of modern life. They feel they are "just a number." In the sacrament of penance, we are *not* just a number. Jesus Christ receives us personally and individually. Priests are instructed to help penitents by giving to each individual all the time necessary.

This personal dimension of the sacrament shows why the Church recommends its frequent use for sins of *all* kinds. Though the obligation extends only to the sacramental confession of all mortal sins annually during the Easter season, regular use of this means of forgiveness is tremendously helpful at all times.

It is one thing to say, "Lord be merciful to me a sinner." But until I identify the particular form that sin takes in *my* life, I am unlikely to do much about it. Sacramental confession helps me identify my own personal sins. In confession I have the opportunity of seeking help from Christ's representative, a priest trained to help people spiritually as physicians help them physically. In the words of absolution spoken by the priest, I experience the forgiveness won for me personally by Jesus Christ. By performing the penance imposed on me by the priest, I express my gratitude and sincerity.

Let me conclude with a personal word. Without the sacrament of penance, I would never have become a priest. Without it, I could not have remained a priest and a bishop. This beautiful, personal encounter with Jesus Christ gives me strength to live, and it will one day give me courage to die. I pray that each of you who reads these words will meet Jesus Christ in this sacrament during the Advent season. You could not give yourself a better Christmas gift. You could not give a finer Christmas gift to him who, on the first Christmas, gave us the greatest gift he could bestow: his Son.

(St. Louis, December 5, 1980)

– ◆ –

Hunger for God

There is a hunger abroad in the land. I see the signs of this hunger all the time: in the letters I receive, in the conversations I have as I move around this great church of St. Louis, in the articles and books I read. It is a hunger for God. People today are no longer satisfied merely to know *about* God. They want to know him in that deep, personal sense in which friends and lovers know one another, in which a wife knows her husband, or a husband his wife. People are hungry to *experience* God.

Our society has made more of the "good things" of life available to more people than probably any society in history. Are people more satisfied? A glance at the morning headlines or the evening TV news tells us they are not. Jesus Christ explains why. "Man cannot live by bread alone; he lives on every word that God utters" (Matthew 4:4). It is not enough to satisfy your *physical* hunger, Jesus is telling us, if you do nothing for your *spiritual* hunger. Saint Augustine (d. 430) was saying the same thing when he wrote: "You have made us for yourself, O God, and our hearts are restless until we find rest in you." The person who has never felt that restlessness is poor indeed.

48

In this and following columns, I want to answer some of the most frequently asked questions about prayer. For it is in prayer that we satisfy our deepest hunger: the soul's hunger for God.

* * *

Q Saying my prayers seems so mechanical. What's the point of it all?

A Many adult Catholics are still praying like children. When we are little, it is natural just to "say" prayers: by memory or out of a book. Those prayers are only *helps* to get us started. They are models for prayer. Merely reciting them by heart or reading them off the page was never meant to be the whole of prayer. If you have not progressed beyond childhood prayer, let me make a suggestion.

Find some time and place where you can be alone and undisturbed for at least five minutes. If you can manage ten or fifteen minutes, so much the better. But don't try too much at first. Take the Our Father, but instead of just rattling it off by heart, take it word by word and phrase by phrase. Think about the words and all they mean. For instance…

God is not only *my* Father, he is the Father of *all* people. That is why Jesus taught us to pray "*Our* Father." Think of his fatherly love. God is stronger than the best father on earth, more loving than the tenderest mother. He is the one who is always there. He accepts us always, in love.

As you think of what each word and phrase of this well-known model prayer means, let your heart go out to this loving Father in love, in thanksgiving, in praise. Tell him how much you *want* to love him, how sorry you are for failing him, how much you need his help. Only when you have exhausted the meaning of one phrase should you go on to the next one. If you do not get through the whole prayer in your prayer time, that's fine. True prayer is not getting through a certain number of words or sentences. It is *spending time with God.*

Q How can I find time to pray?

A We find time for what we consider important. People in love find time for long phone calls, daily letters when they are apart, making and buying gifts for each other. People who claim they have no time for prayer are really saying they do not consider prayer important. Anyone with imagination and goodwill can find *some* time for God at the beginning and end of the day.

In the morning we need to praise God for another day, to dedicate the day to him, to ask his help.

> O God, I praise you today.
> O God, I give myself to you today.
> O God, I ask you to help me today.

In the evening we should give thanks for blessings received, ask forgiveness for sins and failures, and pray for ourselves and others. In addition, some prayer time *during* the day (as suggested above) is essential if our prayer is to be healthy, balanced, and mature.

* * *

Prayer is not a stratagem for occasional use, a refuge to resort to now and then. It is rather like an established residence, for the innermost self. All things have a home: the bird has a nest, the fox has a hole, the bee has a hive. A soul without prayer is a soul without a home....To pray is to open a door where both God and the soul may enter.

– Rabbi Abraham Heschel

Prayer gives a meaning to the whole of life, at every moment, in every circumstance.

– Pope John Paul II

You need not cry very loud. He is nearer to us than we think.

– Brother Lawrence

My soul is thirsting for God....

– Psalm 42:2

(St. Louis, March 6, 1981)

– ◆ –

Q What is the point of praying if God knows our needs before we ask?

A Prayer is not just asking God for things. Petition (for ourselves) and intercession (for others) are only two kinds of prayer. I said last week that prayer is *spending time with God.* We need also to spend time praising him for his greatness reflected in nature and the beautiful people we know. We should thank God for his goodness to us and ask his forgiveness for our failures and sins.

Jesus himself reminds us that "Your Father knows what your needs are before you ask him" (Matthew 6:8). Yet in the Our Father, which immediately follows, he tells us to bring our needs before God in prayer nevertheless. Each time we do so, we acknowledge our dependence on God. That is important. We like to think of ourselves as independent. To pray is to confess that without a power greater than our own, we can never master life's problems or bear its burdens.

Prayer does not change God. It changes *us* by opening us to the action of God in us and through us for others. Job, in the Old Testament book of that time, is a man changed by prayer. Throughout the book, Job confronts God with the agonizing question: "Why should I, who have tried to serve God generously, suffer so terribly?" Job's wrestling with the Lord, in the form of arguments between Job and his "comforters" (who are confident they have all the answers), is really a form of prayer. At the end of the book, Job still has no answer to the mystery of suffering. But he himself is changed and at peace. Job addresses God thus:

> I have spoken of great things which I have not understood,
>   things too wonderful for me to know.
> I knew of thee then only by report,
>   but now I see thee with my own eyes.
> Therefore I melt away;
>   I repent in dust and ashes.
>
> (Job 42:3-6)

Q Many people pray only when they are desperate. Can we expect God to answer prayers like that?

A God never answers our prayers because we are good enough. God answers prayer because he is so good that he wants to share his blessings with us. A prayer of desperation is certainly not the highest kind of prayer. Yet the gospels give us many examples of God answering such prayers. The fifth chapter of Mark's Gospel records three cases: the Gerasene Demoniac, the father of the little girl, Jairus, and the woman who had suffered twelve years from a hemorrhage. Jesus' stilling of the storm on the lake at the desperate request of his terrified companions in the boat is another example (Matthew 8:25).

While fear of impending disaster is certainly not the highest motive for prayer, God can use even an imperfect motive like that to turn our hearts and minds to himself. If you have started to pray again in a crisis, the test of your sincerity is whether you are willing to continue and deepen your prayer when the crisis is past. A good place to begin is with a prayer of *thanksgiving* for help received. To be genuine, however, such a prayer must carry over into generous service of God and others in daily life.

Q I haven't really prayed for so long. Wouldn't it be hypocritical to start now?

A Are you sure this is not just an excuse? While laziness keeps many people from praying, many others are held back because they suspect prayer may make demands on them that they don't want to fulfill. They are right. Prayer *does* make demands on us. Prayer is not tapping into some kind of supernatural power that we can use to get what we want. When we pray, we are opening ourselves first of all to God's power over *ourselves.*

If you have lived apart from God for a long time, then starting to pray again *will* mean changes in your life. You should begin with a prayer for forgiveness in the sacrament of penance (confession). Once you have come back to God in the way he has appointed, the doors and windows of your soul are open for the sunshine and fresh air of his love to fill and flood you.

Remember: you can postpone the encounter with God for a long time, but not forever. You will meet God one day, whether you want to or not. Will he be a familiar friend or a dread judge? The choice lies with you. Making that choice involves prayer.

* * *

Every time I pass a church, I pay a little visit;
So when at last I'm carried in,
The Lord won't say, "Who is it?"

I have lived to thank God that all my prayers have not been answered.
– Jean Ingelow

Prayer does not change God, but it changes the one who prays.
– Sören Kierkegaard

There is nothing that makes us love a person so much as praying for him.
– William Law

(St. Louis, March 13, 1981)

− ◆ −

Q A Protestant friend claims the rosary violates Jesus' warning against "vain repetition." How can I answer?

A Your friend is referring to Jesus' words immediately before he gives us the Our Father: "Do not be babbling on like the heathens, who imagine that the more they say, the more likely they are to be heard" (Matthew 6:7). *The Jerome Biblical Commentary,* a valuable work of contemporary Catholic Bible scholarship, comments on this passage as follows:

> The Lord's Prayer is contrasted not with Jewish prayer but with pagan prayer....The lengthy recital of one's needs is discouraged on the ground that God does not need to be informed of them.

The rosary is a *meditative* form of prayer. During each of the decades, we ponder a scriptural mystery from the life of Jesus or Mary. In its present form, the rosary is at least eight hundred years old. It has been repeatedly recommended by saints and popes and is deeply loved by Catholics everywhere. The rosary is so simple that it can be used by little children, yet deep enough to appeal to learned theologians. During the long hours I had to spend behind the steering wheel of my car as Bishop of Mobile, I often found the rosary a comforting companion. Marine Sergeant Rocky Sickman told us after his release from imprisonment in Iran that he had prayed the rosary every day and drawn strength from knowing his family was using the same prayer back home in Krakow, Missouri.

This centuries' old, deeply loved prayer is an instance, we Catholics believe, of Jesus' promise to send us his Holy Spirit to guide us into all truth. You will find that promise in John 16:13. You might draw your friend's attention to that verse.

Q I liked your suggestion of praying the Our Father slowly, pondering each word and phrase. Can you tell us more about this form of prayer?

A The technical name for it is "discursive meditation." It means using the mind and imagination to ponder the material chosen for meditation; responding with acts of faith, thanksgiving, love, praise, and sorrow for sin; and forming a resolution that grows out of this prayer. The gospels are especially good material. But any Bible verse or passage that appeals to you may be used. Picture the scene. Listen to the words as if they were spoken personally to you. Respond to God's Word in whatever way seems most appropriate: in your own words, or without words, just by lifting up your heart and mind to the Lord.

Your meditation should not become mere reading. Stop reading as soon as you have found a word, phrase, or sentence that speaks to you. Close your eyes and pray over what you have read. Do not return to the text until you have prayed over the material thoroughly, made it your own, and responded to it.

Q What should I do about distractions?

A Ignore them. Distractions are normal. When you become aware that your mind has wandered, simply return to your prayer or to the text (your Bible or spiritual book). It may be that you *come* to prayer distracted. This happens when our prayer time is the only period of the day that is silent. If you keep the radio or TV on all day, you are feeding your mind with junk and trivia. God speaks most often in silence. Cultivate silent times outside of prayer and you will become more open to God at all times.

If you spend your whole prayer time turning away from distractions, you have prayed well. God sees the effort involved. He will never be outdone in generosity.

Q I find prayer a little like dieting. I start well, but give up. How can I keep on praying?

A You must have a *schedule*. People who pray only when they feel like it end up not praying very much at all. Praying when we feel like it is easy. The test of our faithfulness comes when we *don't* feel like praying but keep to our schedule regardless of feelings. Then we are giving something worthwhile to God. The same principle applies in human relations. How healthy would a marriage be in which the partners were kind to each other only when they felt like it?

In making your schedule, aim for an amount of prayer time which you are sure you can *definitely keep*. Ten minutes a day five times a week, faithfully adhered to, is far more valuable than resolving to pray half an hour daily — and then giving up when this proves too hard. It is said that the alpine guides in Switzerland can always spot novice climbers: they start out fast and soon tire. The experienced mountaineer climbs slowly. That is the only way to reach the top. The same principle applies in spiritual things.

* * *

God comes to those who ask him to come; and he cannot refuse to come to those who implore him long, often, and ardently.

– Simon Weil

I will reveal to you the secret of sanctity and of happiness. For five minutes a day, quiet your imagination, close your eyes to the things of the senses, enter within your soul which is the temple of the Holy Spirit, and there say: "O Holy Spirit....Guide me, strengthen me, console me, tell me what to do...I promise to submit to whatever you desire of me and to accept everything you allow to happen to me. Let me only know your will."...If you do this, your life will flow happily, serene and consoled even in the midst of pain.

– Cardinal Mercier of Belgium, 1851-1926

(St. Louis, March 20, 1981)

– ◆ –

Q Prayer used to make me feel so good. Now I feel nothing. Am I going backward?

A The condition you describe is known to writers of prayer as "dryness" or "aridity." Provided this is not due to some serious sin (which should be healed in confession), it is a sign not of backsliding but of *progress*. At first God often encourages us to pray by making prayer easy and giving us many warm, spiritual thoughts and feelings. In time, these are withdrawn. God is challenging us to go on *in naked faith.* Giving up prayer at that point indicates that you were praying more to *get* (for yourself) than to *give* (to God). There can be selfishness even in spiritual things.

Continue faithful in prayer. God will see that you have all the spiritual "experiences" you need — though not necessarily as many as you *think* you need! Often the feeling of being touched by God, or flooded with his love, is given to people who are weak in faith to encourage them. Recently, a priest in his fifties who has made a serious effort to pray for four decades told me he had never had a real "experience" of God. The reason, I suspect, is that this man has unusually strong faith. He may not need the "helps" that God gives to others whose faith is more fragile.

55

Q I used to be able to practice the "discursive meditation" you have described, but now this is impossible. What should I do?

A Provided you are making a consistent effort to be generous with God in daily life, your inability to meditate is a sign that God is calling you to the next stage of prayer: *contemplation.* Discursive meditation is a prayer of the mind, the imagination, and the will. It is an *active* form of prayer. Contemplation is *passive.* It is a prayer not of the mind but of the *heart.* Contemplation is difficult to describe in words. But it is within reach of every generous Christian.

Contemplation, like meditation, begins when we place ourselves consciously in God's presence, asking his Holy Spirit to help us pray. Then, instead of taking a Scripture passage or other meditation material, we take up a short *prayer word* that expresses our faith and love and let it repeat itself within. "Jesus," "God," and "Father" are examples of such prayer words.

The aim is *not* to have thoughts and images, *not* to make acts of faith and love, but simply to rest in the Lord's presence in faith-filled love. We use the prayer word to *silence* our minds and imaginations. God does not need our thoughts. And though thoughts of God are valuable for us, they always fall short of God, who is ultimately unknowable and unthinkable. The anonymous author of the fourteenth century English work on contemplative prayer, *The Cloud of Unknowing,* explains: "By love God can be caught and held; by thinking never."

Two people in love who are separated by distance delight to read each other's letters many times over. As they do so, they constantly discover new meanings, while holding in their imaginations an image of the one they love. Discursive meditation is like that. After years of married life, the young lovers will have less to say to each other. They are happy just to be together exchanging few words, or none at all. Words are no longer necessary to express what is in their hearts. Contemplation is something like that.

Another example of contemplation is the well-known story of Saint John Vianney, the Curé of Ars. Every day he noticed an old farmer sitting in the back of the church. One day Saint John asked the man: "What do you say to God in all the time you spend here in church?" The farmer smiled and answered: "I don't say anything. He just looks at me, and I look at him." The man was contemplating.

There are many good books on contemplative prayer today. One of the best is by the Trappist monk Father Basil Pennington, O.C.S.O., *Centering*

Prayer: Renewing an Ancient Christian Prayer Form (Doubleday: New York, 1980).

* * *

Deep down in me I knowed it was a lie, and He knowed it. You can't pray a lie — I found that out.

- Mark Twain *(Huck Finn)*

In prayer it is better to have a heart without words, than words without a heart.

– John Bunyan

God does not need us to say many words to him, nor to think many thoughts. He sees our hearts, and that is enough for him. He sees very well our suffering and our submission. We have only to repeat continuously to a person we love, "I love you with all my heart." It even happens that we often go a long time without thinking that we love him, and we love him no less during this period than in those in which we make him the most tender protestations. True love rests in the depths of the heart.

– Francois Fénelon

Do not entertain the notion that you ought to *advance* in prayer. If you do, you will only find that you have put on the brake instead of the accelerator. All real progress in spiritual things comes gently, imperceptibly, and is the work of God....Know yourself for the childish, limited, and dependent soul you are. Remember the only growth which matters happens without our knowledge....Think of the Infinite Goodness, never of your own state. Realize that the very capacity to pray at all is the free gift of the Divine Love and be content with Saint Francis de Sales' favorite prayer, in which all personal religion is summed up: "Yes, Father! Yes! and always Yes!"

– Evelyn Underhill

(St. Louis, March 27, 1981)

A Lenten Letter

Dear Friends,

"Come by yourselves to an out-of-the-way place and rest a little," Jesus said to his apostles one day. Mark, who reports the words, tells us the reason for them: "There were so many coming and going that the apostles had no time even to eat" (Mark 6:31).

How often we feel like the apostles: life gets so hectic that we find ourselves running just to stay in place. We all need times of quiet with the Lord. That's why we have Lent. It begins early this year: on February 12, Ash Wednesday.

Traditionally, our Lenten time with the Lord has three elements: prayer, penance, and charity. Let me consider them with you.

Prayer

Have you seen the film about Mother Teresa on public television? One scene shows her in an airplane, answering letters. "Mother, how do you do so much?" someone asks. Mother Teresa's answer is unforgettable: "We begin each day with him. And we end each day with him. That is the most beautiful thing."

Do you begin and end your day with Jesus Christ? Do you make time for him during the day? All of us have times when we grow slack in prayer — archbishops included. Lent is a time to make sure we are nourishing our souls, as we need to nourish our bodies with wholesome food and exercise.

Here are some suggestions for drawing closer to the Lord in prayer this Lent.

- Attend Mass on one or more weekdays.
- Join a small group in your parish for faith-sharing, prayer, or Bible reading.
- Set aside five to ten minutes in your day for private prayer: the rosary, Bible reading, or adoration of Jesus in the Blessed Sacrament in a nearby Catholic church. How fortunate we are to have so many in St. Louis!
- Pray the rosary after dinner with your family. Let the youngest children lead you. They'll enjoy it, and it's excellent training for them.

Penance

We live in a permissive society. Like it or not, we are all influenced to some degree by the "anything goes" mentality all around us. If we never deny ourselves legitimate pleasures, we lose the ability to reject sinful ones.

Fasting is a traditional form of Lenten penance. Some people think fasting is outmoded. Millions fast, however, to improve their health or physical appearance. They call it dieting. During Lent, the Church asks us to fast not just for ourselves, but for God. The emptiness that fasting involves makes it possible for God to fill us with his goodness and love.

On Ash Wednesday and all the Fridays of Lent, the Church requires all Catholics over the age of fourteen to abstain completely from meat. In addition, all Catholics between the ages of twenty-one and fifty-nine should also fast on Ash Wednesday and Good Friday.

If we really want to profit from our Lenten retreat, however, we need to go beyond those minimum obligations. What about forgoing tobacco or alcohol or cutting down on television to spend more time reading, being with the family, or with those we have neglected?

The sacrament of penance should be part of every Catholic's Lent. Make a good confession between now and Easter. It's not just an unpleasant duty we know is good for us. It is a personal encounter with someone who loves us more than we can ever imagine. Jesus is the one to whom we confess our sins. He is the only one who can forgive our sins. The priest is only his representative.

Charity

Repeatedly, the readings for Mass on the weekdays in Lent tell us that prayer and penance are useless unless we are helping those in need. The first reading for the Friday after Ash Wednesday is typical: "Is this the manner of fasting I wish…that a man bow his head like a reed and lie in sackcloth and ashes?…This, rather, is the fasting that I wish…Setting free the oppressed…sharing your bread with the hungry…clothing the naked when you see them, and not turning your back on your own" (Isaiah 58:5-7).

Next Sunday we shall have our annual collection for mission work among our Black and Indian people. And throughout Lent, we shall also have our Rice Bowl offerings for the relief of suffering people all over the world through Catholic Relief Services. I ask you to be generous to both of these offerings, as you always have been. Remember: God will never be outdone in generosity.

Finally, whatever your Lenten resolutions, be humble enough to aim at things you think you can easily accomplish. Modest goals actually achieved are worth far more than heroic sacrifices that are abandoned after a few days. Someone has said: "A little thing is a little thing. But faithfulness in little things is a big thing."

May the Lord help every one of us come closer to him this Lent in these three ways: through prayer, penance, and charity to others. Lent is a beautiful time, a precious opportunity. Use it to the full.

Cordially in Christ,
✛ *John L. May*
Archbishop of St. Louis
(St. Louis, February 7, 1986)

– ◆ –

Nourishing Faith

Almost five years ago we started hearing about something called RENEW. Some priests reported that when they explained how RENEW was intended to deepen and strengthen our Catholic faith, they got reactions like this: "We learned all that in school, Father. Why don't you teach it to the kids?"

The assumption behind such remarks is that religious faith is something like the multiplication table or riding a bicycle: you learn it once and then you've got it — for life. Many people still make that assumption about marriage: two people fall in love, get married, and "live happily ever after."

That's true only in fairy tales. Real life is different. Marriage, like any relationship based on love and trust, has to be *constantly nourished.* Otherwise the relationship withers and dies. How many marriages break up today with untold suffering not only for the spouses but for children and other relatives as well, because the nourishment to love that went on during courtship stopped after the wedding.

Friend: Our Catholic faith is based on a love relationship. It is not just a set of truths in our heads. Faith is an attitude of the heart that goes deep enough to motivate not merely attendance at Sunday Mass but a life centered on Jesus Christ all through the week. Faith, in other words, is a relationship of *personal friendship with Jesus Christ.* Like any friendship, faith must be constantly nourished.

The sacraments nourish our faith, especially holy Communion and penance (confession). All Catholics know that. The sacraments are not

60

merely infusions of a kind of spiritual power called "grace." They are personal encounters with One who loves us more than we can ever imagine.

Our faith is also nourished through God's Word: proclaimed in the church's public worship or read over privately for ourselves or in a group for faith-sharing or prayer.

Friends: Our archdiocese is fortunate to have many such groups. A recent report from our Office of Catholic Charismatic Renewal listed one hundred twenty-four groups meeting regularly for shared prayer and Bible reading.

A March 1985 statement of our American Bishops said that charismatic prayer groups had enabled many people to rediscover "the personal dimension of the faith...the experience of the Church, eucharistic life, the sacrament of penance, Mary's role, and the ancient discipline of fasting. From this has come a new depth of personal prayer, nourished (note that crucial word again) by the two tables of the Lord, the table of his body and the table of his Word."

The Bishops' statement also made an important distinction. "The charismatic renewal witnesses to elements of the Good News which are central, not optional....However the concrete manner, the historic forms in which the charismatic renewal incarnates these necessary elements of the gospel are optional for all Christians.

Catholic, as we all know, means "universal," "for all." One of the beautiful things about Catholicism is that it refuses to force people into a single mold. The Catholic Church has room for the spontaneous joy of the charismatic prayer group, the private and public recitation of the rosary, the silent eucharistic adoration of the Legion of a Thousand Men, the austere chanting of the psalms by a choir of Trappist monks.

Sharing: Many former RENEW groups continue to meet, not for charismatic prayer but for what is called "faith-sharing." Experience has shown that listening, in an atmosphere of prayer and Bible reading, to others' experience of what it means to be a Catholic Christian today — and sharing our own experiences — is a powerful means of nourishing our Catholic faith. Faith is not a private me-and-God affair. It involves not only our "vertical" relationship with God but innumerable "horizontal" relationships with our sisters and brothers in the great family of God that we call the Catholic Church.

Are you nourishing your Catholic faith? Or are you trying to live from the dwindling spiritual capital received in childhood years or decades ago? Lent is the time to think about it.

(St. Louis, February 21, 1986)

–◆–

An Airport Meditation

It won't be long now. Lent is rapidly wearing down, so I want to talk to you very seriously today. I want to talk about a serious subject in a little meditation.

All People: That evening the whole airport was very crowded. Because three or four gates were close together in the area from which my plane was to leave, it was especially crowded — people seated and moving about, luggage piled on the seats and on the floor, coats and jackets and babies in arms, babies crawling on the floor, boredom, anxiety, aimless chatter. When my row number was called, I joined the line moving slowly toward the gate.

Suddenly, between the line and the seated people, a boy of perhaps seven or eight appeared, with braces on both legs, swinging along on crutches, the kind with handgrips and metal braces on the forearm. After he had moved only fifteen feet or so, he disappeared into the crowd and I never saw him again. But I wondered about him. Was he born with some problem? Had he suffered an accident? How was he coping? What was his future?

My thoughts then moved from the little boy to all the other people in the gate area and to those boarding the plane. Who were they? Newlyweds? People going to another city for a funeral or to care for a sick relative? Someone looking for a new job? A travel-weary salesman or businessman? Folks beginning or ending vacations? How much joy, how much sadness, how much tiresome routine, how much sense of adventure, was present on the plane? How many life stories were there, stories confined by crutches or soaring away on wedding rings?

I thought of how often I have been in crowds like that and been, in a sense, all alone with my own concerns — trivial concerns. The little boy had stabbed me with sympathy. But should I not have a greater awareness, a greater sympathy, for all the fellow human beings around me — a feeling that life was being lived around me, my life and theirs dripping away by minutes, our lives going somewhere?

One Man: An airport is only one place where people are. Every day each of us is surrounded by people on the highway, in the supermarket or shopping mall, on the bus, or in the theater. We tend to isolate ourselves from them. They are like shadows with no substance, no emotions, no feelings, no current griefs, no current joys, no life history, no tomorrow. They do not touch us or touch our lives. Sometimes out of the crowd of faceless people, one person or another emerges and catches our attention, perhaps our friendship, or our love. Sometimes we form small circles of inner warmth but isolation from others.

There was only one man who walked through life with his heart open to every person around him — the Lord Jesus. His heart was so delicate, so sensitive, so open, so vulnerable. Because of the way he was, it seemed inevitable that he should open his arms and say, "Come to me all you who labor and find life burdensome and I will give you rest." Inevitable that he should say, "If I be raised up, I will draw all men and women to myself." Inevitable that his heart should literally be torn open for the sake of and for love of all men and women.

He could not pass by the widow weeping over an only son without raising the dead boy to life. When he touched the eyes of a blind man, the ears of a deaf man, the hand of a paralyzed man, the flesh of a leper, he was not touching a diseased member; he was touching humanity; he was touching a person. He was touching a person with love. And it was love that healed. He understood the tears of the sinful woman who wept over his feet. He understood the improbable longing for holiness of Zacchaeus, the tax collector. He understood the desire of the beggar for wholeness, for dignity, for a full share in life. He understood because his mind was not clouded by selfishness, by self-centeredness, by prejudice, by greed or possessiveness. His mind and his heart were totally open to others.

His whole reason for becoming man was to be with us — all of us, to be for us. He was totally faithful to this humanity, freely accepting all of its limitations, even to death on the cross. He was totally faithful to all of us in our humanity, knowing our weakness but going beyond it in love: "Father, forgive them, they know not what they do."

Come: This is the Jesus who gave us the sacrament of penance, the sacrament of peace. He still says "come to me" and "your sins are forgiven," as he did to the suffering people of Galilee. He did it personally then, for each person, and that is why he still wants us to come individually to confession, even though we come together in a communal penance service. He wants to touch you and me. He wants us to hear his words of forgiveness for you and me as the grieving Mary Magdalene did. Confession is something we need. Jesus knows our hearts and our needs. It is sad when we stay away, when we do not let him touch us with his forgiveness.

The time is short. Make a sincere Lenten confession. Come as the prodigal son came in last Sunday's gospel. Come with your sins and your sorrow for them. He wants to press you to his Sacred Heart in his forgiveness and give you peace. Come.

(St. Louis, March 14, 1986)

–◆–

Letting Go

"What is it like, Father, giving a sermon every Sunday?" Hundreds of people are there, all different: young, old, single, married, widowed, divorced. They're there because they want to be or because they think they ought to be. Some will be there next week and the next; some you won't see again for a month. What do you say to all those people week after week?

The question made me think a bit. In a way, I'm always thinking about sermons, but one at a time. The question was bigger than any one sermon. It was about all of them. What am I trying to do here anyway? It may sound a bit old-fashioned, but the simplest answer is: "Helping people get to heaven." That is what we are all about, isn't it?

That last question took on a special force for me this past month with the death of two men in our archdiocese. Each of these men was the father of a large family; each was deeply loved. Yet in each case they and their families finally had to let go of one another. It was a conscious, deliberate decision, one that they had made before and for much the same reason. They had to let go if they were to get on with life.

I have seen little children letting go of their mother's hand on the first day of school. I've watched young men and women hug their folks and say "good-bye" on the first day of college. I've watched a father hug a young bride and give her hand to a waiting groom. More recently, I've watched young husbands and wives embrace and let go as one or the other spouse left for Saudi Arabia. In every case, they were letting go. And in death we let go again, but only to get on with life, our startlingly new life in the kingdom of God.

Christianity reminds us that we must learn to let go. We don't cling to our children but gradually let them go; and there is much love in this release. Jesus reminds us not to cling too tightly to our possessions, lest they weigh us down. "Don't be anxious about what you eat or drink or wear," he urged us. "Seek first the kingdom of God." Prepare to let go of things.

Death brings that lesson home to us with a crash. It is the ultimate letting go, the ultimate act of trust. We can bring nothing with us and no one. It's a graphic reminder of "travel light," "keep it simple," to be about the two tasks each of us was given: to love God with all our heart and soul and strength and to love our neighbor as ourselves.

(St. Louis, June 7, 1991)

–◆–

Mystery

Behold! We bring you good news of great joy. This day a savior is born to you. And this will be a sign to you. You will find an infant wrapped in swaddling clothes lying in a manger.

(Gospel of Luke)

What an odd way for the Savior of humankind to begin his mission. There were no scathing denunciations of our conduct, there was no thunderous summons to repentance. There was just a quiet, nearly unnoticed moment when God's son slipped into our lives. God knew what he was up to. He knew that Mary and Joseph would lose their hearts to the little tyke. The opening gambit in God's saving scheme, it was a tactic he used until the very end.

An infant can neither command nor cajole. Simply by being himself, however, a baby inserts himself into the lives of his parents, entwines himself in their every waking hour and subtly, gently transforms them. Perhaps they had lived only for themselves; now they begin to live for someone else. Not because they must but because they want to, they restructure their time, their priorities, their energies — and all because a child has been born to them.

In his public ministry, the strategy of Jesus was patterned on that of a little child. He insinuated himself into the lives and homes of his listeners, often enough as a supper guest; he entwined himself about their histories. And their way of living and looking at life began to change. Their values, beliefs, and priorities were all transformed. That was the experience of the four fishermen: Peter, Andrew, James, and John. It was the experience of Zacchaeus, the crook, and Magdalene, the prostitute.

How did Jesus do it? By awakening the child in others. "Unless you become like little children," he said, "you will never understand the kingdom of God." A little child hasn't much going for him or her by way of wits and virtues. But then neither have we, certainly not enough to barter our way into the kingdom of God. What Jesus taught us was that we do have the power of a child over the heart of an indulgent parent. As he said: "When you pray, say Abba [Father]...." It's the secret of a child, the secret of the kingdom.

(St. Louis, December 20, 1991)

– ◆ –

As the Democrats in New Hampshire keep telling us, these are difficult days. Unemployment, the national debt, the trade imbalance — all the signs are grim indeed. It is times like these that try men's souls — and make them go to church.

But somehow that is not happening. Some of our old pastors used to say that Mass attendance always improved in days of depression or of war.

But today veteran pastors lament the empty pews on Sunday, and so do many grandparents, complaining about their children and grandchildren. "Father, what can I do?" So many sigh, "They just won't go to church."

How to explain it? Why the dramatic change? My guess is that large numbers of Catholics no longer feel "obliged" to go to Mass on Sunday. While I know of no Catholic moral theologian who would say that it is a mortal sin to miss Mass on any given Sunday, all will say we can lose our souls by not going to Mass on Sunday; we can lose them even in this life. We can lose them to different forms of idolatry, to the "spirit of the age."

In every age and every place, men and women have felt a profound need to worship God, to acknowledge their dependence on him, to praise him and thank him. This instinct is rooted in our very being, our sense of creaturehood. If we do not worship God, we shall worship something else. We shall worship money, power, possessions, pleasure, work, status. We may even end up worshiping ourselves, centering our lives on ourselves. When we have done this, we place the weight of our lives on something too fragile to support them. When we need them most, these strange gods crumble beneath us. If we do not praise God, we shall end up praising ourselves. And that is a dismal thought indeed.

If we are not in regular touch with the Word of God proclaimed in the Mass, if we are not nourished by the bread of life, we can lose our moral bearings. We move from that high ground from which we see who we are and where we are going as part of the pilgrim people of God. We are, Scripture tells us, not mere creatures but the beloved children of God destined for eternal life with him. He summons us to the table of his Son so we may find strength to pattern our lives on his, to be filled with his Spirit, to follow him in this life and into the next. If we ignore the summons, his voice grows distant, our strength begins to fail, and we can lose ourselves in a society where luxuries have become necessities that we exhaust ourselves to possess. Jesus said, "What will it profit if you gain the whole world and suffer the loss of your own soul?"

If we do not worship God, we impoverish ourselves, surrendering our glorious heritage as God's children to go our separate ways, until we find ourselves locked in ultimate isolation. God did not command us to keep holy the Sabbath because he needed us; he did so because he knows how desperately we need him.

Excuses, Excuses: Excuses I've heard for not going to Mass:

> **1.** I prefer my own private conversation with God. I get a great deal more out of a quiet walk in the woods thinking of him than I do out of Sunday Mass.

Response: On Sunday, God invites us to the eucharistic table of his Son, who said, "Do this in memory of me." He is prepared for refusals, of course; he has had enough of them to sympathize with any parent whose children prefer to raid the refrigerator and eat in their room rather than join the family for supper.

> **2.** I'm turned off by hypocrites who pretend to be holy on Sunday and spend the rest of the week being their ugly selves.

Response: The Mass is about and for sinners; at least that's the way Jesus saw it ("...that sins may be forgiven.") After a lifetime of missionary work, Saint Paul concluded we are all sinners; and he was among them. "The good

I want to do, I do not," he said. "The evil I don't want to do, that is what I end up doing." We are all in that same leaky boat. As I recall the parable, God invited the "nice" people to his banquet. When they turned him down, he started beating the hedgerows for the beggars and the thieves. The Eucharist is for people like us who need it, not for some mythical person who deserves it.

3. Someone told me I don't have to go to Mass on Sunday.

Response: I wish I knew who that "someone" was; he or she was wrong. Church law does require attendance at Sunday Mass. The law echoes the ancient command of Jesus at the Last Supper: "Do this in memory of me."

4. I don't need Sunday Mass.

Response: Yes, you do; we all do. There's profound need in all of us to thank God, to praise him, to love him. The word *eucharist* means "thanks." Jesus offered thanks and praise to God before he broke the bread and shared the cup. He commanded us to do the same. In the Eucharist, we are one with Christ. Our weakness is joined to his strength, our darkness is penetrated by his light. United to his Son, we are infinitely pleasing to God. Apart from Christ, we are little more than passing, often annoying, curiosities. "Who are we that you should notice us?" asked the psalmist.

5. Sunday is the only chance I get to rest and catch up.

Response: Perhaps we had better take another look at our lives and our priorities. Jesus said, "Could you not watch one hour with me?"

(St. Louis, February 14, 1992)

- 4 -
MARY

Mary is hailed as a preeminent and singular member of the Church, and as its type and excellent exemplar in faith and charity. The Catholic Church taught by the Holy Spirit, honors her with filial affection and piety as a most beloved mother.

This sacred Council earnestly exhorts theologians and preachers of the divine Word to abstain both from all false exaggerations as well as from a too great narrowness of mind in considering the singular dignity of the mother of God....Let them assiduously keep away from whatever, either by word or deed, could lead separated brethren or any others into error regarding the true doctrine of the Church.

(Constitution on the Church, #53, 67)

October is the month of the holy rosary. I just wonder what that means here in our Diocese of Mobile. Why not try this? After supper, before leaving the table, the whole family could join in praying one decade of the rosary. Each member of the family in turn could narrate the mystery of that decade and what it might mean for us today (this is the heart of the rosary). Then all could join in the prayers of the decade. The mysteries and prayers are right out of the Bible, you know. Sometimes

I wonder if some of us won't inspire the same comment uttered by a little boy at a wake: "Doesn't Uncle Joe look funny in that casket with a rosary in his hands?"

(Mobile, October 9, 1970)

– ◆ –

Advent Lady

On my way to Rome, I spent several days in German Rhineland. Since I was driving, I was able to wander off the beaten path. So I stopped in at many a rural parish church as well as the neighborhood churches in the cities and the glorious major cathedrals.

It was a joy to see in every one of those churches, large and small, a tasteful shrine to our Lady with fresh flowers and burning candles. In so many, there were also devotions before the evening Mass, with good attendance of both young and old praying the rosary.

Seeing that beautiful devotion to our Blessed Mother made me wonder whether a visitor here would be impressed by our love of the mother of Jesus. More important, are our children learning to love Mary as we did growing up? Have we lost some of our veneration for this beautiful Lady who is so much a part of Catholic tradition the world over?

Advent is a time when we need to think of her in a special way. During this time of preparing and longing for Christmas, she is surely our model — she who of all people was absolutely unique in waiting for her Son, who would also be her Savior and Lord. Imagine the wonder and prayer in her heart during those nine months before that first Christmas. Her meditation on the ancient prophecies of Israel and the Lord's words to her through the angel should be an inspiration and example to us through these weeks of Advent. The Bible says that "she pondered all these things in her heart." We need to take some time for the same kind of quiet and wonder during these days of Christmas shopping, hustle, and bustle.

During this beautiful time of Advent, we might pray the ancient prayer of the Angelus around our supper table with special devotion. This is the prayer that focuses on the great mystery of this time.

About thirty years ago, Pope Pius XII put it this way:

But when the little maid of Nazareth uttered her fiat to the message of the angel…she became not only the Mother of God in the physical order of nature but also in the supernatural order of grace she became the Mother of all who would be made one under the headship of her divine Son. The Mother of the Head would be the Mother of the members. The Mother of the vine would be the Mother of the branches.

(Mobile, December 8, 1978)

– ◆ –

Pilgrim's Progress?

Since July 1 nearly everyone in greater St. Louis has heard of the Pilgrim Virgin statue. The arrival of this statue (a replica of the original carving of our Lady of Fatima), and its subsequent exhibition at many of our parishes, has been broadcast to our metropolitan area by the press, radio, and television. As I said in my letter of welcome to this program and to this statue, I am always happy with any effort to foster true devotion to our Blessed Mother.

Authentic: I consider it a serious responsibility in our archdiocese to teach and to guide so that we will have true devotion to Mary. Accordingly, I do feel an obligation to speak clearly right now while the Pilgrim Virgin statue is being taken from parish to parish in our community.

The Catholic Church has spoken very specifically about devotion to Mary in recent years because there has been some careless and foolish talk about this beloved Catholic tradition. Some have exaggerated, some have minimized, what we believe and practice. The Church has responded with very precise statements of what we really believe about Mary.

Sources: These doctrinal statements are principally: (1) *Lumen Gentium,* the Vatican II teaching on the Church, including Mary's role. (2) *Marialis Cultus,* the encyclical of Pope Paul VI, stating the Catholic teaching fully and clearly for people of our time. (3) *Behold Your Mother: Woman of Faith,* the pastoral document of the American Bishops reemphasizing devotion to Mary in our country.

These documents give the following characteristics of Catholic Marian doctrine and devotion: it must be *scriptural* and *liturgical.* The Catholic belief on Mary can be found primarily in the Bible and in the official worship of the Church (liturgy). From the scriptural account of Mary's Annunciation and Visitation, God's Word presents Mary as blessed among women, whom all generations would revere. She is the Mother of the Lord, whom he gave as the Mother of the Church on Calvary and Pentecost. Could anyone say anything more sublime about Mary?

We must also be *ecumenical* in our teaching about Mary. Other Christians share the Bible with us, so we must emphasize its teaching rather than local Catholic devotions that appeared over the years. We must also avoid "vain credulity" in speaking about our Lady, lest non-Catholics be misled as to our beliefs. Accordingly, tales of how the Pilgrim Virgin statue wept in Las Vegas, Nevada, how doves sat at its feet for weeks without food and drink, how the statue goes where it chooses, and so forth, are misleading in my judgment. Even if such sensational stories (all of which I heard on radio news accounts) could be verified, they do not represent Catholic belief about Mary. Compared to what the Bible says about Mary, such claims pale into insignificance. The Fatima message of Mary — a plea for prayer, more faithful Christian living of vocation, penance of peace — is in full accord with what the Bible says of this beautiful woman.

Finally, we must speak of Mary in truly *anthropological* terms. In smaller words, she must be preached as a woman we can identify with in modern conditions. She was a human being who lived by faith. The Bible says she was blessed because she believed. She believed even when she did not understand. She pondered all these things in her heart and said, "Be it done to me according to your word." We are all called to do the same.

So she is the first Christian, the beautiful model of all Christians, who are also called to live by faith.

To Sum Up: I welcome the Pilgrim Virgin statue, but I hope its coming will be an occasion to profess our belief more clearly and our love more faithfully with the one holy Catholic Church. Let us never mislead any other Christians. Pope John Paul II has visited Guadalupe, Knock, Czestochowa, and now Aparecida in Brazil, but he always preaches what the Bible and the universal Church say about our Lady. He recalls with gratitude the various local devotions and traditions about her. They are beautiful but not officially part of Catholic faith. The clear, authentic Catholic doctrine about Mary, as set out above, is what we must always emphasize with him. I ask that this be done in every parish welcoming the Pilgrim Virgin statue in this archdiocese.

Mary the dawn, Christ the Perfect Day,
Mary the gate, Christ the Heavenly Way!
Mary the mother, Christ the mother's Son.
By all things blest while endless ages run. Amen.

(St. Louis, July 11, 1980)

– ♦ –

Month of May

As you might expect, I am a bit partial to the month of May. You must admit, it is beautiful. Along with the delightful weather, there are so many joyous occasions — anniversaries, graduations, first Communions, confirmations, ordinations, religious professions, and so forth. It is truly a beautiful but busy time of year.

Another thing I like about May is that it is the month of Mary. And the month begins on May 1 with the feast of Saint Joseph the Worker. So I thought it might be helpful to think a bit today about these two people who were closest to our Lord and Savior, Jesus Christ.

Mary: Our Lady is the perfect model of a believer. She put all her trust in God and dedicated her whole being to carrying out his will. When she gave her "yes" at the Annunciation and became the mother of Jesus, the rest of her life was devoted to the person and the work of her Son.

Because she believed and because she responded obediently to the word that God addressed to her, she became the new Eve, the new mother of all the living, the mother of all believers.

Because Mary heard God's Word and responded to it, the Word became incarnate in her. She did not run away from life and its demands. She accepted life freely and eagerly. She was not a timid woman. Rather, she proclaimed for all to hear that God vindicates the humble and the oppressed, that God also dethrones the proud and powerful. (Read Luke 1:46-55.)

In her *Magnificat,* we find these two kinds of people. On the one hand, there are the poor, the lowly, the sick, the downtrodden, the unfortunate. On the other hand, there are the proud and the arrogant, those who feel no need of God. The lowly recognize their dependence on God. The proud assert their personal power and claim an independence from God.

Mary is first and foremost among the poor. She contrasts her lowliness

73

with God's greatness, power, holiness, and mercy. She rejoices that God is God, and Mary is Mary. Through prayer, Mary comes to know who she is: both lowly and blessed. She also comes to know who God is: the Holy One, the merciful Father, the all-powerful God, the Great One of Israel.

Mary is called blessed by all generations not only because she carried the Lord within her but also because of her great faith. Saint Luke describes her not only as the Mother of the Lord but also as the first of the disciples. We rightly honor her as the Mother of the Church.

God remembers his people. No matter how difficult our lives may become, we can be confident that God is with us. He never abandons his people. That is what Mary tells us.

I encourage you, during the month of May, to think about Mary and her role in the history of our salvation. In a special way, I commend to you the rosary. The rosary is a prayer in which we reflect on the events in the life of Jesus and Mary and their meaning for us today. It is a prayer that helps us to increase our personal devotion to Jesus. It is a prayer that also draws us closer to Mary.

Joseph: We have no recorded words of Saint Joseph. The New Testament makes it clear that there was entrusted to Joseph the care of the two persons most radically important to the salvation and well-being of all humankind. The task of being foster father to the Son of God was important, but it was also delicate. Joseph's son was his Messiah and Savior and Lord. Joseph had to be master of his household and servant to his Lord.

Joseph was also husband to Mary, the true mother of the Son of God, a woman of unparalleled beauty, a woman from whom he received love and to whom he gave love, a warm, human love, yet from whom he was always somehow removed by God's wish and by a sense of reverence. Joseph was someone whom God chose for his task because his love was total and totally unselfish.

Joseph is the patron of the Church itself. The Church calls upon Joseph to care for it and provide for it as he once cared for and provided for Jesus. Down through the centuries, the Church has known persecution and oppression. It has been aware of corruption in some of its members. It has been aware of internal dissension and lack of unity. The Church knows itself to be human and needy in its members. And it calls upon Joseph, through his intercession, to be its official protector.

Joseph is patron of Christian families. The Church asks Joseph to take care of all families as he once took care of the Holy Family. The Church sees in the family the fountainhead of human life, the basic means of preserving human society and the Church.

While there is no historical evidence, Joseph is presumed to have died in the arms of Jesus and Mary. For him, the inscrutable darkness of death was relieved by the presence of the consoling love of Jesus and Mary and the assurance that beyond the darkness, he would once more meet his Messiah-Son. So the Church has proclaimed Joseph the patron of the dying — as the intercessor to whom we may turn when all our strength fades, when our hold on life ebbs away, when we face the moment of complete and final surrender to God.

From the teaching of the Church, we can see why Joseph is regarded as the greatest of the saints, after Mary — wordless, humble, ordinary, workingman, mortal — but the greatest.

Beyond his official titles, Joseph might also be taken as our model of contemplative prayer. He was called in the night to take Jesus and Mary and flee into Egypt in order to escape Herod. As he walked under the stars in the soft sand of the desert beside the mule that carried Mary, there must have been times when he carried the Infant Jesus in his arms, when he felt the warmth of his little body, sensed the beating of his small heart, when he somehow knew that he held the peace of God, the love of God in his arms. As the years passed and he lived always in the presence and the company of Jesus, as he experienced the exquisite delicacy of divine love expressed in human terms, he must have felt himself always more and more deeply bonded to the God who was his son. From Mary, whose spirit always rejoiced in God her Savior, who always said, "Holy is his name" and "Let it be done to me as you say," he must have learned how to know and respond to the divine Goodness. We need to learn to pray like that, too.

(St. Louis, May 16, 1986)

– ◆ –

"Behold Your Mother"

Jesus spoke those words from the cross, and we Catholics have understood them to be directed to us and all Christians. So during this month of May, the month of Mary, we should think about our Lady and all Christian people. For example, just listen to these words:

Sing o ye people, sing ye the praises of the Mother of God....She is the holy Temple, the Receiver of the Godhead: the instrument of virginity, the Bridal Chamber of the King, wherein was accomplished the marvelous mystery of the ineffable union of the natures which come together in Christ.

Those quotations are taken from the liturgies in the Orthodox tradition. The Roman Catholic Church, the Orthodox Church, and the ancient Churches of the East are united in their devotion to the Theotokos, the Mother of God. This title was assigned to Mary in the early Church to emphasize her motherhood of God, proclaiming both the human and divine nature of Christ.

Protestants: Throughout history, this truth has been acclaimed as part of our belief in a triune God. Even the Protestant Reformers — Luther, Zwingli, Calvin, and Wesley — held fast to this image of Mary.

We are in the midst of the Marian year called by Pope John Paul II for all Christians to focus on Mary's role in salvation history. We are encouraged to prepare for the anniversary of Christ's coming two thousand years ago by following Mary's example as both bearer and follower of Jesus Christ. We see Mary as our model to say "yes" to God's call in our lives. We follow her example as disciples of her Son.

In his encyclical *The Mother of the Redeemer*, Pope John Paul II points out the many ways the Churches of the East have honored Mary in liturgy and art. He sees this devotion as a source of unity between east and west. In the Church's ecumenical endeavors with the Protestant Churches, he hopes that Mary could be a sign of unity rather than division among all Christians. Throughout the document, he turns to Scripture as the basis for ecumenical dialogue on the Virgin Mary.

At midpoint in the encyclical, the Pope writes: "The journey of the Church, especially in our own time, is marked by the sign of ecumenism: Christians are seeking ways to restore that unity which Christ implored from the Father for his disciples on the day before his Passion: 'That they may all be one; even as you, Father, are in me, and I in you, that they also may be in us, so that the world may believe that you have sent me' " (John 17:21).

He continues: "Christians know that their unity will be truly rediscovered only if it is based on the unity of their faith." He points out that Mary, who is the model of "this pilgrimage of faith," is to lead them to the unity that is willed by their one Lord. He also writes: "It is a hopeful sign that these

Churches and Ecclesial Communities are finding agreement with the Catholic Church on fundamental points of Christian belief, including matters relating to the Virgin Mary."

Right Here: In the light of the encyclical and in the light of the National Lutheran/Catholic Dialogue's present focus on Mary, our Archdiocesan Council of the Laity has planned an archdiocesanwide ecumenical Scripture study program on the Blessed Mother during this month of May in this Marian year. It is going on right now in Roman Catholic and Lutheran parishes but is open to all Christians. The program was developed by Father Francis X. Cleary, S.J., in cooperation with Lutherans and other Christians.

We hope to promote a renewed devotion to Mary, centered on the Scriptures we share. Plan to take part in this Scripture study on Mary, the Mother of God and encourage your Christian neighbors to join you.

Learn more about the beautiful mother described in the following poem by Ann Weems, a Presbyterian writer:

Mary, Nazareth Girl

Mary,
   Nazareth girl:
What did you know of ethereal beings
   with messages from God?
What did you know of men
   when you found yourself with child?
What did you know of babies,
   you, barely out of childhood yourself?
God-chosen girl:
What did you know of God
   that brought you to this stable
   blessed among women?
Could it be that you have been ready
   waiting
     listening
       for the footsteps
     of an angel?
Could it be there are messages for us
   if we have the faith to listen?

                       (St. Louis, May 13, 1988)

Mary and the Poor

Here it is August 15, the beautiful summer feast of our Lady's Assumption in this year of Mary, so proclaimed by Pope John Paul. In many countries this day is called Our Lady's Day of the Harvest. Rural people through the centuries associated this feast with a bountiful harvest as summer nears its end. Very appropriately, they recall on this day how Mary was welcomed by her Son into the eternal joy of heaven. Jesus said that the just would be gathered as a beautiful harvest into the Lord's barn. Mary is the first fruit of that glorious harvest in her Assumption into heaven.

It is good to recall those old associations of this day. Very often our Lady is pictured today as the beautiful queen welcomed by her royal Son. Christian art often portrays her garbed in resplendent blue and white bordered in gold. Often a crown is put on her head. Here is certainly a place for that kind of tradition, especially on this day.

But sometimes I wonder about that emphasis and also the alleged appearances of Mary in certain apparitions (the present frenzy over Medjugorje). Recently, in going to a family funeral, I drove through the little Wisconsin town of Necedah. Out of curiosity I stopped at the nearly forgotten Shrine of Our Lady of the Rosary to which people flocked thirty-five years ago because of reported apparitions of our Lady, which have since been disproved totally by the Diocese of LaCrosse. The same is true of Veronica Leuken's description and "messages" of Mary in Bayside, New York. On and on it goes. The Church has always viewed such phenomena with healthy skepticism.

Today, in this Marian year, we are asked by Pope John Paul in his recent encyclical to see our Lady as she appears in the Bible. We might also recall her one Church-authenticated appearance in the new world (lest I seem to be totally skeptical of nonbiblical Catholic tradition).

Guadalupe: The apparition of Our Lady of Juan Diego at Tepeyac outside Mexico City in 1531 (Our Lady of Guadalupe) illustrates Mary's self-identification with the poor. The way she appeared to Juan Diego has been perpetuated in the miraculous picture she left in the tilma, or cape, of Juan Diego after he spilled out the December roses. Mary appeared to Juan as a dark-complexioned Aztec woman, speaking in Juan's own language and dialect. She called Juan *xocoyote mio,* "my little son." She said that she was the merciful mother of his people. Mary came looking like an Indian, speaking like an Indian, expressing concern for the poor Indians — no crown or royal robes for her.

Besides the miracle of the roses in December and the image on the tilma, two other miracles followed upon the appearance of our Lady: first, a massive conversion of the native population; second, a conversion on the part of the Bishop of Mexico City to whom Juan Diego has been sent. Bishop Juan de Zumarraga changed his whole attitude toward the Indian population. He began to see — as it were through the eyes of Our Lady of Guadalupe — the indigenous people as people of dignity, worthy of respect and of care.

For all of us who are ordinary, who are "lowly," who are not mighty, who are not rich — Mary is near. We are all her "little sons" and "little daughters." Heavenly Queen though she is, she has lived the pilgrim way of the lowly. She shows us how to live.

I think that is what she teaches us on this Assumption day.

(St. Louis, August 14, 1987)

Mary and Today

Now and then a preacher blasts the mothers of the 1990s for their failure to imitate the Virgin Mary. Their children are going astray because the kids lacked the inspiration a "Mary-like" mother might give them. As such a recent harangue droned on, one young mother whispered to another: "Sure, it was easy enough for her. She had only one kid and he was God."

What, if anything, does Mary have to say to the contemporary family with its not-too-traditional profile: The single-parent family, the family where the parent is separated, divorced, widowed? This is the family that knows the pressures of tight finances and growing needs. The stress of coping alone.

Stress: Mary certainly had her share of stress. God's call meant a radical disruption of her own plans for the future. The angel asked her, in effect, to become an unwed mother. She agreed at great risk to herself and to the utter consternation of her fiancé, Joseph. She gave birth in a stable far from whatever small comfort her own home might have offered. And if shepherds and Magi came searching for the child, so did the soldiers of Herod.

It was beneath the cross of Jesus that Mary knew her greatest pain. Not only did she lose a son prematurely; she saw him betrayed and destroyed by violence. When he breathed his last breath and she held him in her arms, she was a childless widow, one of the most forlorn figures in Jewish society.

What was Mary's response to the pain she encountered? The biblical texts show us a woman who grappled with each stress-filled situation. Her "yes" at the Annunciation was not passive acquiescence but a readiness to take on all her consent implied. In her active, struggling response to suffering, Mary stood in a long line of Jewish women: Esther, Susanna, Judith.

Like them, she yielded neither to despair nor self-pity, the greatest temptation of those who know real suffering. When she stood beneath the cross, at the very moment of her greatest loss, she opened her arms to embrace the beloved disciple as her son. In the face of her most intense suffering, she was able to think of others.

Most importantly, Mary "let go." She trusted herself to the God who loved her absolutely and unconditionally. Little wonder that the Second Vatican Council saw her as a "sign of sure hope and solace for the pilgrim people of God" — the Mother of the Church. May is the month especially devoted to her. So may it be in our archdiocese.

(St. Louis, May 11, 1990)

A letter reporting a conversion experience and deepening of faith during a visit to Medjugorje brought the following response:

Why have I not promoted pilgrimages to Medjugorje or at least that devotion? I know that many of our people have gone there and some of our priests have also. I have decided to wait until I knew more about the whole phenomenon. Even more, I wanted to wait for the teaching of the Yugoslavian Bishops and especially our Holy Father on this matter. The letter is quite impressive. Some people have been similarly moved by Medjugorje and others have been slightly so. I have read quite a bit about these alleged apparitions, which seem quite different from Guadalupe and Lourdes, where our Lady did not show up day after day to a group of visionaries over a period of years. She has never been so talkative before. But this tiny hidden place in a communist led country is the kind of place you would expect her to choose. Her alleged message is simple and orthodox, apparently repeated over and over again with nothing new — no special secrets, and so forth, which makes me wonder why one should have to go all the way to Yugoslavia for the conversion this Lady experienced. Why not to one of our retreat houses with a Bible in hand? What the sacred Scriptures and the official teaching of the Church say about Mary and her Son seems to me eminently more beautiful than anything I have heard from Medjugorje. But at Guadalupe and at Lourdes, there was also a skeptical bishop. And they did not understand the approach of our Lady either.

Last February 8, the local bishop in Medjugorje met with the Pope to report the study just completed by all the Yugoslav Bishops. They concluded that "it cannot be confirmed that supernatural apparitions and revelations are occurring at Medjugorje." The Pope accepted the report and promised to give a more authoritative response "in due time."

Meanwhile, I am happy for our letter writer today and for others who have written and spoken to me along similar lines in recent years. But I continue to reserve judgment. I am not convinced. We have other "seers" these days like the clearly spurious visionary of Bayside, New York. We have the alleged claims of Sister Lucy of Fatima, warning of imminent worldwide tragedy if all the bishops of the world, together with the Pope, do not consecrate Russia to the Immaculate Heart of Mary. She claims that Mary told her that. None of this has anything to do with the faith of the Roman Catholic Church, and I am afraid we are not helped by it in any way.

There is a counterpart to all this in the hysteria abroad today among fundamentalist Protestants in their prophetic biblical interpretations about Armageddon and the "end times." The Middle East war fits right into all this apocalyptic theorizing that has arisen again and again through the years in our country. We need to stay with Jesus, who said of the end of the world, "No one knows, however, when that day and hour will come — neither the angels in heaven nor the Son, the Father alone knows....Watch out then, because you do not know the day or the hour" (Matthew 24:36, 25:13).

We need to stick with this word of Jesus and the teaching of his Church, which says the same thing.

(St. Louis, March 1, 1991)

- 5 -
STEWARDSHIP

People should regard us as servants of Christ and stewards of the mysteries of God.

(1 Corinthians 4:1)

As generous distributors of God's manifold grace, put your gifts at the service of one another, each in the measure he has received.

(1 Peter 4:10)

"All things are lawful, but not all things are expedient. All things are lawful, but not all things edify" (1 Corinthians 10, 23; cf. 6, 12). This teaching of Saint Paul comes to mind following the legalization of church bingo in our state.

Let me say straight off that I voted for Proposition 3 and not just "to keep Grandma off the streets," as the bumper stickers put it. I did so because I don't know which is worse: making criminals out of otherwise law-abiding citizens engaged in a harmless pastime for a good cause or the widespread acceptance of a situation in which the law is openly flouted with impunity.

The passage of the measure makes me uneasy nonetheless. Will we now see outside Catholic churches the enormous sign "BINGO!" which disfigures too many Catholic churches in some states, dwarfing the parish name and Mass schedule? I pray not. Church bingo seems to me an apt example, in today's world, of Paul's category of things that are lawful but not always expedient.

For financially hard-pressed pastors and parish councils who see no other way than bingo to pay the bills incurred in doing the Lord's work, I have great sympathy. I also have understanding. I know, too, the burdens of maintaining the Lord's work in worship, education, charitable action, and evangelization. Surely, the temptation to close the financial gap through bingo is strong. However, I suspect that even its staunch defenders would be greatly relieved if it were possible to raise the necessary funds in some other way.

"A More Excellent Way": Is there a better way? I am convinced there is. It is called "stewardship." Contrary to a widespread impression, stewardship is not concerned solely with fund-raising. It is neither a gimmick to shake people down for money nor a quick and easy solution to all church financial problems.

Stewardship is a total concept embracing all areas of life. It is a central theme of the Bible, which tells us that we are not owners of our time, talent, and treasure. We are stewards, called to manage these gifts for a limited time, responsible to God who entrusts them to us.

The Catholic teaching most of us grew up with emphasized obligations: Sunday Mass, some form of daily prayer, avoidance of at least the more serious sins, and some measure of church financial support. For all too many of us Catholics, this means tossing God the loose change that is left over after we have taken care of our needs and as many luxuries as we think we can afford.

All these obligations were defined in minimum terms. So it is easy to see why many Catholics suppose that once they have satisfied their minimum obligations, the rest of their time, talent, and money is theirs to do with as they please. God, in such a view, remains on the fringe of life. And a religion of minimum obligations generates no joy.

The Center: Stewardship aims to change all this by moving God from the fringe of life to the center. To people accustomed to thinking solely in terms of minimum obligations, this seems threatening, as if the level of obligations was being raised so high as to crush them. In fact, precisely the opposite is the case. Only a religion that puts God at the center of life can generate the contagious joy we see in Christ's most devoted followers, from the pages of the New Testament down to Pope John XXIII and Mother Teresa in our day.

Stewardship of money involves a radical shift in the traditional Catholic approach to fund-raising. We usually list church needs and ask people to meet them. Essentially, this is begging. The stewardship approach starts not with institutional needs but with something even more important: the personal need of each of us to return to God a truly grateful portion of our income in thanksgiving for all the good things he gives us.

A grateful portion must be the first portion. When I decide that the first portion of my income belongs to God and his poor, I am making a faith-decision: I am trusting that what is left over after I have given God "his" share will be enough for me and my dependents. Giving from what is left over after taking care of my own needs and pleasures involves no faith at all. It is a simple arithmetical calculation.

Stewardship of money says that more important than the Church's needs is the need of the giver to give. Those who meet this personal need are filled with joy and grow spiritually. Their faith is deepened. They discover another way of worshiping God: by being good stewards of their money. Many people have found that practicing stewardship turns money, for the first time in their lives, into a source of joy and blessing rather than a worry. When a substantial number of people become good stewards of their money, the Church's needs are fully met, with a surplus for expansion. Far more important, however, than these financial benefits is the spiritual growth experienced by those who live as good stewards of their time, talent, and treasure. Meeting church financial needs through bingo often concentrates not on people but on dollars. It can deprive people of spiritual growth by withholding from them the good news about a vitally important central element in our lives: our money.

The principles of stewardship are theologically sound. They flow from the biblical and Catholic doctrine of God as creator and all of us his stewards. Stewardship thinking is badly needed in American Catholicism today. I would hope that the Church of St. Louis would lead the way in the years ahead.

(St. Louis, November 14, 1980)

—◆—

Lots of letters come in day by day. Some of them could never be quoted here. But this one I must share with you. Here it is almost word for word with only the names withheld:

Dear Archbishop May,

Though a few weeks late, we wanted to share this miracle with you. Several weeks ago we listened to your taped homily on the Archdiocesan Development Appeal. We had been discussing our finances and what our gift could be this year. As we listened to you, especially your reminder that the pledge was truly an act of faith and not simply what we could see we could afford, we returned home and prayed about the Appeal. Following this, we made a pledge of $100 per month — considerably more than we actually felt we could afford and placed it in the hands of our Lady, hoping our "act of faith" would be truly one of faith.

To our surprise and delight at how the Lord works, within one week we received an unexpected raise that provided an extra income of exactly $100.54 per month. (We're not sure what the 54 cents is for!) So we praise God and thank him for his many gifts. We pray that God will continue to bless you and make your leadership fruitful in building up the Church. We wanted you to know that your words and your love are very powerful and draw us to live more fully Christian lives. We thank you.

In Christ,

Mr. and Mrs. _____

(South St. Louis)

I have rarely heard the spirit of tithing or stewardship expressed more strikingly. We all need to trust the Lord that he will care for us if we make our tithe to him first. We need to give to him of our "first fruits" each month in faith instead of waiting to see what is left over for him at the end of the month after we have taken care of ourselves. Doing that takes faith, and that is part of what Catholic living means.

(St. Louis, June 12, 1981)

– ♦ –

Q What is this tithing all about? I heard that the Cardinal of Chicago has suggested it in place of bingo. Do you agree?

A Many Catholics probably consider tithing "something Protestant." Some Catholics aren't even sure how to pronounce the word. It rhymes with "writhing." If tithing is Protestant, then only in the sense that Bible-reading is Protestant: something that rightly belongs to all Christians but which Protestants have preserved more faithfully than we Catholics have.

Tithing means returning to God the first portion of the good things he gives us. A tithe, in modern terms, is the first ten pennies of every dollar of income for God and his poor. In Bible time, tithing was compulsory. The Jewish farmer and the shepherd returned to God the first fruits of field and flock out of gratitude and to express the conviction that everything came from God and belonged to God.

This was the religion that Jesus learned and practiced. He would have been shocked at the practice of so many of his followers today who return to God not the first fruits but the leavings: the loose change (sometimes only some of the loose change!) that is left over after taking care of all their own needs and as many luxuries as they think they can afford.

Today, with income taxes and the welfare state, the obligation of tithing has lapsed. What has not lapsed, however, is our duty to use our money and possessions responsibly. As the American Bishops said in 1977:

> We are absolute owners of nothing; rather, we are stewards of all we receive and we must see such resources responsibly.

Tithing is a way of doing this. Like praying the rosary, Bible reading, making a novena or retreat, or family devotions or weekday Mass (none of which are compulsory), tithing is something that helps to deepen our Catholic faith and to live it more fully. How so?

- Deciding to give God the first portion of our income, and to take care of our needs out of what remains, is a faith decision. We are making an act of faith that what is left over after we give God "his share" will be enough. Giving God leftovers involves no faith at all.
- Tithing enables us to use our money to express our faith. This is the sacramental principle: using something material as the vehicle or instrument of the spiritual — to express our gratitude for God's blessings.
- People who tithe consistently find that money ceases to be a cause of worry and becomes a source of joy.

Here, from my files, are testimonies from two laypeople supporting what I have just written. A woman who prints and sells artistic greeting cards writes:

My business began back in 1971, but it wasn't until 1979 that I began to tithe — and it was then that the business really started to grow. My husband and I were reviewing our records in March for our income tax. (Putting four children through school and college wasn't too simple!) We discovered to our amazement that my cards had earned over ten thousand dollars that year. Glory be to God! That was when we decided to return to him the first portion of what he had given us.

I can remember perfectly the thrill of writing those first checks: five hundred dollars for our parish, the other five hundred dollars for two other charities I was interested in. Actually, I didn't even feel it was mine to give. I still don't today when I'm writing those checks. That is the wonderful thing about tithing. You figure the first ten percent belongs to the Lord, and without hesitation, off it goes to do its work. There is nothing to equal it!

A husband on a small income writes:

Every Sunday at Mass when the collection basket came my way, I tossed in one dollar...until a year ago. I had a small family and no debts, except a small mortgage on my house. My annual salary was in excess of eighteen thousand dollars, so I could certainly afford to give more, but I was blinded by materialism. I did not want everything on earth, but I thought there were many things I had to have to make me "happy." These had become the driving force and center of my life.

Then a layman spoke at Mass one Sunday about giving the first ten pennies of every dollar to the Lord and his poor. That same week I was shocked by the death of a friend at age thirty-seven. I realized that I could not hold on to the worldly goods I was striving for, even if I lived long enough to attain them.

I decided to increase my offering to five dollars a week and found that giving more did not cause me pain, as I had always thought. It gave me pleasure! These feelings have increased as I see how my parish has been able to reach further out to those in need.

Does the Lord give back to us more than we give? I prayed that if this was so, I would receive spiritual blessings and increased faith...and my prayers were answered. In addition, within ten months of my first increased offering, my salary was raised more than I gave! This enabled me to increase my giving farther toward the goal of a full tithe.

Sacrificial giving (as opposed to the "tip" that I used to give) has enabled me to release the pressure associated with living in and for the future. It has brought me closer to living my days as God gives them to me — one by one.

If more Catholics tithed, there would be no need to raise money for the Lord's work through gimmicks and gambling. I agree fully with Cardinal Bernardin that we need to tithe and get rid of bingo and Las Vegas nights. More important, however, is the personal enrichment experienced by all those who really put God first. The testimonies above are examples.

"Who tithes?" More people than you might think. Wouldn't you like to get on the same team? Catch us if you can!

(St. Louis, June 13, 1986)

At this time of year, we realize again the beauty of our state of Missouri. It is time to enjoy it, appreciate it, and protect it. Sunday, June 5, has been declared "Environmental Sabbath," a day to give thanks to the Lord for our good earth. Such a feast for our planet fits right into our Catholic liturgy at this beautiful time of year.

On Christmas Eve, 1969, as *Apollo 8* circled the moon, on-board cameras televised the mother planet, 231 thousand miles away. Captain James A. Lovell remarked that the earth looked like a "grand oasis in the big vastness of space."

Then Major William A. Anders started reading:

> In the beginning, God created the heaven and the earth. And the earth was without form and void; and darkness was upon the face of the deep....

The three space travelers took turns reading the creation narrative from the first book of the Bible, finishing with "and God saw that it was good."

To millions of viewers watching the image of the cloud-covered ball that was being beamed into their homes from *Apollo 8,* the point was obvious: like the three astronauts in their frail craft, earth, too, is isolated and fragile — the only body in the universe that is known to support life.

"The heavens declare the glory of God" (Psalm 19:1).

The Fragile Balance

The image of earth as an isolated island of life, with a closed life-support system very much like that of a spacecraft, is no illusion. Years before the moonshot, Ambassador Adlai E. Stevenson had made the same point in his last speech to the United Nations:

We travel together, passengers on a little spaceship, dependent on its vulnerable resources of air and soil; all committed for our safety to its security and peace; preserved from annihilation only by the care, the work, and, I will say, the love we give our fragile craft.

The planet is littered with the ruins of civilizations that have ignored or scorned that fragility:

- North Africa, the garden of the Roman Empire, is today a land of dead cities, buried under silt and sand. Overgrazing, uncontrolled lumbering, and poor farming practices eroded the region's top-soil.
- Turkey's cities of Ephesus and Tarsus were thriving seaports in biblical times. Both are now landlocked due to environmental abuse.
- The Fertile Crescent of the Bible no longer exists. Lebanon's cedars have almost all been cut down. Since the time of the Hebrew patriarchs, human mismanagement of soil has filled in the Persian Gulf for a distance of one hundred eighty miles.
- Greece, Spain, and even pre-Columbian America also bear the scars of humanity's lack of respect for earth's delicate balance.

Human beings may have dominion over the works of God's hands. But the decaying ruins on our planet bear witness to the fact that humanity's domination is not absolute.

"Draw me up an account of your stewardship" (Luke 16:2).

What We Can Do

As a private individual, a citizen, a consumer, and a contributor to pollution, each of us can take a number of steps to reverse the trends about us. This checklist is a partial guide to our options:

- *Moderate your lifestyle.* Conspicuous consumption is wasteful, and in a world of undernourished people, unthinkable.
- *Buy only what you need.* Americans make more garbage than anyone else on earth. When shopping for packaged foods, electrical gadgets, and luxury items, show a little restraint.

- *Don't litter.* Without becoming a nut about it, pick up some litter that is not your own. Don't be shy about indicating your disapproval of litterbugs.
- *Keep garbage tightly covered.* Starving a rat helps everybody.
- *Keep noise down.* Blow your horn sparingly. Keep radios and TV sets at a moderate volume. Use noisy appliances at decent hours.
- *Teach your children to respect their world.* With proper guidance, youngsters can become environment-minded.
- *Don't be taken in.* A "politics of tokenism" can rely on grand gestures, with high public-relations value, instead of grappling with environmental problems. Lasting solutions will be difficult, expensive, and slow in coming.
- *Report violations.* Keep a phone list of city, state, and federal agencies that deal with air and water pollution. Report abuses.
- *Vote.* Support candidates with constructive platforms that include reasonable solutions for pollution.
- *Give your support.* Your time and money are needed by responsible groups that are pressing for effective legislation on federal, state, and local levels; for lawsuits against flagrant polluters; for environmental lobbying.
- *Get involved.* Join a conservation group. Start a cleanup campaign. If there is a block association working to improve your neighborhood, join. If not, start one.

Where Faith Comes In

"Reason," claims Joseph Sittler, a Lutheran theologian, "says that destroying clean air is impractical. Faith ought to say it is blasphemous."

For people of faith, all things belong ultimately to their Creator. They exist for the benefit of humanity, but they are held in trust. They obey laws that are not of our making, laws that we ignore or violate at our peril. There can be no license to abuse the goods of our earth — and no exemption from the consequences of doing so.

"To the Lord belong earth and all it holds, the world and all who live in it" (Psalm 24:1).

Prayer for God's Good Earth

Father,
You looked on everything that you had made
and saw that it was good.
But we have squandered
the riches of creation.
We have laid the ax to the mighty forests.
We have despoiled the green hillsides
and wasted earth's mineral wealth.
We have fouled the air,
littered the countryside,
and polluted lakes, streams, and oceans.
Voices have been raised to stop us
from squandering our inheritance.
May we heed them.
May we heal the earth.
And one day, may we look on our planet
and say with pride,
once again,
"Behold, it is good."
Amen.

(St. Louis, June 2, 1989)

- 6 -
CATHOLIC EDUCATION

Bishops should take pains that catechetical instruction – which is intended to make the faith, as illuminated by teaching, a vital, explicit and effective force in people's lives – be given with sedulous care to both children and adolescents, youths and adults.
(Decree on the Pastoral Office of Bishops, #14)

Here it is — back to school time. I know this is a happy time for mothers, and I hope it will be for all our students, too.

First of all, our Catholic schools are alive and well in the Mobile Diocese. Almost every seat in every school will be filled. No schools have been closed in the diocese, and one new school has been built at Holy Trinity.

Very soon new boards of education will begin meeting in the three deaneries of the diocese. Perhaps the most encouraging trend: the number of Sisters involved in all these works of education has increased considerably over last year.

This continued development of our educational program costs a great deal — and not just in money. There is a tremendous amount of blood, sweat, and tears required from all — pastors, principals, faculties, parish councils, school boards, and so forth. Besides that, there is the cost in cold hard cash. Regretfully, our tuitions have gone up almost all across the board and still the parishes and diocese have to subsidize Catholic education on every level. But I feel it is worth it all, and as long as all of you agree, we intend to make every effort for Catholic education throughout this diocese.

Finally, we must intensify our commitment to meaningful racial integration in all our schools. I believe this is especially necessary today when there is a growing backlash for resegregation of public schools on the part of many white people and some black separatists. Despite pious protest about devotion to quality education, much of the feverish politicking in this election year is obviously appealing to the subtle scheming of many people to get back to segregated neighborhood schools. This movement and the flight to segregated private schools are part of the same basic pattern when just the opposite is so vitally needed — the honest and open dedication to equal educational opportunity for all our children, white and black. Certainly, we should expect no less from our leadership community, and yet we find even some prominent Catholic families in the fight to segregate schools, especially on the secondary level. And I would match our Catholic high schools with any local private schools for academic achievement.

As Catholics, I think we should be honest when we talk about quality education. Quality education for whom? In this day and age, does not quality education include teaching little children to know and respect and work with people who are different? In fact, is not the failure to do this a denial of extremely vital education for children who will be the next generation of Americans? How is such segregation education training for life — Christian and American life?

(Mobile, August 25, 1972)

– ◆ –

The Basics

Well over a century ago in England, the great Cardinal Newman said, "We want a laity...who know their religion, who enter into it, who know just where they stand, who know what they hold and what they do not, who know their creed so well that they can give an account of it, who know so much history that they can defend it."

That is a big order, and it is the reason for all our religious-education programs from preschool on up to adults. But we want far more than an academic knowledge of the Faith in these times. We want Catholics who hear God's Word and keep it, people who put the gospel to work in every action of their daily lives, whose joy and concern for others are so radiant that all will recognize them as Christ's disciples by the love they have for one another. To achieve all that, the American Bishops have emphasized three basic approaches.

Prayer: Catholics must be a praying people — when they come together in the name of the Lord and when they close their door and pray to the Father in secret. All Catholics should know and pray the great old prayers: Our Father, Hail Mary, Apostles' Creed, Act of Contrition, the rosary, and so forth. But memorized formulas are not enough. Spontaneous, informal prayer and thoughtful spiritual reading are just as important. Prayer groups growing everywhere today are bringing this richness and variety into Catholic life more and more.

Liturgy: As emphasized in preceding columns, the center of our worship as Catholics is the Mass and the sacraments. More and more, all Catholics are taking a greater share in the liturgy — in reading, song, music, and in all the beautiful programs of family participation in baptism, first confession and communion, confirmation, the anointing of the sick, holy orders, and holy matrimony. Compare the preparation and involvement of the family and parish in these sacraments just ten years ago and today. There has been beautiful growth.

Bible: Undergirding all our basic beliefs as Catholics is the Holy Bible. Vatican Council II has called for a renewal of Bible study and preaching. You have noticed how that has been carried out in our liturgy and in all our religious-education programs. A love of the Bible and fidelity to the traditional teaching of the Catholic Church belong together. Both constitute the source of our basic beliefs as Catholics, who must be Bible Christians always.

In Practice: Our Catholic faith is lived every day, not just on Sundays. Several weeks ago we recalled the Ten Commandments of God, and today we state the specific precepts of the Catholic Church as proposed by the Bishops of the United States:

1. To keep holy the day of the Lord's Resurrection; to worship God by participating in Mass every Sunday and holy day of obligation; to avoid those activities that would hinder renewal of soul and body, for example, needless work and business activities, unnecessary shopping, and so forth.

2. To lead a sacramental life; to receive holy Communion frequently and the sacrament of penance at least once a year (annual confession is obligatory only if serious sin is involved); minimally, to receive holy Communion at least once a year, between the First Sunday of Lent and Trinity Sunday.

3. To study Catholic teaching in preparation for the sacrament of confirmation, to be confirmed, and then to continue to study and advance the cause of Christ.

4. To observe the marriage laws of the Church; to give religious training (by example and word) to one's children; to use parish schools and religious-education programs.

5. To strengthen and support the Church: one's own parish community and parish priests; the worldwide Church and the Holy Father.

6. To do penance, including abstaining from meat and fasting from food on the appointed days.

7. To join in the missionary spirit and apostolate of the Church.

On Easter Sunday we are all asked to renew our baptismal vows and profession of faith. After doing so, we might say the following from the Rite of Confirmation:

> This is our faith. This is the faith of the Church. We are proud to profess it in Christ Jesus our Lord.

(Mobile, March 21, 1975)

– ♦ –

Q Why do you ask Catholics to subsidize inner-city schools when many of the students are non-Catholic and have no intention of becoming Catholic? Many Catholic parishes in the city and county are having a difficult time paying our own teachers a just wage.

A First of all, many of our converts each year do come to the Church from our inner-city parishes and especially from those which have parochial schools. But our motivation in maintaining these schools is not primarily to increase the numbers or the income of the Catholic Church.

We believe we must follow Jesus, who did not help only those who were Jews or prospective converts to Judaism or who could help that faith in one way or another. He helped the pagan Samaritans and Romans and all those most in need, regardless of religious loyalty. And he was criticized for it.

Certainly, the black children in our inner-city schools are most in need of equal education opportunity. Their parents search out our schools to give them a better chance in life, and they sacrifice to do so. (Tuition in these schools is often above the tuition in our more affluent parish schools.) Our Catholic schools care for our own, but I am proud that our parishes also freely help to subsidize our struggling inner-city schools. Presently, we are reappraising our work in these schools to achieve maximum effectiveness and economy. We hope to announce plans soon. Our inner-city schools do great good for many deserving black families and for the common good of this entire community. They teach as Jesus did.

(St. Louis, January 20, 1984)

– ◆ –

Beacon of Hope

That title is the theme of Catholic Schools Week. It is appropriate. Our Catholic schools are a beacon of hope for the years ahead.

It was quite the vogue about ten years ago to prophesy the inevitable demise of Catholic schools. The prophets of doom were accorded a hearing everywhere. Today religious schools of all denominations are alive and well. I am happy to say that such is also the case with our Catholic schools here in our Archdiocese of St. Louis.

Facts: All kinds of hearsay slips trippingly off many a tongue whenever schools are mentioned, so it might be helpful to review some official data.

- Our Catholic-school system in the St. Louis Archdiocese is the tenth largest in the United States (our archdiocese ranks twentieth in the overall Catholic population).
- The St. Louis Archdiocese is number one in the nation in Catholic-school enrollment in proportion to Catholic population. Our local commitment to Catholic education is evident.
- We now have 65,785 students in our 178 Catholic-elementary schools and 34 high schools. Then there are also the students in our local seminaries, Catholic colleges, and St. Louis University.
- An additional 25,785 students are enrolled in part-time Catholic education in our parish schools of religion. So there are well over 100,000 young people served by Catholic education here in our archdiocese.
- There are presently over 3,700 teachers: priests, religious, and laymen and women comprising the faculty in our full-time schools. Another 1,450 teachers serve in our part-time programs.
- On the parish and local level, thousands of people serve on individual school boards, volunteer in libraries, lunchrooms, and playgrounds, and help Catholic education in so many other ways.

So much for facts and figures. How quickly we review them, how rarely do we ponder their deeper significance.

Significance: What does this data review mean to us? Catholic people have provided a tremendous educational asset for this overall community. One of every five students in St. Louis City and County is in a Catholic school. In several other counties in this ten-county archdiocese, the ratio is higher. This year alone Catholic schools in this archdiocese are saving Missouri taxpayers more than 190 million dollars. More valuable than money is the education provided for so many young Missouri people, the productive citizens of tomorrow.

For our Catholic faith community, Catholic schools are also an invaluable asset. Recent research (McCready's *Young Catholics)* confirms conclusively past studies that today Catholic-school graduates are the active parishioners and the faithful families in the Church. The growing sacrifices of our people in maintaining our Catholic schools are worth it all. Our St. Louis Catholics remain committed to our schools. Our enrollments have stabilized, with first grade our largest class. Our Catholic schools are truly a beacon of hope for our Church and our community in the years to come. Full speed ahead!

(St. Louis, March 20, 1984)

– ◆ –

Another new start is well underway now in all our Catholic schools. It was encouraging to see them begin a new school year with no great fanfare in contrast to school strikes and turmoil around us.

I salute all our administrators, teachers, and staff that make it possible. They represent a remarkable blend of professional competence and dedication. All these people are worth far more than we are able to pay them. Their sacrifice is part of a miracle that continues to make our Catholic schools available to so many of our young people.

The other part of the miracle is those parents and parishioners who continue to supply the funds to keep our schools going. I know personally of many families whose effort is nothing short of heroic. Congratulations for having your priorities straight! And there are many folks without children in school who are the unsung heroes in many of our parishes. I just want to sing your praises right now.

Years ago in Washington at a national symposium, the Librarian of Congress said of Catholic schools, "Practically and financially they should never have gotten started, are impossible to run today, and ought not survive the demands of the future — but I suspect they will!" Thanks for proving him right. It is a miracle.

(St. Louis, September 14, 1984)

Our Schools: Past, Present, and Future

While the subject of schools is on the front burner these days, I want to say up-front once again that I strongly support Catholic schools at all levels. I firmly believe that Catholic schools give fine academic training, discipline, religious and moral formation. I believe that Catholic schools have a strong, positive impact on the adult life of those who have attended.

Already I hear parents saying, "What about tuition?"; teachers saying, "What about salaries?"; pastors saying, "What about cost to the parish?" I know that these are problems. I worry about them. I have no magic answers.

Financing education has been a problem for schools, public and private, since the time of our Founding Fathers. For solutions, we must all work together. What is important is *conviction* of the value of Catholic schools, the will and desire to give our children the very best foundation for a happy and productive life as adults and for a happy eternity.

History: During the nineteenth century (1800-1900), education became a very high priority for all Americans. At first, schools were one-room or small schoolhouses with one teacher. Many were started by churches and later were state supported "common schools," or public schools. Religion and Bible study were an important element in the curriculum of all schools. Disputes arose over what beliefs would be taught and what versions of the Bible would be read. Many of the schools were directed by the Protestant majority, and Catholics began to establish their own separate schools.

In the 1830s in New York, most parishes had schools that were usually in the basement of the church for about five thousand children. The major problem for these schools was finances. In 1838, Bishop John Hughes began a two-year battle to gain public funds from the New York Common Council. In this effort he was not successful.

Despite this setback, various factors contributed to the growing commitment to a separate Catholic-school system. The earliest factor was a strong anti-Catholic sentiment on the part of many U.S. citizens. Another factor was the influx of immigrants from Europe, who wanted to preserve not only their religion but also their language and culture. Many Catholic schools were German, French, Polish, Slovak, Czech, or Lithuanian. Many of these immigrant groups brought with them their own priests and nuns. A factor that made such a commitment realistic was the great number of women religious who were willing to teach for minimal salaries or even for nothing. In 1900 there were 40,340 women religious in the United States, mostly teachers. Of 119 religious communities, 91 were European or Canadian in origin.

The three Plenary Councils of the U.S. Bishops — Baltimore, 1852; Cincinnati, 1858; Baltimore, 1884 — were very strong in their support of Catholic schools, placing strong obligations on pastors to provide schools and on parents to enroll their children in Catholic schools.

Over the years the Catholic system, like its counterpart, the public-school system, has become more professional and sophisticated, more competently organized and supervised.

Future: The question arises: Since anti-Catholicism (while it has by no means disappeared) has abated, since we are no longer an immigrant Church, since we can and have taken our place in the mainstream of American life, since we wish to maintain friendly relationships with people of all beliefs, since the number of women religious teachers has been drastically reduced, since the two-hundred-year-old problem of financing has not gone away, since public funding seems remote, do Catholic schools still have a value?

I strongly affirm their value. Over the years, public schools, once ardently religious, have become secular and legally areligious. I see the inculcation of religious, spiritual, and moral values as having a very significant importance. In our amoral, areligious, undisciplined society, serious grounding in moral and spiritual values is more important than ever. I see the Catholic school not only as a place where teaching and training in skills takes place but also as an environment conducive to healthy growth, an atmosphere intimately related to parents and families and to the local Church. Studies by sociologist Father Andrew Greeley demonstrate that Catholic schools are academically superior, that they send more young people to college and to advanced studies than do public schools. His studies show that Catholic schools strongly influence the future behavior of their students. They significantly help their students acquire a sense of community, a social sense, and a commitment to social justice and provide a choice in education to minority and poor families. (They also enhance the life of the parish.)

This column is about Catholic schools. Nonetheless, I realize that many of our young people, for one reason or another, go to public schools. I believe that as citizens and taxpayers we should all be interested in excellence in public schools. I would encourage parents of children in public schools to take an active part in public-school boards and PTA groups. I would likewise strongly urge these parents to see to it that their sons and daughters attend the Parish School of Religion or religious-education programs in their parishes. While the PSR program does not involve the same amount of time or constancy as a school, the programs are nevertheless excellently organized and can be of very great help to your daughters and sons.

Cooperation: Of the thousands of youths heading for the classrooms in the St. Louis area this week, one of every four will be going to private schools, most of them parochial.

The contributions of parochial schools in the metropolitan area are significant. Many sections of the city have literally been saved by their presence. The quality of education they provide prompts increasing numbers of parents to choose them for the education of their children. Missouri taxpayers are saved at least $150 million each year because of them.

The quality of life depends greatly on a dual system of strong schools — private as well as public. Private and parochial schools are not places for the wealthy. Many of the students come from homes in which parents often deny themselves the necessities of life in order to pay tuition.

Nonreligious benefits from government should be available to all children, regardless of the school they attend. Freedom of choice in just about every aspect of American life is considered a fundamental right; freedom of choice in education is often penalized. For example, safety of children traveling to school in Missouri is a concern only if they travel to a public school. Although revenues are allocated according to the total number of students residing in a given district, the money is spent only for the benefit of the public-school children.

Unfortunately, discussion about the use of public money for children in the nonpublic schools often is viewed as a win-lose situation. Anything the children in private schools gain is a loss to public-school children. This doesn't have to be the case. There are all kinds of win-win possibilities if we ever get to the point where education of all children is considered an urgent priority in this city, in this state, and in this nation that values freedom of choice. Despite some unfortunate decisions, the U.S. Supreme Court has acknowledged that

> parochial schools, quite apart from their sectarian purpose, have provided an educational alternative for millions of young Americans; they often afford wholesome competition with our public schools; and in some states they relieve substantially the tax burden incident to the operation of the public schools. The states have, moreover, a legitimate interest in facilitating education in the highest quality for all children within its boundaries, whatever schools their parents have chosen for them.

(St. Louis, September 2, 1988)

— ◆ —

Myths and Facts

For just about a month now, almost seventy-three thousand students, from kindergarten through college, have been back in Catholic schools in our archdiocese. In this column, I'd like to salute them, their dedicated, hardworking teachers, and the tens of thousands of parents and others whose sacrifices make this great achievement possible.

Are those sacrifices worthwhile? Especially when free public education is available through high school and when public colleges cost far less than private ones? Some people will tell you they're not. For them, and for all of you, I've got good news. It comes from a book by two non-Catholic sociologists, James S. Coleman and Thomas Hoffer, *Public and Private High Schools: The Impact of Communities* (Basic Books).

The authors' research has uncovered facts that clearly refute several popular myths about our Catholic schools.

Myth: Catholic high schools do better than their public counterparts because they get rid of problem students.

Fact: Far from expelling problem students, Catholic schools have a dropout rate that is lower than in other schools. Moreover, they are far more likely to retain those with disciplinary and academic problems from sophomore to senior year. The dropout rate in public high schools from sophomore to senior year is fourteen percent. In private schools it is twelve percent. In Catholic schools it is (would you believe it?) three percent.

Myth: Catholic schools, lacking the financial resources of their public competitors, cannot compete academically.

Fact: The achievement of sophomores to seniors in Catholic schools, depending on the subject matter, is between one and two years beyond the two years' achievement of public-school students. Moreover, Catholic high-school graduates are more likely than their public-school counterparts to go on to college, to stay in college, and to do well there.

Chiefly responsible for the success of our Catholic schools is something called "social capital." This is the sociologist's way of saying that Catholic schools come out of, and are supported by, a community agreed on common values. Such values are lacking in public and other private schools.

"In many, if not most public schools," sociologist Father Andrew Greeley has written, "there is no value consensus at all. In the private schools, there is, perhaps, value consensus but not an ongoing network of relations outside the school. Only the religious schools (and some special schools in special situations) seem to have both value consensus and preexisting social networks that can be activated to sustain and support both the school and the student in the school."

The common values of the Catholic community help explain another fact uncovered by the Coleman-Hoffer study: "Parents are more likely to be active in the Catholic schools than are parents of either public or other private-school students. They are more likely to have attended a parent-teacher conference or a PTA meeting, visited classes, or volunteered to work in the schools."

The bottom line, according to Father Greeley: "The greater success of Catholic schools cannot be attributed to greater financial resources of either parents or schools but seems rather to be the result of the greater social resources of a community that shares not only values but also relationships."

Here in River City

St. Louis Catholics are justly proud of our Catholic-school system. If the network of Catholic schools and colleges in the United States is unique in the world (and it is), our local achievement is unique in the country. Although St. Louis ranks only twentieth in Catholic population among all American dioceses, we have a higher percentage of students in Catholic schools than any other diocese. Philadelphia, which has the next highest percentage, outstrips us in Catholic population almost three times.

This great heritage from the past is no reason for complacency. On the contrary, it challenges us to continued effort. None of us thinks our Catholic schools are perfect — or even as good as they could be. As we rededicate ourselves, however, at the start of a new school year to the never-ending task of maintaining and improving our schools, we can be proud of our accomplishment. The sacrifices we make are not in vain. They are deeply worthwhile. To all who make those sacrifices — teachers working for less than they could earn elsewhere, parents and others whose gifts support our schools — I say, from the bottom of my heart: "Thank you — and may God bless and reward you richly."

(St. Louis, October 2, 1987)

- 7 -
LAITY

The laity are called in a special way to make the Church present and operative in those places and circumstances where only through them can it become the salt of the earth.

(Constitution on the Church, #33)

Bishops, pastors, and priests...should remember that laypeople also have their own proper role in building up the Church. Therefore as brothers they should work with laypeople in the Church and for the Church, and show a special solicitude for lay people in their apostolic works.

(Decree on the Apostolate of the Laity, #25)

Perhaps you've read that the Holy Father has asked the next Synod of Bishops that will meet in Rome next year to discuss the vocation of the laity. As you know, too, we are having Synod 10 right here in our archdiocese. One of the big changes in Church life over the last two decades has been the rediscovery of the role of the laity. Some of us can still remember hearing that Catholic laypeople were supposed to "pay, pray, and obey." An exaggeration? Of course. But one whose effects still linger on.

"The Church," for many Catholics, still means the clergy. "He went into the Church" means "He became a priest." "Why doesn't the Church do something about it?" means "Let the bishops take care of it." Even in gatherings of the baptized, the Church is often not recognized as present until the priest arrives.

But that is not authentic Catholic teaching. The Second Vatican Council reminded us that though there are different functions in the Church, there is a fundamental equality among all the baptized.

> The chosen people of God is one: "One Lord, one faith, one baptism" (Ephesians 4:5). As members, they share a common dignity from their rebirth in Christ. They have the same filial grace and the same vocation to perfection....All share a true equality with regard to the dignity and to the activity common to all the faithful for building up the Body of Christ.
>
> *(Constitution on the Church, #32)*

Witness to World: How do laypeople fulfill the call to perfection that we all received in baptism? Vatican II gives a clear answer: in daily life, both at home and in the workplace.

> The family is, so to speak, the domestic Church. In it parents should, by their word and example, be the first preachers of the faith to their children. They should encourage them in the vocation which is proper to them, fostering with special care any religious vocation.
>
> The laity...seek the kingdom of God by engaging in temporal affairs and by ordering them according to the plan of God. They live in the ordinary circumstances of family and social life, from which the very web of their existence is woven. They are called there by God so that by exercising their proper function and being led by the spirit of the gospel, they can work for the sanctification of the world from within, in the manner of leaven. In this way they can make Christ known to others, especially by the testimony of a life resplendent in faith, hope, and charity.
>
> The laity are called in a special way to make the Church present and operative in those places and circumstances where only through them can she become the salt of the earth.
>
> *(Constitution on the Church, #11, 31, 33)*

That heavy, "official" language needs to be brought down to earth. A person who has done so quite successfully is Father Walter J. Burghardt, S.J. He inspired us priests with a beautiful vision of our role in the Church at our convocation in September. Here is Father Burghardt's "translation" of the Council's teaching about the vocation of the laity.

We were sent on mission the moment we were baptized. For Christ baptized us not simply for our own salvation...but to transform the world on which we walk, in which we work. Lay mission territory is where the laity live and move and have their being. For, with rare exceptions, only lay Christians can bring Christ to law, office, and legislature, to media and medicine, to public school and private industry, to executive suite and union hall, to the thousand and one areas of human living seldom open to the ordained. And note well: in these areas the laity are not replacing a shrinking clergy, are not substitutes waiting for the first team to come back on. These are the laity's grounds; here is their area of action; here *they* are the Church, by right and duty.

("Is Being 'Catholic' Worth Saving?":
Georgetown Magazine, Spring 1986, page 9)

Are laypeople called to express their faith *only* in the world? Don't they have a role in building up the Church as well? Of course they do. I hope to deal with that topic in this space next week. See you then!

(St. Louis, October 31, 1986)

Kenneth Guentert is a Catholic layman in San Jose, California. In an article in *U.S. Catholic* last January, he reflected on the difference between lay and priestly roles.

If priests preside over the literal Eucharist, the transformation of bread and wine, the laity presides over the symbolic Eucharist, the transformation of the world....The task of transforming the world — of making peace, feeding the hungry, sheltering the homeless, caring for the sick — is not a priestly task. It belongs to the nurses, the realtors, the farmers, the secretaries, the judges, and the unskilled.

Guentert sees a shortage today not just of priests but of qualified laypeople as well. A "qualified layperson," he explains,

is any nonprofessional Catholic with the imagination to connect the creative work of his or her life to the creative work of God. Every occupation — from automaking to repairing power lines — has some connection to God. Every task — from diapering a baby to spreading compost on the garden — has some connection to creation. Sometimes a negative connection (as in dumping toxic waste, for example).

Guentert is right. The hour or so that laypeople spend at Mass on Sunday is supposed to empower and inspire them for the call we all received in baptism: to make Christ and his Church present in daily life.

Does the lay vocation end there? Of course not. The English Cardinal Hume of Westminster believes we still need to emphasize that the laity's principal role is to be found "in the conscientious discharge of family responsibilities and in daily life at work in society." He adds, however:

> It would be a mistake to insist too rigidly on a distinction of roles. It is unhelpful to assign to the clergy an exclusively "churchy" role and to the laity exclusively a secular one. Laity have a role within the life of the Church as well as within society.

Inside Too: This takes us into what today is called lay ministry — the involvement of laypeople in the ministry of the Church. Few areas of Church life have undergone such rapid development in recent years as this one. Little more than two decades ago the role of laypeople in the Church was mostly limited to housekeeping tasks: counting the Sunday collection, running bazaars and other fund-raising events, and maintenance of the church plant and grounds.

Consider, by contrast, the many ministerial roles open to Catholic laypeople today:

- Reading the Scriptures at Mass
- Leading the intercessions at the prayer of the faithful
- Distributing holy Communion in church and to the sick and shut-ins at home
- Preparing engaged couples for holy matrimony
- Pastoral ministry in hospitals and priestless parishes

In addition to these activities and many more like them, laypeople contribute their expertise and views in consultative bodies at all levels: parish and deanery councils, our Archdiocesan Pastoral Council, and now in the eleven committees preparing our Archdiocesan Synod, which will meet in 1989.

Responsible for these developments was the rediscovery at the Second Vatican Council, which met in 1962 to 1965, of an ancient Catholic truth: the fundamental importance of baptism. Sadly, there are still Catholics who think of baptism as a kind of religious vaccination. In truth, baptism commissions us for the Lord's service. There are not two classes of people in the Church — active and passive — corresponding to the clergy and the laity. In baptism, we were all given active roles.

Vatican II explicitly recognized the laity's unique role in the Church. It commanded the Church's pastors to "make willing use of laypeople's prudent advice...confidently assigning them duties in the service of the Church, allowing them freedom and room for action...[and] encouraging them to undertake tasks on their initiative" (*Constitution on the Church,* #37). Bishops especially are to "recognize [the laity's] duty and right to collaborate actively in the building up of the Mystical Body of Christ" (*Decree on Bishops,* #16).

The Council told laypeople to look to priests "for spiritual light and nourishment," but "not to imagine that [their] pastors are always such experts, that to every problem that arises, however complicated, they can readily give...a concrete solution, or even that such is their mission" (*Church in the Modern World,* #43). The lengthy hearings that preceded the two pastoral letters of American Bishops — the 1983 *Pastoral on Peace,* and its forthcoming sequel of *Economic Justice* — put into practice the Council's recognition of lay expertise.

Despite the great strides we have made, however, the old attitude that "Father knows best" dies hard. Sometimes priests resist change; quite as often, resistance comes from laypeople. All of us, clergy and laypeople, need to recall that the Church is not ours, but Christ's. The parish does not belong to the pastor or the diocese to the bishop. Neither do diocese or parish belong to the laypeople. All of us together are servants of a common Master. We have "one Lord, one faith, one baptism; one God and Father of all, who is over all and through all and in all" (Ephesians 4:5f).

(St. Louis, November 7, 1986)

— ◆ —

Parishes in the Laity's Life

(Address to the Bishops' Synod in Rome, October 5, 1987)

I. Introduction

For almost two years in preparation for the Synod the Church in the United States has been engaged in dialogue. The focus: the life, needs, hopes, and gifts of the laity; and the many ways in which laymen and women generously and creatively contribute to the mission of the Church.

During these two years the National Conference of Catholic Bishops' delegates to this synod have been listening to the two hundred thousand men and women who have participated in our consultation. And we have tried to listen to those whose voices are muted: the otherwise silent ones; people on the fringes; the alienated and, yes, the angry ones. We have learned from this listening, convinced again that the Spirit of God is active among the faithful. It has been a serious and sacred conversation. As we reviewed all the materials collected during this consultation process, a single theme emerged cogently and consistently. We have chosen to express this under-lying theme as "co-discipleship for the mission of the Church in the world." This includes four basic theological concepts:

1. We are all disciples of Jesus Christ.
2. All of us share responsibility for carrying out his mission.
3. The Church's mission is the extension of Jesus' proclamation and promotion of the Good News in the service of the kingdom.
4. While the Church's understanding of its own nature is described in Vatican II's dogmatic constitution *Lumen Gentium,* its mission to the world is best expressed in the pastoral constitution *Gaudium et Spes:* "the role of the Church in the Modern World" (40-42).

As we have reflected and prayed with the laymen and women of our country, as we have analyzed their concerns and expressed needs, the following facets of Christian life emerge:

— The relationship that exists between the Church and the world and that relationship to the kingdom of God.

— The role of women in our Church.

— The spiritual life of our laity and their own experience of faith.

When our people talk about God's presence in their lives, the primary place they identify is their family. Next is their parish. That is my topic today.

II. The Parish: Communion, Community, Mission
1. Communion

"Every day the Church gives birth to the Church." So says Saint Bede. Every generation must proclaim what the first generation of Christians proclaimed; and when a new generation of Christians receives that proclamation in faith and love, the Church is again generated.

The Eucharist is the prototypical representation of the Church. Or as *Lumen Gentium,* No. 26, states, "The Eucharist makes the Church, and the Church makes the Eucharist." And as the council also noted, eucharistic assemblies are called "churches" in the New Testament. Parishes represent the first and often the most crucial experience individuals have of the church. The diocesan and the universal church is realized for most Catholics in the parish.

In the presynod consultation within the United States, after the family, the parish was most often cited as the place where people experience God's presence. In the preaching of God's Word and in the sacraments, especially the Eucharist, people meet the Lord.

In the average U.S. Catholic parish about one thousand Catholics, half of all the parishioners, assemble each Sunday for the Eucharist.[1] Another few hundred will not let a month go by without joining them.[2] A little more than sixty percent of them are women,[3] but the men who are present are as likely as the women to take part in other parish activities as well.[4] It is largely social activities that broaden most parishioners' participation in parish life, but three of every ten registered parishioners will be present for two or more parish events besides the Sunday liturgy.[5]

2. Community

Most laypeople who participated in our consultation regard small communities within the parish as vital in deepening their life of faith and enabling them to fulfill whatever ministry God has for them.

---

1 There are over 19,000 parishes in the United States. The median size of these parishes in approximately 2,000 Catholics (cf. *Parish Life in the United States,* final report to the Bishops of the United States by the Parish Project, November 1982; U.S. Catholic Conference Office of Publishing Services, page 23. Hereafter this report is cited as *Parish Life.*). Estimates vary concerning church attendance by Catholics, hovering around half of all U.S. Catholics each week. One reliable report puts the weekly rate of attendance at 53 percent (cf. George Gallup Jr. and Jim Castelli, *The American Catholic People,* Garden City, NY, Doubleday, 1987, page 26. This is hereafter referred to as Gallup-Castelli.).

2 Gallup-Castelli, page 28.

3 Cf. David Leege and Joseph Gremillion, eds., Notre Dame Study of Catholic Life, Report No. 2, page 6. Hereafter they are cited as CPL.

4 Cf. Philip J. Murnion, "Parish Leadership," *The Parish in Transition,* David Byers, ed., Washington: USCC, 1985, page 62.

5 Cf. CPL, No. 3, page 6.

Small communities are proliferating in our parishes. The RENEW program has been most fruitful in this development in the U.S.A. So has the de Sales program of small-group prayer, study and action. The Rite of Christian Initiation of Adults gives promise of continued growth in small-group work along with many other programs in our country.

These communities provide the ongoing formation of the laity in prayer, Scripture study, life-sharing and outreach to the needs of society.

Our laity seek this community experience within, or at least along with, their regular parish experience. Since most of our parishes, especially in cities, are large, such small groups are more and more necessary for productive Catholic life. Parish councils in most of our parishes have led in encouraging shared responsibility by our laypeople.

Our young people especially are searching for meaning, for belonging. In the United States, growing numbers of young adults are serving as volunteers in both domestic and foreign missions — a result of their formation in these small groups. Small communities put a human face on our Church.

It is a matter of concern to us that these groups not be content with supporting individuals in their private lives but also empower members for the mission of Christ in the world. Greater recovery of the observe-judge-act method can help to underscore the fact that private faith must have public consequences.

3. Mission and Ministry

The Council's description of the laity includes their participation in the mission of the church to the world.

The laity of the United States see the development of lay ministry as integral to their faith. They recognize clearly the essentially unique role of the ordained minister, but they have a strong sense of their share in the mission of Jesus Christ and the Church by virtue of their baptism. Very few persons mention the lack of ordained priests as the primary reason for lay ministry — collaborative ministry is their high priority — codiscipleship.

There is no desire to replace priests or to take over traditional "priestly" work, but there is a desire to contribute all that laypeople can so that priests can concentrate on their primary pastoral roles. Our people see this role in the work of ecumenism in our religiously pluralistic country, in evangelism, in bringing Catholic values to the professions, in government, in the marketplace, and above all, in family life.

The parish exists not for itself, but for the mission of Christ. And so people are called forth to minister to one another in the parish community as well as to those around them where they live and work.[1] The parish remains the primary means for encouraging and equipping Christ's faithful to exercise their "obligation and right to strive so that the divine message of salvation may more and more reach all people of all times and places."[2]

To join in spreading the message of salvation is to share in the work of evangelization and human development and to see the relationship among the two.[3] It is primarily the vitality of the parish community itself, in all the ways already described, that in the Catholic style is the instrument of evangelization and the source of understanding and encouragement for the work of human development. Describing and expressing the communion of all God's children and the sacramental potential of all human action, parishes, through their liturgy and teaching, their work of hope and charity, and their opportunities for reflection and mutual support, remain the most reliable resource for the mission of the Church.

The parish as a medium for people's participation in the mission of the Church throughout the world needs more consideration.[4] Through their parishes, Catholics in the United States continue to offer ever increased financial support for the Church's mission in the world through the Society for the Propagation of the Faith, the Catholic Relief Services, and many other forms of mission aid. Nonetheless, we must continue to find ways, spurred on by our own recent pastoral letter on the missionary work of the Church, to foster a sense of solidarity between Christ's faithful in individual parishes and the people of the world and between evangelization and the work for human development. Some individual parishes have done remarkable things to express these relationships, such as individually operating health stations in sections of Africa or twinning with a parish in the Third World. We need to keep fostering a sense of the solidarity of all of Christ's faithful and of all of the human family. There is a great tradition of this in

1 NCCB Committee on the Parish.
2 Canon 211.
3 This was especially developed in the Vatican II Decree on Missionary Activity, *Ad Gentes*, e.g., Nos. 11-12.
4 The NCCB has addressed this concern in its recent pastoral letter on the Church's missionary work, *To the Ends of the Earth*.

parishes partly because our people are from all parts of the world; we need to keep celebrating and expanding this tradition.

Conclusion

In the light of the preceding considerations, I respectfully propose for discussion the following questions:

How can national or regional lay movements work more effectively through parishes rather than apart from them?

How can we nurture in the proliferating small communities of faith in our parishes a true sense of the diocesan and universal Church?

How can we most effectively bring the ministry of our people within the parish into lay service to the needs of the world?

(Origins, 17 [1987] 353, 355f)

(Report to the Bishops' Conference on the Synod)

The Synod was a time of listening and learning for all of us. During the first days of this collegial gathering, bishops and invited observers from around the world had an opportunity...to share their insights. We heard stories of cruel oppression and contemporary martyrdom. We heard stories of courage and faith on the part of laity, priests, religious and bishops. What we heard were vivid, concrete examples of co-discipleship.

It was interesting for us to learn that the concerns of American Catholics are shared by laity in most areas of the world. Questions like How can parishes be vital centers of spirituality and mission? What kind of spiritual formation do laity need or want? How can women's gifts and competencies be more fully incorporated into the life of the Church at every level? In exploring such questions together, we discovered many areas of shared faith, commitment, and concern.

We listened to hundreds of interventions and we spent hours in small working groups. A number of topics surfaced then, for example, Catholic laity's involvement in the political arena; spirituality and formation; the need to clarify ministries; the importance of marriage and family in lay life and in the life of the wider Church; appreciation for the contribution of youth to the life of the Church; and recognition of the parish as "a community of communities." But two in particular could be called major.

1. The role of women in the Church very quickly became a principal concern of the synod. Interventions from bishops all over the world and reports from the *circuli minores* emphasized the need to address this issue forthrightly and now....There is a serious and profound need to admit women to decision-making positions at all levels of the Church, including the international level. Interventions of the U.S. delegates often asked specifically for this and also that the ministries of acolyte and lector be open to women. Bishops from other countries requested serious study of the diaconate for women....Opening nonordained ministries to all Catholics, in keeping with local circumstances and pastoral judgments, is a matter of principle based on the radical equality of all the faithful in baptism.

Even though specific recommendations such as the above are not to be found in either the message from the synod or in the propositions presented to the Holy Father, the synod did reinforce the conviction growing in the United States: namely, the issue of women's role in Church and society must be addressed effectively by the Church in the United States.

2. The other topic which held central place at the synod was that of lay movements and their relationship to the local church. The issue is this: Over the past years, especially in Europe, large lay organizations have emerged, deeply committed to various forms of the apostolate and so centrally organized that they operate in parishes and dioceses oftentimes independent of local responsibility and accountability. For some, these are signs of the direction of the Holy Spirit in our times; for others, their charism needs to be discerned on the local level by the bishop and their apostolate endeavors coordinated by him with the other efforts in his diocese.

Our discussions recognized that the charisms of the Spirit can be and often are present in these new lay organizations. But it was generally underlined that the local bishop also has the responsibility and charism of discerning the role of a particular movement in his pastoral plan of his diocese. The bishops in synod also urged that these movements incorporate a more profound commitment to justice and to the service of the poor.

Message to the People of God

A message from the synodal fathers was drafted....What is perhaps most noteworthy about this message is a *Gaudium-et-Spes* consciousness, that is, a recognition that the church lives and moves and has its being in the world (as well as in God), for the world, too, dwells and breathes — abides — in God. Our own theme of co-discipleship has found a place in this message, not so much in words as in tone. The synodal fathers address the lay faithful in a spirit of humble solidarity, recalling the words of Saint Augustine, "Christian with you; bishops for you." The message reminds not only the laity of their call to holiness but of our call, as bishops, to serve the laity.

Follow-up

I think it is necessary to consider the synod in terms of our pastoral life and mission at home: in our country, in our dioceses, in our parishes, in our homes. And ultimately, it is up to us to make concrete whatever inspiration and insight we have gained from this synodal experience of shared prayer and discussion....I think at this time we can say, as an episcopal conference, the following:

1. We are committed to continued consultation with the laity, building on the dialogue and mutual respect which has grown between laity and bishops, not only during the preparation for the Synod but in the last several years as we prepared our major pastoral letters on peace and the economy. In doing so, we must make creative use of existing structures and explore development of new ones.

2. We will promote study and research into spirituality and formation, including the laity in these efforts.

3. We will commit ourselves to cooperation with women, welcoming their involvement and leadership both in Church and society. We look to the pastoral letter on the concerns of women now being prepared by our conference as a significant contribution to this effort.

4. We will make every effort to build on the global awareness of the lay vocation and mission which this synod has strengthened, promoting a mission consciousness.

5. We will study the themes of this synod, through appropriate NCCB-USCC committee structures and locally in our diocese and parishes.

6. When the Holy Father issues a statement on the laity, we will energetically use the appropriate resources of the conference to implement the statement.

Conclusion

The last part of the Message of the Synod is a series of appeals. In one of these, the synod fathers implore young men and women with these words: "You carry on your shoulders the hopes of the world and the Church. Do not allow yourselves to be frightened by the world you see." We might paraphrase that for ourselves. We carry with us the hopes, the needs, the trust, the fears, as well as the generous contributions of the lay faithful who form the vast body of our Church. The laity have cared enough to dialogue with us in great candor and great charity. We must not allow ourselves to become frightened by what we see and hear, but rather we must allow ourselves to look to Christ who dwells within the *christifideles* as surely as he does with us, to listen to him and how we might create a more just and loving world and a more responsive Church.

(Origins, 17 [1987] 447f)

"Stand Still and See the Salvation of God"

(Address to the Leadership Council of Catholic Laity, St. Louis, March 6, 1992)

You have asked me to speak about "tensions within the American Church, and ways for both bishops and laity to respond lovingly and creatively."

I would like to address these tensions in three areas:

1. With regard to the role of the laity in the inner life of the Church;
2. With regard to the laity's mission to the world outside the Church;
3. With regard to the role of women, within the Church and in society at large.

1. The Role of the Laity Within the Church. A recent incident in one of our parishes illustrates a form of tension between clergy and laity that I believe is widespread in American Catholicism today. The pastor concerned is a priest who values lay participation in parish life and consults with those to whom he ministers before making important decisions.

At a parish council meeting, criticism of a decision by the pastor crystalized in the objection, heatedly expressed by a young woman: "But Father, it's *our* parish."

The pastor replied: "No, Mary, it is not your parish. And it is certainly not my parish. It is the Lord's parish. We all serve him."

At the next council meeting, when tempers had cooled, the pastor explained his response as follows: "Last month as we sat around this table, we were told: 'It's our parish.' If the 'our' in that statement is *inclusive,* then I affirm the statement a hundred times over. But that was not what we heard here last month. 'It's our parish' really meant, 'ours, not yours.' What was really being said was something like this: 'It's our parish, Father, not yours. And if you don't do what we want you to do, we're going to cut off your water and you can have your parish all to yourself."

The story has an ironic postlude. Many months later, when discussion in the council turned to the parish's financial problems, one of those who had been most insistent that the parish belonged to the parishioners and not to the pastor turned to him and remarked, with obvious satisfaction: "Yeah, you're broke." The man was only too ready to turn the parish over to the pastor when it was a question of finding the funds necessary to do the Lord's work.

That violates not merely logical consistency but — what is far more important — a fundamental principle of the gospel: Jesus' teaching that ordinary worldly standards cannot apply among his followers: "You know how among the Gentiles those who seem to exercise authority lord it over them; their great ones make their importance felt. It cannot be like that among you. Anyone among you who aspires to greatness must serve the rest; whoever wants to rank first among you must serve the needs of all" (Mark 10:42ff and parallels).

Those words of Jesus are directed first of all to the Church's officeholders. We are the ones most susceptible to the temptation of lording it over people rather than serving them. Indeed, in Luke's Gospel, Jesus' words are the response to an argument among the Twelve at the Last Supper about "who should be regarded as the greatest" (Luke 22:24).

And yes, in the preconciliar Church, too many pastors thought of the parish as theirs to do with as they pleased — an attitude that merely replicated, at the parish level, that of many bishops toward their dioceses.

You cannot correct this unchristian attitude, however, by substituting for it the idea, taken over from secular democracy, that Church officeholders are delegates of the people bound to carry out the wishes of those they represent. The pastor in the parish, the bishop as pastor of his local Church, the pope as pastor of the universal Church, represent not the people they serve but the Lord.

Consultation is important. And a pastor, at any level of Church life, must have weighty reasons for overriding the results of such consultation. Sometimes, however, the service a pastor owes to his people requires that he do just that. Fortunately, such instances are rare. If a pastor frequently acts against the advice he receives, it is a sign that something is wrong: with the pastor, with his advisers, perhaps with both.

Vatican II emphasized that there is a real equality of all the baptized. But this does not cancel the fact that some in the Church have real spiritual authority over others. How else can we make sense of Peter's treatment of Ananias and Sapphira in Acts 5? They were the unfortunate couple, you recall, who fell down dead at Peter's feet because they lied about the amount of money received from the sale of property and subsequently donated to the Christian community.

If in today's Church the unchristian argument about "who should be greatest" involves not just the clergy but increasingly the laity as well, this is in large measure because, following the Council, we neglected to show those who serve on our newly introduced consultative bodies how to exercise their role in accordance with the standards of the gospel rather than those of secular democracy.

How do we respond "lovingly and creatively" to the tensions that have resulted from this neglect? By renewed efforts at Christian formation and by deeper conversion of heart on the part of clergy and laity alike.

2. The Mission and Role of the Laity Outside the Church. The involvement of laypeople in Church life — not merely in consultative bodies but in the liturgy and works of charity — is one of the big success stories of the postconciliar Church. Too often, however, this success has been purchased at too high a price: neglect of what the Council clearly and repeatedly says is the laity's primary role: "To make the Church present and operative in those places and circumstances where only through them can it become the salt of the earth" (LG 33) — in other words, in the secular world.

Only a minority of laypeople will ever be members of Church consultative bodies, lectors, ministers of Communion, and the like. All laypeople, however, are called, the Council says, to "work for the sanctification of the world from within as a leaven" (LG 31). How well are we preparing laypeople for this, their primary mission? Inadequately, at best.

If you doubt that, I suggest you ask yourself two questions. How often have you heard of workshops for parish council members, lectors, or ministers of Communion? And when did you last hear of a Church-sponsored workshop to help business people, public-school teachers, trade-union activists, members of the military, engineers, lawyers, or health professionals "make the Church present and operative" in their respective spheres of work, Monday through Friday?

The signers of the 1977 *Chicago Declaration of Christian Concern* stated:

> While many in the Church exhaust their energies arguing internal issues, albeit important ones, such as the ordination of women and a married clergy, Christians who spend most of their time and energy in the professional and occupational world appear to have been deserted.

Little has happened in American Catholicism in the fifteen years since that protest was first launched to render it obsolete.

Still valid as well is the *Declaration's* further complaint:

> Many priests and other Church professionals have acted as if the primary responsibility in the Church for uprooting injustice, ending wars, and defending human rights rested with them. As a result, they bypassed the laity to pursue social causes on their own rather than enabling Christians to shoulder their own responsibility....The impression is often created that one can work for justice and peace only by stepping outside of the ordinary roles as a business person, as a mayor, as a factory worker, as a professional in the State Department, or as an active union member and thus that one can change the system only as an *outsider* to the society and the system.

Time was when Catholics *were* outsiders in American society. Today we are insiders. In a host of publications, Andrew Greeley has given the sociological data to support that statement. We need to take far more seriously than we have yet done the concluding plea of the *Chicago Declaration*: "In the last analysis, the Church speaks to and acts upon the world through her laity. Without a dynamic laity conscious of its personal ministry to the world, the Church, in effect, does not speak and act."

3. The Role of Women in the Church and in Society. Few topics arouse so much heat and so many tensions in American Catholicism today as this one. Dealing with these tensions lovingly and creatively demands renewed attention to our twofold call as Catholic Christians: the call to be counter-cultural and the call to give full weight to Church tradition.

There is much in the agenda of contemporary feminism that we Catholics can support. The demand for equality before the law, equality in the marketplace, and equal job opportunities: these are matters of simple justice. We cannot support legalized abortion. In the face of a culture which says that the right of the unborn to life can be overridden by the right of their mothers to self-fulfillment and happiness, we must defend the right to life of society's weakest and most helpless members: babies in the womb. In the face of a culture which claims that abortion-on-demand contributes to women's liberation, we must continue to insist that abortion is the ultimate exploitation of women by irresponsible men.

The call to be countercultural also means being vigilant about feminist demands which diminish respect for women who choose to be full-time mothers and housewives or that erode legal protections for such women. Equal access for women to jobs is one thing. Quite another is a legal or social system that leads women who forgo gainful employment in favor of motherhood and child rearing to think that they have chosen second-best.

The call to be countercultural also rules out arguments for the ordination of women based on embarrassment in the face of a culture which charges that in refusing to ordain women, the Catholic Church is denying them equal rights. If women are ever to be ordained in the Catholic Church, this must be for *theological* reasons; not because we are embarrassed at the charge of today's sophisticated opinion that in this matter, as in that of abortion and many others, we Catholics are unenlightened, behind the times, and just not "with it."

It is no secret that there are some theologians who think there *are* theological arguments for the ordination of women. This position is sharply rejected by our present Holy Father. Precisely because the argument for women's ordination seems persuasive to so many in our culture, I ask you to consider that the rejection of this argument by the Church's present leadership is not due merely to obscurantism or cultural influence (Polish, Italian, or whatever). The fundamental motive is something far more important, something with which we Americans do not have much ex-perience: *respect for Church tradition.*

A two-thousand-year-old tradition of ordaining only men, especially when coupled with the conviction, which continues to prevail in the Church, that this reflects the Lord's will for his Church, cannot be changed by majority vote. That is the way of American democracy. It is not the way of the Catholic Church.

Change in a matter so fundamental to the Church's life will be possible (if it ever comes, which we cannot predict with certainty) only in the face of *an overwhelming consensus of the people of God that the Spirit is calling us in this direction.* I see no such consensus even in American Catholicism. In the worldwide Church, it is not even on the horizon. In this situation it is neither loving nor creative to demand that American Bishops, or bishops anywhere, should support the ordination of women.

Conclusion

Amid all this talk of tensions, it is easy to become dispirited. And I haven't even mentioned further sources of tension and worry, such as the decline in religious vocations, in church financial support, and the anomaly of a Church whose leaders plead for economic justice in the marketplace but too often find themselves unable to extend this justice to their own employees.

There are plenty of people today who cry alarm, who castigate Church leadership for refusing to follow their demands. Such voices come from both left and right. Bishops find themselves mostly in the middle — perhaps not a bad place for people who are supposed to be centers and guardians of the Church's unity.

I find few of these criers of alarm creative. Nor are some especially loving. What we need in today's Church, above all, is renewed confidence in the providence of God, who is able to write straight on the crooked lines of our unfaithfulness.

A man who had that confidence, and can help us regain it today, was John Henry Newman. I hope that beneath his serpentine prose you can hear the authentic note of Catholic faith.

> Christianity has been too often in what seemed deadly peril, that we should fear for it any new trial now. So far is certain; on the other hand, what *is* uncertain, and in these great contests commonly *is* uncertain, and what is commonly a great surprise, when it is witnessed, is the particular mode

by which, in the event, Providence rescues and saves His elect inheritance. Sometimes our enemy is turned into a friend; sometimes he is despoiled of that special virulence of evil which was so threatening; sometimes he falls to pieces of himself; sometimes he does just so much as is beneficial, and then is removed. Commonly the Church has nothing more to do than to go in her own proper duties, in confidence and peace; to stand still and to see the salvation of God.

(Newman's *Biglietto* speech in Rome, May 12, 1879;
cited from W.R. Neville [ed.],
Address to Cardinal Newman With His Replies,
1879-1881 [London 1905], pages 69f)

- 8 -
PRIESTS

Bishops should always embrace priests with a special love, since the latter to the best of their ability assume the bishop's anxieties and carry them on day by day so zealously. They should regard the priests as sons and friends and be ready to listen to them.... They should be solicitous for the spiritual, intellectual, and material welfare of the priests so that the latter can live holy and pious lives and fulfill their ministry faithfully and fruitfully.... With active mercy bishops should pursue priests who are involved in any danger or who have failed in certain respects.

(Decree on the Pastoral Office of Bishops, #16)

Appointing priests to their various assignments is one of the most important responsibilities of a bishop. Perhaps it causes him more concern than almost anything else. I know that much of a priest's personal welfare and happiness, and so much of the people's needs, can only be served by the appointment of the right man for the right place. Such decisions are usually the result of hours of consultation and prayerful consideration. The priests' own personnel board (five priests elected by their fellow priests) are a great help in this process. But, ultimately, the buck stops here. The final decision and responsibility rests with me. So please pray for me in this awesome task.

After being appointed a bishop, I had the privilege of having an audience with Pope Paul VI, along with several others who had received similar appointments. The Pope said words I have never forgotten: "You have good priests in America. Above all, as bishops, be good to your priests."

(Mobile, September 14, 1970)

– ♦ –

Here we are — the night before Christmas and all through the land, every pastor is smiling with things well in hand! The missalettes have been spread through the pews with care, in the hope that parishioners all soon will be there.

Christmas is different for priests. For many of them, as here in Alabama, it is not a day spent with all the family, a day of well-fed recuperation from the weeks of shopping and cleaning and mailing.

Priests are often surrounded by hundreds of people at many crowded Masses in big parishes. Or they are weary from the miles of driving from church to church, from midnight on, in the mission areas. And early in the afternoon, after the last usher has put away his collection basket and the last church door is locked, the priest is so very much alone. His family may be across the country or across the ocean. It is a tired time, a time for long, quiet thoughts, a time of memories of Christmas past.

(Mobile, December 24, 1971)

Proper Garb

Here in our archdiocese, I have been generally gratified by the clerical garb of our clergy. This is not the case everywhere in our country, I assure you. So as the summer comes on, I hope that we will keep up our good manners and image. A clerical shirt and collar are certainly acceptable in an informal setting around the parish. But please notice that at receptions, wakes, ecumenical and civic gathers, and so forth, gentlemen, and especially professional men, dress in a suit coat and tie. Clergy should do no less in wearing a coat and collar out of respect for all present and more so for our own calling. Casual sweaters, jackets, and just a short-sleeve clergy shirt are a bit gauche. We should not be stuffy, but we should always appear as gentlemen, properly groomed and dressed. Our people deserve to be proud of our appearance. We represent them and their Church on all such occasions.

(Notanda, May 21, 1982)

Clergy Appointments

They come every year at this time in considerable number and then as needed all through the year, too. Many folks may wonder about all this, so just a few words of explanation may be in order.

It is helpful for every priest to have experience in a number of different appointments, especially in his earlier years of priestly service. Accordingly, associate pastors usually serve a limited number of years in each appointment.

Pastors are often changed also — sometimes at their own request, sometimes because of parish or personal needs, sometimes when deaths or emergencies create a vacancy, and so forth. The same is true for our clergy in administrative and teaching positions. No priest is ever given a position for life or an indefinite period, since all must be subject to regular review.

Who does the review? Our priests elect six of their peers according to age groupings, to serve on our clergy personnel board. Throughout the year, this board meets regularly to consider needs presented by our parish councils and our priests and deacons. Our auxiliary bishops, vicar general, and chancellor often add to the consultation. From this process, recommendations are made to me and I make the tentative decision.

The final stage is confidential consultation with the priest to be appointed in case he wishes to raise some consideration that may not have been seen. If not, he is expected to accept the appointment in keeping with the promise of obedience every priest makes to his bishop on his ordination day. Then I make the official appointment in personal letters to the clergy concerned, and the announcement is made in the *St. Louis Review.*

Naturally, there will be delight and disappointment for many people reading the clergy appointment list. It is ever so. But I assure you that we do try hard to meet the needs of all — our clergy and our people. It is a big, tough job, one of the most serious responsibilities I bear as archbishop. In case you are wondering right now about a particular appointment, read and ponder the following. This piece appeared in a national column some years back, as a clergyman's application for an open pastorate.

Dear Friends:

Understanding your pulpit is vacant, I should like to apply for the position of pastor.

I've been a preacher with much success and also I have had some success as a writer. Some say I'm a good organizer. I've been a leader most places I've been.

I'm over fifty years of age. I have never preached in one place for more than three years. In some places I have left town after my work has caused riots and disturbances. I must admit I have been in jail three or four times, but not because of any real wrongdoing on my part. My health is not too good, though I still get a great deal done.

The churches in which I have preached have been small, though located in several large cities. I've not gotten along well with religious leaders in towns where I have preached. In fact, some have threatened me and even attacked me physically.

However, if you can use me, I shall do my best for you.

(signed)
The Apostle Paul

(St. Louis, May 27, 1983)

Personnel Problems

One of the problems that I have to deal with occasionally is what should be done when a priest — pastor or associate — and his parishioners seem to be on a collision course. I don't mean simply when a parishioner has a difficulty with a priest and asks me to reconcile the matter. That's easy. I just send the letter of complaint to the priest involved and ask for some response. Usually that opens up communication between the person and the priest, allows misapprehensions to be corrected and peace to be restored. And the matter is handled at the local level, where it should be since none of us here in "the round house on Lindell" can really know all that is going on in a given parish.

The real problem comes when for one reason or another, a priest and the people he serves just don't get along anymore. Complaints come in and as chief pastor of the archdiocese, I do have to consider the matter.

These words are addressed to the laity involved in such problems; I regularly communicate with the priests through a special newsletter I send them. Believe me, I do know that in these unhappy cases — fortunately relatively few — there is plenty of soul-searching to be done by both sides.

I would first remind all concerned (as Saint Paul did) that the Christian community is a community of love. What sort of sign do we give to the world of the love of Christ if we cannot bear with one another? Love does not mean a silent acceptance of injustice or other moral weakness. But it does mean that all parties to the problem attempt to put aside personal hurts to come to an acceptable solution. It also means that we put up with the same human weakness that we expect to be tolerated in ourselves.

In addition, many people fail to realize that there is no way that a pastor can satisfy all members of the parish community. We sometimes receive complaints about a pastor, some upset because he is too slow with change and some upset because he is moving too fast. Often, dissatisfaction with a priest reflects divisions within the parish itself, divisions that the parish community need to address honestly.

I would also ask our people to be understanding of the background of the priests serving them. Priests whose seminary education was received prior to the mid 1960s were taught a somewhat different outlook on theology, liturgy, and also on the rights and responsibilities of laypeople, than priests ordained later. We have attempted to update in our clergy continuing education programs, but that is not easy and many priests feel conscience-bound to some of the forms of ministry that many parishioners today find patronizing and stifling. On the other hand, men ordained since the mid 1960s come out of the seminary and, in attempting to implement what they have been taught, find opposition and misunderstanding from people whose religious formation leads them to dislike and even fear some of the things that younger priests say and do. Again, the Christian community needs love and understanding, as it always has.

Finally, suppose there is a priest who is often wrong about many things in his ministry and, despite admonition, simply cannot change. Should he simply be moved to another parish or would that only move the problem somewhere else? He might well be a man of prayer, of personal and quiet charity, and a man of many other virtues. Would it be a reasonable and Christian act to remove such a person from ministry? Can there not be better solutions within the parish community?

Again and again I must insist on patience and understanding from our priests toward parishioners of one particular mind-set. I know that our people are also products of their religious education and parish customs. Change is harder, much harder, for some than for others. Priests need to understand that in their people. I tell them that often. Today I have pretty much the same message for our people as they size up their pastors.

All of us involved in these difficult situations have responsibilities. I am aware that I have primary responsibilities to both our priests and people. I stand willing and ready to take the necessary steps to assure insofar as possible that our parishes will have the leadership and the example they have a right to expect. Saint Paul asked the early Church to "bear with one another's weaknesses." That is what I would ask of the Church of St. Louis in 1983.

(St. Louis, August 5, 1983)

— ◆ —

"Let's Hang Together"

Things are getting tight in clergy assignments to meet the needs of all our parishes and institutions. There will have to be some changes in emergencies that may be hard to understand — especially for our people. We really ought to work together to help our people. It is distressing when we do just the opposite. For example, a priest is transferred after consultation in which he clearly wanted the move, which was obviously a promotion as perceived by him and me. The next Sunday he tells the people he is leaving with a broken heart and only because of his obedience to the archbishop. Loving people write the cruel ogre on Lindell for what he has done to their dear priest and to them. Should I tell them Father asked out? You would not appreciate my doing that, even though it would be true. Changes are often hard enough for all of us. Why do they have to be even more traumatic because of pulpit dramatics? Let's hang together — or we shall all hang separately.

(*Notanda,* September 7, 1983)

— ◆ —

Q I know of "resigned" priests and nuns living in St. Louis, a couple in our own parish. I am wondering what our attitude about this should be.

A Over two years ago, I established the Archdiocesan Committee for the Reintegration of Resigned Religious and Priests. The goals of the Committee are

1. that all members of the archdiocese understand the status of dispensed priests and religious.
2. that parishes and institutions of the Church use the availability and talents of these fellow Catholics for service in the Church.
3. that all resigned clergy and religious be given every help for return to active ministry or proper dispensation by the Church and every opportunity to live a full Catholic life whenever possible.

A dispensation by the Church is necessary for the full reintegration of resigned priests and religious and the utilization of their talents in the parish. As long as there is no scandal in the local community, every priest who has been properly dispensed should be free to offer his services to the Church as any other layman. His background, education, and experience obviously should enable him to contribute much more fully than many lay Catholics. The same holds true for resigned religious. I am aware of a number of dispensed priests and religious who are serving on both parish and archdiocesan committees.

Old Soldiers: Remember those nostalgic words of the late General Douglas MacArthur: "Old soldiers never die; they just fade away." It seems he meant that military professionalism just never dies in many a proud man. While the soldier in such a man never dies, there comes a day when the man fades away.

It is much that way with priests. They, too, are used to living under discipline, living in service. And no matter how old they get, the priesthood in such a man never dies, even though his health, his life may fade away. To him, after all, was said on ordination day what Saint Paul said of Jesus, "You are a priest forever in the order of Melchisedech."

We have many priests. From time to time, I am privileged to visit Regina Cleri (Queen of the Clergy), our home for twenty-seven aged and disabled priests at 4540 Lindell Boulevard. It is always a joy for me to share a holiday or special celebration and join them at supper. They keep up remarkably on what is going on in the archdiocese and back up all we are doing by their daily prayer and sacrifice. I always come home encouraged and edified.

Besides the retired clergy at Regina Cleri, there are others who live at the Little Sisters of the Poor Home and a few who live with family or on their own. Priests who require full-time nursing care receive it at our new Mary Queen and Mother Nursing Home near Kenrick Seminary.

Then we also have other senior priests who come to the age when the Church asks them to offer a letter of resignation from pastoral administration. (Since Vatican Council II this has been asked of priests and bishops at age seventy-five.) We have a growing number of pastors who are still able and anxious at that age to continue serving in a parish, even though they are relieved from the administrative responsibility of the pastorate. Naturally, I am happy to encourage that trend. We need them.

(St. Louis, January 13, 1984)

Better Homilies?

Do you remember those pre-Vatican II times when the sermon at Mass was often simply omitted on steamy summer Sundays? Today that would be shocking. The homily is considered an integral and essential part of Mass.

Is preaching important? Judging by my mail, it is — to many people. Surveys of why Catholics attend Mass, or stay away, confirm this impression. For a high proportion of Catholics, it seems interesting and meaningful that homilies that relate to their daily lives are important.

Mark Twain remarked once that everybody talks about the weather, but no one does anything about it. Sometimes I think we could say the same about homilies. Granted, the first responsibility rests on preachers. But listeners share this responsibility. Too many Catholics who endure bad homilies do nothing but complain to their fellow sufferers.

"He was up there so long, I shook my watch to see if it was still running."

Or that old canard: "Our pastor has two homilies. One is on money. The other I haven't heard yet."

Those are cheap shots. Such critics risk nothing and accomplish nothing. They become accessories after the fact. Would you like to raise the level of preaching in your parish? Here are some suggestions.

- Get to church early enough to look through the readings before Mass — or read them at home beforehand. Reflect on them, as you would on a letter from a loved one. Pray about the thoughts they suggest. When the now familiar words are read aloud, allow them to penetrate your consciousness.

- Pray for the homilist and for all who will hear his words, yourself included. Ask the Holy Spirit to guide the words that are spoken and to open the hearts and minds of those who listen.
- Prepare to hear God's Word by joining heartily in the singing, responses, and prayers. No one can be an active listener to the homily who is passive during the rest of the Mass.
- Try to find one point in the homily that is meaningful to you or helps you in your life. Pray about it before you leave church and during the week. Mention it to a family member or a friend. Even a mediocre homily has *something* of value in it.
- Let the preacher know when something he said hit home or helped you. Tell him what you would like to hear about in the future. Even critical comments show interest.

A prime reason for bad preaching, it seems to me, is that we priests, unlike our Protestant colleagues, are so seldom held accountable by the people who sit in the pews, pay our salaries, and furnish our housing. Admittedly, this is a touchy area. But I'm convinced we can improve.

We could take our cue from Saint Francis de Sales, who wrote: "A spoonful of honey will get more results than a barrelful of vinegar." When you hear a good homily, do you let the preacher know how much it meant to you? A few words at the church door after Mass are good. A phone call or a note later on are better. We all need affirmation. Sermon preparation, like all creative work, is a lonely and difficult task. We preachers need to hear about it when we've done a good job. It makes all the hard work of preparation worthwhile — and encourages us to keep giving our best.

Yes, and we need to know, too, when we fail. If you can't find the courage for a personal conversation, you could write Father a note. Get others to do the same. You will be doing yourself and your fellow parishioners a favor. Be sure to sign your name. Anonymous letters go into the circular file — where they belong. Try to make your criticism positive. Let Father know you appreciate what a difficult task he has, that you know he wants to improve. If you have heard him do better in the past, tell him that too.

Preaching *is* important. Sometimes, however, I think we have unrealistic expectations. The Sunday homily should nourish our faith for the coming week — not for life. Most homilies are like most meals: good, plain fare, but not especially memorable.

Father William J. O'Malley, S.J., a high-school teacher in Rochester, New York, helps us to have realistic expectations about preaching. He writes:

> Jesus was the greatest teacher who ever lived: "No man ever spoke as this man speaks" (John 7:46). Yet Jesus was a complete failure till fifty days after he had departed the scene. When he died, he had at best one hundred disciples. Of the twelve most committed, one turned him in; his favorite denied even knowing him (and not to a soldier with a knife at his throat but to a waitress); and all the rest, save John, turned tail and ran, deserting him at the precise moment when he most needed them. Even at the very end, at the moment of Jesus' ascension, after three years of listening to him preach, after having experienced the tragedy of the crucifixion and the triumph of the resurrection, their very last question to him was: "Are you, uh, going to restore the kingdom to Israel now?" Despite all his hammering away at their selfishness, all his demands that they take the last place, that they look to serve and not be served, they still want to know whether they can go shop for thrones and get measured for the gold lamé robes.
>
> ("Ten Commandments for Homilists":
> *America,* July 30, 1983, page 47)

Not the least difficulty about preaching is that the preacher himself is at risk. His own words can rise up to condemn him. Knowing this caused Paul to fear "that after preaching to others I should find myself rejected" (1 Corinthians 9:27). So keep on praying for us preachers. We need your prayers — more than I can tell you.

(St. Louis, June 20, 1986)

— ♦ —

Alleluia Day

Next Saturday, April 25, promises to be an occasion of special joy for our archdiocese. At ten o'clock in the morning, I intend, God willing, to ordain the former Episcopalian priest W. Larch Fidler IV to the priesthood of the Catholic Church in St. Anselm's Church, Creve Coeur.

Larch and his wife, Grace, are the proud parents of a five-year-old daughter, Catherine, a kindergarten pupil at the Academy of the Visitation.

Larch joins the other priests of our archdiocese in virtue of a policy instituted by Pope Pius XII in the early 1950s. This permitted the ordination to the Catholic priesthood of a number of married convert clergymen in various European countries.

A "Pastoral Provision"

In 1980 our present Holy Father, Pope John Paul II, responding to the petition of several married Episcopalian priests in this country, established a "Pastoral Provision" permitting these men to become Catholic priests. Cardinal Law of Boston oversees the process as "Ecclesiastical Delegate of the Holy See."

Father Fidler is the first priest to be ordained in St. Louis under this Pastoral Provision. We hope that he will be followed soon by Gregory Lockwood, another married candidate, a former Lutheran pastor, who is now preparing for ordination. Nationally, thirty-six married convert clergymen have become Catholic priests. The bishops in whose dioceses they serve report overwhelmingly about their positive reception by priests and people and about the fine work they are doing. Some seventy more married convert clergymen are preparing to follow them.

A Change in Celibacy?

The popes from Pius XII onward have emphasized that permission for the ordination of married convert clergymen is by way of exception. It constitutes no change in the centuries'-old rule of the Latin or Western Church requiring a promise of lifelong celibacy by all those ordained to "major orders" (deacons, priests, bishops).

The Catholic Church respects the different discipline of the Eastern Churches (the Orthodox and Eastern-rite Catholics in communion with the pope). From the earliest centuries, they have ordained married men. They, too, however, forbid those who have received major orders to contract matrimony afterward. So a married Orthodox or Eastern-rite (Catholic) priest whose wife dies may not remarry. The same rule applies to married men who are now ordained as permanent deacons — and of course to the married convert clergymen who become Catholic priests.

This explains why the Church cannot readmit to priestly ministry priests who have resigned in order to marry. Like all Catholic priests (except those ordained after marriage in an Eastern rite), they were ordained with a promise of lifelong celibacy, made only after years of preparation and reflection. Convert clergy made no such promise. They married in good faith. Their decision to enter the Catholic Church entailed great sacrifices by them and their families. Their ordination as Catholic priests reflects the Church's recognition of their courage. It offers no basis for those of us who were ordained with a promise of celibacy to expect that we can abandon our commitment without consequences.

A Lonely Road

It is difficult for those of us who have been part of the Catholic household of faith from infancy to appreciate the hard and lonely road those who come to us from other faith communities must walk. The difficulties are compounded when the convert is an ordained clergyman, with pastoral responsibility for others. Overnight he loses home, salary, medical insurance, pension rights, and all security. In place of the support of loved ones and the whole Catholic community, which accompanied us as we journeyed to priesthood, the convert clergyman (and his wife if he is married) faces at best lack of understanding from many of those near and dear to him. Not infrequently he must endure bitter resentment and charges that he is breaking his previous ordination vows and betraying a sacred trust.

The convert clergyman accepts these sacrifices gladly for the sake of conscience and truth. He has received a call like God gave to Abraham: "Leave your own country, your kinsmen, and your father's house, and go to a country that I will show you" (Genesis 12:1). He follows in the footsteps of the apostle Paul, about whom the Lord said: "I myself shall indicate to him how much he will have to suffer for my name" (Acts of the Apostles 9:16).

Welcome

One of the most beautiful things in the life of a Catholic priest is the welcome we receive from people to whom we may be total strangers, but who see in us not the weak, sinful men we are but the Lord whose uniform we wear and whom are proud to serve. From my first assignment at St. Gregory Parish in Chicago in 1947 until my unforgettable reception here in

St. Louis in March 1980, I have experienced again and again this wonderful, sometimes almost unbelievable, love of God's people.

I know that you will extend this same welcome to Father Fidler and his family as he begins his priestly ministry among us.

(St. Louis, April 17, 1987)

– ◆ –

Morale of Priests

The past few weeks have been the worst I have ever seen in the treatment of Catholic priests by the media. I personally believe much of it was orchestrated as a reaction to the Vatican *Instruction on Homosexuality*. The counterattack was to try to portray the Catholic priests in America as heavily homosexual in orientation and practice. I have made a study of these various instances and noted that almost never has there been any data to back up the allegations. There have also been widespread insinuations of heterosexual infidelity to priestly vows on the part of a majority of priests in our country. I believe that we have all suffered greatly from this kind of treatment, and I have spoken of it with news people across the country. As we all know, however, it just takes a few accusations to besmirch reputations, and it takes a great deal of work to try to repair the damage. This kind of thing makes it all the more imperative that we be fully united among ourselves in our support for one another. In three different dioceses, I have been impressed by the honesty, integrity, and fidelity of the vast majority of our clergy. I believe that most of our people feel that way about us also. But they are embarrassed, scandalized, and confused by the kind of things they hear these days. Obviously, it is all the more important for us to be aware of what we are facing right now. In our sex-saturated society, we are clearly the sign of contradiction, and we need to expect to be treated as such.

(*Notanda*, March 13, 1987)

– ◆ –

"Nothing to Fear"

The elders among us remember those words of President Franklin Roosevelt from his first Inaugural Address. At the depth of the Great

Depression, the President's message to all Americans was: "We have nothing to fear but fear itself."

I think the same words need to be addressed to every one of us clergy here in the Archdiocese of St. Louis at this particular time.

We do not live in a vacuum, of course, and our experience is that of many priests in various parts of the world. This is why our Bishops' Conference addressed the issue in its booklet on the morale of priests. This is also why the 1990 Synod of Bishops will address the priesthood from the perspective of priestly formation, not only the formation of candidates for the priesthood but also the ongoing continuing education, formation, and support of priests themselves.

In my years here, I have talked a lot about being a Vatican II diocese. In doing so, I have tried to follow the position of John Paul II, who says the same thing. There are probably some among us who feel that the Council's teaching is depleted, that is, both the Church and society have moved beyond it. There are others, however, who are committed to what has been labeled the "restoration." Their desire and intention is to restore things to what they were *before* the Council. For them, the Council may have been a well-intentioned effort, but it has not turned out too well. There are still others — the majority perhaps — for whom Vatican II is only a name. They do not fully understand the significance of the Council and often fail to see its relevance to their daily lives.

It is my conviction that we do not fully understand all the implications of the Council's teaching and, for that reason, have not adequately implemented it. While much has changed in the past quarter century, it takes more than a single generation to assimilate fully the teaching of an ecumenical council, especially one whose purpose was primarily pastoral and that addressed so many important topics and concerns. To fulfill this task, we must be faithful to the values of both the old and the new; one cannot be emphasized at the expense of the other. Such a comprehensive approach to conciliar teaching, I believe, will prevent us from becoming preoccupied with single points in isolation from all the rest. It will enable us to see the full beauty and relevance of our heritage as it has developed under the influence of the Holy Spirit from the apostolic age to the present.

But even as we consider the larger agenda of the Church, let us focus on our immediate future, as priest-leaders in this particular Church. How should we proceed? How do we avoid becoming a hostage of the voices of doom — whether from the left or the right — who would engage us in a battle that is enervating and ultimately, by its very nature, destructive?

We priests often — and correctly, I might add — think that our work has become more and more complex. We also see the multiplication of our responsibilities. But we are not alone as we confront the complexity and expansion of our ministry. Other people face similar situations, for example, in education, healthcare, and government.

Perhaps I have said it too often, but we priests, diocesan and religious, in this archdiocese need to count our blessings again and again. We have all we need here to do a good job. There is no valid reason for us to be afraid of the years ahead in priestly ministry. We have nothing to fear but fear itself. We need to accentuate the positive and eliminate the negative. The vocation numbers crunch will be a self-fulfilling prophecy if we let it happen.

We do not have to fear the priest shortage. We do need, however, to pray to the Lord of the harvest, and we need to recruit suitable fine young people. I meet them in my rounds, and you know them better than I. Many write me of their love for the Church and their families. They care for the Church.

We need to speak straight to them about priestly vocations. The Pope does so. In every confirmation homily, I challenge the candidates to pray over their vocation, to consider priesthood and religious life. Do you do that in your preaching? On a regular basis? Why are we afraid to do so? We have nothing to fear but fear itself.

Our seminaries are doing well in their new start. They are working hard and showing good results already. But most of the recruiting job is up to you and me. Our young people need to see priests happy to be priests and anxious to have young men following in their footsteps. In June, I was in Monterey, Mexico, on NCCB business. I went to the seminary to see four hundred students, with five hundred expected next year. In July, I was in Mexico City and spoke to the Archbishop of Guadalajara who has nearly one thousand in his seminary in an officially anticlerical, anti-Catholic, struggling country. There are young Americans among these students. Now I know some of the sociological reasons, and so forth, in this situation, but I am convinced that there are plenty of vocations right here also.

We have to do our part and say with Jesus, "Come, follow me." They do that south of the border. There are also dioceses in the United States doing the same. There is no reason why we should not be one of them. Our seminaries here — prep, college, and theologate — should also be full. There is nothing to fear in our vocation picture but fear itself.

Priorities

Now and then I have been asked by many of you to state my "vision" for the Church of St. Louis, to list my priorities. To some degree, I have been reluctant to do so since I have said simply that we must be the Church of Vatican Council II. Pope John Paul states his pastoral plan in beginning his pontificate in similar words. But maybe I should respond more specifically. So here goes:

(1) *A richness and a depth in our liturgical celebrations.* Vatican II states: "The liturgy is the summit toward which the activity of the Church is directed: at the same time it is the fountain from which all her power flows." The liturgical celebration is a microcosm of the parish as priests, deacons, ministers, and participants all come together to worship God, each playing his or her own proper role in the celebration. In my years here, I have been happy to see an enriched liturgy throughout our archdiocese. But we still have much to do as I have continued to emphasize. We must become, before all else, a holy, priestly people.

(2) *Outreach to our overall community.* I have called for this in our evangelization, communications, and ecumenism. I hope I have given this example in our local Church in being available around the area to community and ecumenical groups, to radio and TV, and in my weekly column. We have established our radio-TV center and redeveloped our paper and ecumenism office.

Our outreach in service to the poor has been expanded through reorganization of Catholic Charities and its many new services, from inner city agencies to our outlying office for rural poor. Housing and legal aid programs have been organized and expanded in recent years, and this approach will continue.

(3) *Racial harmony.* Our St. Louis community remains divided along racial lines. Until Catholics in West County, rural Missouri, and North St. Louis all truly join in the effort to overcome separation by race, nationality, poverty, or other extrinsic cause, the body of Christ is lessened by our divisions.

Our Human Rights Office has been expanded, our Focus reorganization of our schools, and especially the coming of Bishop Steib have shown our commitment to heal racial division, the running sore of this community.

(4) *Shared responsibility.* Vatican II taught us to appreciate the unique gifts of each member of the Church and use those gifts at every level of archdiocesan life. Priest, religious, or layperson, male or female, of whatever social, ethic, or economic group, all must have every opportunity to fulfill the calling of their baptism and confirmation in the Church and within their state of life.

We have therefore emphasized parish, deanery, archdiocesan pastoral councils, school boards, and soon will complete our first Synod in nearly forty years. We should not be surprised or shocked at the human weaknesses of other members of our parish and archdiocesan communities. We need to be familylike in this Church of St. Louis in the loving, quarreling, growing, accommodating style that every family knows.

Our parishes are full of prayerful people, good liturgies, generous priests, and other leaders. Our people support an excellent religious-education system, an almost unmatched Catholic healthcare system, strong programs in support of human rights, human life, and the special needs of special groups like the elderly, the young, and the separated and divorced, which extend beyond the Catholic community and contribute to the common good. We should have more knowledge of these efforts and support them even more strongly.

(5) *Vocations.* Compare above and recall the reorganization of our seminaries and our organized vocation efforts. Now we are moving into the prayer and recruitment efforts in our clergy and people, which must be the foundation of all this work.

(6) *Stewardship.* All of these efforts must be supported. Accordingly, I have tried through these years to use and develop our material resources as carefully as possible. I would just cite the reorganization of our development appeal, our insurance program, revolving fund, data processing and accounting, parish stewardship program, estate planning, our stabilized school situation, and so forth. We have made careful progress and we shall continue this overall plan to be good and responsible stewards.

(*Notanda,* August 4, 1989)

Celibacy Today?

"There has to be something wrong with a fifty-year-old unmarried male." According to the current issue of *Time*, that is a widespread analysis of our new Supreme Court nominee, David Souter.

USA Today, reporting the failure of numbers of clergy to live their vow of celibacy and pointing to the priest shortage, mentions "experts" who say that "the Catholic Church's practice of clerical celibacy is out-dated."

Opinion polls indicate that significant numbers of Catholic clergy and laypeople favor "optional celibacy." Why, they ask, cannot the pope and the bishops accept the inevitable?

Origins: Where did this idea of clergy celibacy come from? Most other Christian churches do not have it.

Jesus was celibate. He called for absolute renunciation from his disciples, even to the point of giving up wife and family (Luke 14:26). He mentions the possibility of leading a celibate life for the kingdom of God (Matthew 19:12). Saint Paul, a celibate, counsels that way of life, especially to foster commitment to the Lord's service without any reservation (1 Corinthians 7:32-34).

In that spirit, celibacy arose in the Church. Gradually, it was emphasized more and more, and finally after centuries made obligatory for clergy especially in the rise of monastic orders in the West. Again and again obligatory celibacy for clergy was attacked in the Church. In the Eastern Church, it was required only of bishops, but in the Latin Church, it was maintained for all priests despite concentrated opposition in the ninth through eleventh centuries, at the time of the Protestant Reformation, during the Age of the Enlightenment and the period of modernism. The Catholic Church continued to treasure clerical celibacy as something precious through the inspiration and power of the Holy Spirit. This stand has brought misunderstanding and violent opposition off and on throughout Catholic history. It is doing so again in our time.

Today: Nor is it only the celibate vocation that is under grave pressure today. The vocation to marriage is in at least as serious a crisis. The percentage of marriages that end up in separation or divorce is far higher than the percentage of priests or religious who do not persevere in their celibate call. Celibacy is ordinarily viewed in relation to marriage, and there is a striking parallelism in the changes affecting both forms of life today. In both, there is a shifting from an institutional emphasis toward a personal one. While marriage is still esteemed by many, the partners in marriage are more and more regarded from the viewpoint of personal pleasure and fulfillment. The celibate vocation likewise is passing from a largely institutional to a more personal emphasis. Its validity for the priest is increasingly seen in the degree to which it enables him to fulfill himself personally. There seems to be no other consideration.

Through the years, I have learned from leaders of other faiths with whom I meet regularly that marriage is no solution to problems of clergy life. I know denominational leaders who envy Catholic freedom from the many difficulties of clergy life that plague them.

Is clerical celibacy outdated today? In our sex-saturated society, maybe it is more needed today than ever. The Pope has made that very point and so have the American Bishops.

(St. Louis, August 10, 1990)

From the Pews

How often you hear those exciting words, "Today we have a letter from the Archbishop." It is true that I do send you a letter from time to time. However, I also receive letters — at least as many. I thought that you might like to read some of them. Here is the first.

Dearest Father John,

As I write these lines, I am asking our Mother Mary to ask Jesus to send you a special blessing. I was delighted to read in your *Review* column that bishops read the letters that are sent to them. Sometimes I feel that you are so far away that I cannot say to you what is in my heart and that, if I did, it would be a great imposition on your very busy schedule.

This last week I was so touched by your plea to us to pray and fast for peace. I felt that it truly came from your heart. It was with great thankfulness that I obeyed. Please do not be afraid to call us back to prayer, fasting, and penance. Our long and rich history gives us many saintly models to follow. Surely, we should not be above such things just because we live in the twentieth century. True paths to Jesus have withstood the test of time. It is only our selfishness and arrogance that make us believe that we have more up-to-date ways to reach God, which are easier.

For anyone who is reading Scripture and the newspapers today, it is becoming more and more evident that the world as we know it is beginning to crumble. The house that we've built on sand cannot last forever. If this is so, then the people of God need to build themselves up so that we can face what lies ahead unafraid. Nothing is going to happen (whether it be wars, economic hardships, natural disasters, and so forth) that should make us anxious if our eyes remain on the Lord and if we are building peace in our families. Even the Church will not be exempt from trouble.

If we were physically overweight, we could put ourselves on diets and begin exercise programs. Can we do less when our spiritual life is in danger? In every age, God has sent prophets to call his people back when they have strayed. He will do so now. What I am asking is that you be one of those prophets, even when that means that you will be labeled as "old-fashioned" or "behind the times." Truth is not always fashionable.

Perhaps you wonder why I ask you this. Why don't I just reform my life and leave others to follow their own way? As a member of the body of Christ, I am not permitted to let everyone do "his own thing." By virtue of my baptism, I must not only seek a private relationship with our Lord, I *must* reach out to my brothers and sisters. Because I have been given the gift of faith and had it nurtured by others, so I must do for others as well. We are all in this together.

Challenge your people. Call them to more. Be the voice of Jesus in St. Louis. Speak with urgency, for our time is growing short. It is with great love and respect that I end my letter. My prayers are with you as you carry the heavy burden of your office. When you feel overwhelmed, please know that there are those of us "out in the field," so to speak, who support you and thank God for your faithful service to us. May you be filled with the sense of peace, which only comes from trust in our Lord.

Respectfully,
Just One of Your Flock

(St. Louis, February 15, 1991)

— ◆ —

As announced last week, I am trading place with all you aspiring columnists. So here is our guest columnist this week who sent me this letter last October from Columbia, Missouri.

To Priests of the St. Louis Archdiocese
c/o Archbishop John L. May

Dear Fathers,

In view of the fact that I know how strongly you feel about unsigned letters, let me explain right up front that I have no intention of signing my name to this letter. That's because who I am is not important right now. Who *you* are is what makes a difference.

And just who are you? You are a tall or not-so-tall, slender or not necessarily slender, blond-, red-, brown-, black-, or gray-haired individual...or you have no hair at all. You have blue, brown, green, gray, hazel, or almost black eyes. You've been a priest for a matter of months or for years and years! You're nice or maybe you're a little crabby. Fresh and enthusiastic or maybe weary and worn out. A magnificent administrator or you aren't that terrific at it! You still wear a cassock, or you wouldn't be caught dead in one. And, really, none of that makes a whole lot of difference. Because none of that is *who you are*. It's just *what we see with our eyes*. And sometimes what we see with our eyes isn't how it actually is!

It's *what we see with our hearts* that makes a difference. Then, who are you when we see you with our hearts? You are a man who has dedicated his life to the Lord and his Church. You may have had plans to be a lawyer...or a doctor...or a businessman. You may have dreamed of marrying the girl next door or an unnamed someone you didn't have the chance to meet. You may have pictured yourself with a yardful of children and a garageful of cars, bicycles, lawn mowers, and snow blowers. You may have thought about taking over a family business or starting one of your own. But, no matter what those dreams were, somewhere along the way, the Lord asked you to set it all aside and follow him a different way. No wife, no children, no white picket fence, no steps up the corporate ladder. No certitude that someone would be there when you came home after a tough day at the office — no promises for your old age. No assurance that you'd always live with people you get along with or that you would work with people you enjoy.

He simply asked you to be there for his Church. To take a step beyond that call of duty, to share so fully in his plans that you would not have time for the warmth and security of a family and all the responsibility that requires. He asked you to be a priest. More important than his request that you become a priest was your answer. You said "Yes!" And, in doing so, you entered into a relationship with God, his Church, and his people unlike that of any other vocation in the world.

When we see you with our hearts, we see a man who presides at daily liturgies, day in and day out, whether you're "in the mood" or not. We see a man who starts early in the day and ends late at night. Someone who wants to be with us when there is a crisis or trauma. Someone we call when things aren't the way we think they should be at the parish, but whom we forget to call to say "Everything's going fine, Father!" A man who will listen to our problems and our sins so we can go home feeling fresher and free-er and reconciled with our God. A person to baptize our babies, anoint our dying, marry our daughters to "Prince Charming," and balance the books, mend the parking lot, tuckpoint the church, and heat the school.

We want you to be prayerful in your approach to life, gentle in the reconciliation room, dynamic at the pulpit, reverent at the altar, understanding in the parlor, delightful at a cocktail party, compassionate, concerned, gracious, kind, forgiving, chaste, charitable, loving, and a well-developed, well-mannered, and well-rounded human being.

Remarkably, you are many of those things with extraordinary frequency. And, when you aren't, you are a "theme show" on *Donahue, Oprah, Geraldo, Sally* or some other vehicle of sensationalism. Not because priests are bad and fifty percent of you do thus and so, seventy-five percent have done whatever, or ninety-two percent have at one time or another wondered if there is a God. But because you are unique and the world wonders. How can he really be celibate at a time when "sex makes the world go 'round?" How can he possibly be willing to live in a room or two of a rectory with other men, relinquish the materialism that pervades our lives, give of himself for something as intangible as a "kingdom yet to come"? How can he be in his right mind and be as committed as he says he is when we're into an "as long as it feels good" mentality? You make headlines when you make a major error...not because it's a common, everyday event and when one commits an indiscretion, the whole bunch of you are probably doing the very same thing behind closed doors. You make headlines because you stand for God in a godless world, because you strive to be Christian in a worldful of false idols and you are different. You make headlines because somehow it maybe makes some people feel a little less guilty for their own lifestyles when even the good guys falter now and then.

Maybe you make the world a little uncomfortable because you represent something difficult. Your presence is a reminder that the world isn't how it ought to be, but it might be a tad uncomfortable for us to do something about it! Your sense of commitment is a constant reminder for us all of our call to follow him also. I don't think the headlines should read, "Father So-and-So Made a Huge Blunder and Let's All Shake Our Heads in Disgust!" The headlines should read, "Priests Ad Infinitum Give and Give of Themselves to Make God's Kingdom Right Now! Let's Give Them Our Love and Support!"

Thank you for all the times you are there for us! Thank you for all the times you live your priesthood to the fullest. And thank you, too, for the times when you sin like all the rest of us and you pick yourselves up and try again. Thank you for your prayerfulness, your priestliness, and your plain humanness. And thank you for all the times you work together with us and for us in an attempt for us to walk a little closer with our God!

When we look at you with our hearts, we see something very, very special. That's who you are!

Gratefully with prayers,
Anonymous

Now wasn't that a thoughtful meditation on the priesthood in today's world? We priests should be especially grateful for that tribute. And I hope some of your parents and grandparents call it to the attention of some of our young folks. They may get a thought about their own future. The Lord calls in many different ways.

(St. Louis, February 22, 1991)

- 9 -
RELIGIOUS VOCATIONS

Bishops should foster priestly and religious vocations as much as possible and should take a special
interest in missionary vocations.

(Decree on the Pastoral Office of Bishops, #15)

Through most of its history, our diocese has been dependent on vocations from across the U.S.A. and from Ireland. Almost half of our diocesan clergy hail from the Emerald Isle, and four of our large parish schools are taught by Sisters of Irish communities. There are growing indications these days that the number of these vocations from American and Irish sources may be reduced sharply in the years ahead.

Meanwhile, we must do more to develop vocations here in our own diocese. Much was done in the past, and we do have a number of Alabama priests, Brothers, and Sisters; but we have never had enough. After all, we are an old Catholic community for the most part, with a wealth of tradition, Catholic education, solid family life, and so forth. Why should we not stand on our own feet? Why cannot our young men and women serve their own people? It is either that or we shall be closing many of our parishes, schools, hospitals, and other works of charity in the generation ahead.

We had better think about it and "pray that the Lord of the harvest send forth laborers into his vineyard. The harvest is great, but the laborers are few."

(Mobile, September 25, 1970)

Future Priests

If I survive (and I often wonder), ten years from now there will be a new archbishop here. I certainly do not want him to inherit an archdiocese with a horrendous clergy shortage. You do not want to live and work in such a situation either, I know. (This all applies to both our diocesan and religious clergy.)

What I am about to write does not reflect just my own thoughts. It comes from other bishops also in various parts of this country who are pondering and praying over this matter as never before. What I write again is not rah-rah cheerleading. It is what I firmly believe. So here goes.

Catholics are all talking about the crisis in vocations. I believe there is a crisis in vocations. However, I believe with all my heart that the crisis in vocations is primarily that there are too many people who have convinced themselves that there are no vocations. I am totally convinced that the Lord is still calling generous young men and women — and those not so young — for service as priests and Brothers and Sisters.

The Church belongs to Jesus and, therefore, he who is its spouse and its savior is going to have the greatest possible interest in its survival — which he has promised — and in its continual ability to do what he has sent it to do. For that reason, I believe without any hesitation that the Lord is still calling servants into his Church to guide and shepherd and lead and care for this Church of his. If the Church is his, therefore, then surely with a brother's love he is not going to let us flounder or be abandoned. He himself has instituted the priesthood as essential to the life of his Church. He himself has willed that the authentic witness to the values of the gospel that he gave his life to proclaim would be manifest through priests who give their lives to serve as he did.

This is why I say that I am not convinced there is any real crisis in vocations except within us — a crisis in our confidence, a crisis in our wills, a crisis in our faith that the Lord will take care of us. Now I do not believe that I am a pollyanna on all of this. I know full well that the picture is different in different communities and in different parts of the world. I can really only speak with some limited authority in the area of the diocesan priesthood because, as a diocesan bishop, I understand that vocation more than I do the others. But I believe generally the same about religious vocations of men and women.

Let us look at three of the problems that can be instrumental in creating the so-called vocation crisis. Now here once again may I remind you that my definition of the vocation crisis is not that we have no vocations but that too many people have convinced themselves that we have no vocations.

The first of the three problems is the *present culture* of our modern society — the constant screaming of the world. The TV commercials, the radio, the newspapers, the magazines, the lyrics of the popular songs — all these combine to create a total conspiracy against anyone accepting an absolute value and against anyone being willing to give up anything for a good cause. Everyone wants to do it his or her way. We have forgotten that there is a very special grace in doing it God's way — in accepting an absolute value and living up to its demands, in being willing to accept a cross, a hardship, a sacrifice for the greater good. This is not just a mentality that affects religion. It is a mentality that affects every walk of life, and all of us recognize it as a tremendous handicap in the growth of values and in the development of real character, indeed, in every sphere of human activity. Sometimes it is called excessive personalism, and it is truly present in most of the developed societies of the world.

The second major problem that I see is the fact that we are *no longer supporting the choice of a priestly vocation.* Let us be totally honest. Even our family-support system is often absent for vocations. It is absolutely true that one of the difficulties in promoting vocations today is a lack of support from the societal systems that are so important in our lives. The most important of these, without a doubt, is the family, and we too often find in the family a lack of affirmative, positive joy when a youngster reveals that he believes that God is calling him to be a priest. This is an almost universal problem. We find it even among very fervent Catholic people who somehow fear for their sons in the priesthood. We can speculate on their reasons but hardly deny them.

The third problem is, I believe, that there is a real link between the lack of vocations and the *lack of the use of the sacrament of penance.* The fact that there are fewer confessions today means that there are fewer moments when young people have a chance to bare their souls to a thoughtful and understanding priest. How many vocations were stimulated because a priest began to realize that a young man was living a life of special virtue and made it a point to talk to him about the Lord and the possibility of his calling to priestly service.

In the face of these baffling problems, there are success stories. Consider two dioceses, Metuchen in New Jersey and Orange in California. (There are others also, but I mention them because they are of roughly equal size and on opposite ends of the country.) In the last few years both have had remarkable growth in the numbers of priests ordained and in seminarians. For example, in 1982, Metuchen ordained two, in 1986, fifteen. Why?

First, in all their preaching and teaching, they tried to make the vocation to the priesthood attractive. They tried to demonstrate that the priesthood is a great life, not a life of total joy, not a rose garden, not a retirement farm, but a life of accomplishment and of satisfaction and of service.

Second, they made it demanding. They made it clear that the priesthood would be a life of tremendous challenge for these young men, a life lived in the pattern of the Lord, who came to serve, not to be served.

Third, they involved the priests. The greatest vocation director is the priest in the parish or the priest in the reconciliation room or the priest in the pulpit or the priest on his day off. If his life is filled with natural virtue crowned with a supernatural faith and hope and love for God, then he is infinitely more valuable than the most cleverly designed poster or the most intricately organized program. Priests cannot leave this work to a couple of their confreres appointed as "vocation directors."

Above all, throughout both dioceses there is an intensive program of prayer for vocations. That intention is emphasized constantly in the homilies of the bishop and in every eucharistic celebration in every parish. All the people throughout the diocese are aware of this need and pray for priests now and in the days ahead. It is all part of a new awareness, a new attitude, a new start.

We can do the same thing here — *if we really want to.* We have even greater advantages than the dioceses mentioned. I believe we have a rich heritage of vocations, solid family life, and excellent seminaries right here.

This I know, that every harvest depends on four essential factors — on good soil, on sunshine, on rain, and on cultivation. God gives us three out of the four just through his bounty. He asks us to add the cultivation sometimes, and this is nowhere more clear than in the area of vocation apostolate. We must put our hand to the plow and continue to work at it, knowing that the Lord of the harvest has already planted the seed, that he has given the sunshine and the rain, that the soil is good.

The Lord still says, "Come, follow me." He does his part. He asks us to pray and do ours for workers in the harvest. We need to cast off our negativism, our lethargy, our cynicism. We can do what these other dioceses have done. In these next ten years we will. (In 1997 we will move back into the rejuvenated Kenrick building because by then the number of seminarians in our college and theologate will demand it. Young men see visions and old men dream dreams. That is my dream.)

(Notanda, July 31, 1987)

– ◆ –

Good Shepherds – Tough Times

In last Sunday's gospel, we heard the words of Jesus: "I am the good shepherd." We prayed in all our parishes for priestly vocations last Sunday, for priests who will be the good shepherds in the years to come.

Our Priests: Last week on April 11, I met for a full day with over four hundred of our diocesan priests for personal discussion of our priestly life and ministry. I was very happy with our meeting. Once again, I was most favorably impressed with the overall spirit of our priests. It was edifying and encouraging for me.

When Jesus called himself the good shepherd, his hearers knew that the shepherd was not the romantic figure depicted in our stained-glass windows and on holy cards, cuddling a cute little lamb in his arms. In Jesus' day, the shepherd's life was hard. He had to be out in all kinds of weather, constantly on the move, protecting his weak and timid sheep from wild animals, thieves, and from their own tendency to stray from the flock and get lost — or worse.

Jesus is "the good shepherd": the one who never deserts his flock, who works not for pay but for love. There is an almost personal bond between this shepherd and his flock. "My sheep hear my voice. I know them, and they follow me."

Since Jesus' Resurrection and Ascension, he has had to depend on others to do the shepherding for him: parents for their children, teachers, priests. A wise bishop said once: "The Good Shepherd is in residence in every parish and every rectory. He just looks different in each place."

Good Shepherd Sunday has been designated by our Holy Father as Vocation Sunday. Obeying Jesus' command, "Pray the Lord of the harvest to send laborers into his harvest" (Luke 10:2), we prayed last Sunday in a special way that many of our young people will hear and heed the call of the Good Shepherd to priesthood and the religious life.

Tough Times: These are not the best times for the Lord's shepherds as their numbers shrink. A recent report on priestly morale says that many priests feel "trapped, overworked, frustrated....Loneliness is often mentioned by priests as cause for anxiety and pain....It is devastating to morale for priests to feel isolated from one another, not understood by their superiors, and left alone before criticism and complaint."

With few exceptions, we love being priests. If we had to choose over again, with the experience life has brought us, we would choose priesthood. If we were to die tonight, we would die happy men, proud to have been chosen for the greatest service in the world.

Without the support of wives and children (and the many burdens of family life), Catholic priests depend heavily on the affirmation and love of those they serve. Priests are deeply grateful for this support.

Catholics, on the other hand, who attack and criticize their priests, take on before God a terrible responsibility. God alone knows how many priests have given up ("just doing the necessary" or actually leaving the priesthood) because they just couldn't take it anymore: the petty accusations, constant criticism, and sullen resentment of some of those they try to serve. Priests are aware of their many faults, but most of them try to do their best. They hang in there day by day, year by year, for life as they promised on the day of ordination.

Pope John Paul II says: "The fostering of vocations cannot be considered a marginal activity of the parish." Please pray, therefore, for many religious vocations in our archdiocese — and that we will provide the support young people need to answer the call of the Good Shepherd.

(St. Louis, April 21, 1989)

— ◆ —

151

Q Last week I heard a radio discussion about the diminishing number of priests expected in future years. Where do we stand?

A Our situation statistically is not as alarming as the numbers mentioned on the program, but we also will have to cope with a worsening shortage of priests in the foreseeable future. Despite our excellent vocation program and our reorganized seminary system, we are not ordaining enough priests to replace our clergy who retire and die each year. Right now there are forty-one St. Louis students in the four final years of preparation at Kenrick Seminary. Even if every single one perseveres to ordination, they could not fill the need for priests in the next four years in our two hundred fifty-four parishes, in our schools, and in other institutions. Obviously, we must do much better in the decade of the 1990s because meanwhile our Catholic population is growing. Also we have some religious-order priests having to give up their care for some of our parishes.

Remember, Jesus talked about this situation: "As he saw the crowds, his heart was filled with pity for them, because they were worried and helpless, like sheep without a shepherd. So he said to his disciples, 'The harvest is large, but there are few workers to gather it in. Pray to the owner of the harvest that he will send out workers to gather in his harvest' " (Matthew 9:36-38). Following that instruction of the Lord, I have directed our priests to lead prayer for vocations at every Sunday Mass, to have a holy hour for vocations weekly in every parish but at least every month, regular prayers in all our schools, and so forth. We should also fast and abstain from meat every Friday for this intention and pray the rosary. We must get serious about doing what our Lord asks of us — praying for vocations!

More: Recently I read the words of Mother Teresa explaining that her vocation was due primarily to the example of her parents. I think I can say the same. My parents never pushed me to priesthood, but they were always supportive and grateful to have a priest in the family. Some night at supper why not ask yourselves as parents the following questions:

- Do the young people in your family hear frequent criticism or ridicule of priests or Sisters?
- Do you ever give them any reason to believe that foregoing marriage to serve God's Church is worthwhile, good, and exciting?
- Most important of all: if your son told you tonight that he wanted

to be a priest or Brother — or your daughter that she wanted to be a Sister — how would you react? Overjoyed, thrilled? Or sad, disappointed, even angry? What reaction do you think your children expect if they were to make such an announcement?

• What values are you giving your children by the way you live: Is having nice things a big priority? The fancy car or van, the boat or other recreational equipment, expensive clothes?

• If you are a mother of young children working outside the home, is this out of necessity? Or is it really for the extras the second income will buy?

Religious vocations come from families in which children learn from the example of their parents the beauty of sacrificing for others. Today's decline in religious vocations is closely connected with the acceptance by Catholics of "consumerism": the idea that happiness depends on money and the things money can buy. That cruel falsehood actually cheats young people by giving them false values and false goals that bring only frustration, disappointment, and unhappiness.

Finally: Here is a suggested prayer for all our parents on this Vocation Sunday:

> God, our Father, by bringing life into the world, we are sharers in your creation. We turn to you to give us faith, love, and a spirit of sacrifice in our home which will allow our children to hear you. Give them the grace to live their Christian vocation according to your call. Whether they are called to be married, single, priest, Sister, or Brother, help us to say a joyful "yes" and to have the courage to let go of their lives. May our family life extend beyond our home and be a blessing to others as we grow in love for you and for one another. Strengthen daily our desire as a family to have a part in making your kingdom come. Through Christ your Son we pray. Amen.
>
> (St. Louis, January 26, 1990)

— ♦ —

Think Positive

Several weeks back I had a marvelous experience. It was the ordination liturgy on Saturday, January 12, when ten new priests were ordained in our cathedral. It has been some years since I ordained that many in one ceremony. I hope it will not be long before I can do it again. Much of that will depend on you. I am afraid we worry too much about the priest shortage and we don't do enough about it.

Call: Vocation, of course, simply means a "call." Every one of us received God's call when we were baptized. Baptism made us God's daughters and sons forever. Baptism and its completion in confirmation give us the gift of God's Holy Spirit, who enables us to fulfill our fundamental call as Catholic Christians by living a life that proclaims what we truly are: sisters and brothers of Jesus Christ, heirs with him of God's kingdom.

God calls us also to a *state of life:* to marriage, to the single state, or to serve him and others as priests or as religious Sisters or Brothers. We pray especially these days for these *religious vocations.*

"Every community may rest assured of this," Pope John Paul writes. "The Lord does not cease to call! But at the same time we also know for certain that he wants our help in making his call known." How can we help? The Pope makes three suggestions:

- "Be a vibrant community."
- "Be a praying community."
- "Be an inviting community."

A vibrant community is one whose members care about one another and affirm one another. Do you speak positively about priests, deacons, Sisters, and religious Brothers? We certainly don't want you to put us on pedestals. But young people will never be able to hear the call of the Good Shepherd to a religious vocation if those who have already responded to that call are constantly mocked and criticized. We need to talk up religious vocations and to support the men and women who have received them. Have you ever discussed this matter with your children, your grandchildren? The first seminary or convent is often a Catholic home.

A praying community: God knows our needs, of course, before we ask. He wants us to ask nonetheless. Each time we do so, we are reminded how much we need him.

Jesus tells us to pray specifically for religious vocations: "The harvest is rich but the laborers are few, so ask the Lord of the harvest to send laborers to his harvest" (Luke 10:2). Prayers for vocations should be offered at Mass in all parishes. Holy hours, rosary, or prayers at home are also part of our "new start."

An inviting community doesn't wait for people to volunteer. It regularly seeks out suitable candidates. "Talking about vocations in a general way," the Pope writes, "is not sufficient to lead young people to commit themselves to a consecrated life.... These calls must be explicit and personal. This is the method Jesus used." Priests especially must follow the Lord's example in inviting promising young people to consider a priestly or religious vocation.

I also ask each of you reading these words to help in a very specific way. Look around at your acquaintances, your friends, your relatives, who have not yet chosen a state of life. Which of them might make a fine Sister, a priest, a religious Brother? Perhaps someone you know is just waiting to be asked. Send the names and addresses of those you think might be suitable to Director of Vocations, 5200 Glennon Drive, St. Louis, MO 63119. Your suggestions will be handled in confidence; you will not be identified. We shall contact those whom you suggest, however, asking them tactfully to consider whether God may not be calling them to serve the Lord and his Church. We would never pressure anyone. But we should respectfully invite recommended individuals to *consider* a religious vocation. The early Christian communities used to do so. It is about time for us to do the same.

How about you? Don't say, "I'm not good enough." God knows that already. He doesn't always call those who are fit. But he always fits those he calls. Only two things disqualify a person. Jesus, the Good Shepherd, cannot use anyone who won't work or can't love. All other shortcomings can be remedied, however, with goodwill, perseverance, and prayer. Ask any priest for advice. Or write me and I will put you in touch with someone who can help you. We need *you* and we invite *you*.

If the Lord is calling you to share in his work as shepherd, you must be ready for discouragements and setbacks. Our test of a vocation is willingness to undergo the drudgery it entails. But it isn't all drudgery. I can't promise you glamor or riches or visible success. But I can promise you deep, abiding joy — the joy that comes from knowing you are part of the greatest service in the world.

I know. The Good Shepherd called me. I answered his call forty-four years ago. I have never regretted it. Not one single day.

(St. Louis, February 1, 1991)

- 10 -
ECUMENISM

Bishops should deal lovingly with the separated brethren, urging the faithful also to conduct themselves with great kindness and charity in their regard and fostering ecumenism as it is understood by the Church. They should also have a place in their hearts for the nonbaptized so that upon them, too, there may shine the charity of Christ Jesus, to whom the bishops are witnesses before all.

(Decree on the Pastoral Office of Bishops, #16)

Just look in your telephone book. In the classified section's listing of churches, there are thirty-two different Christian denominations in the Mobile area. Across the U.S.A., there are more than two hundred separate sects of Christians.

All these churches profess belief in the Lord Jesus and use basically the same holy Bible. Most of their members share the same primary doctrines, and sometimes they would have a hard time explaining how their denominational faith differs from that of the folks in the church across the street.

Many of these churches are heroic monuments built at great cost over many years. Others are most modest — the gift very often of pitifully poor people. Most of these buildings are used one or two days a week and then for a few hours at a time.

Some people would say this is all part of the American way, the free-enterprise system in religion, another evidence of liberty in our great country. The fragmented state of the Christian Church is all of that, perhaps, but it is also much more.

This situation is a disgraceful, wasteful, stubborn scandal, directly contrary to the mind and will of Jesus. At the Last Supper, he prayed that his followers would be one, as he and his Father are one, that all Christians would be one in him. And then he said why: in order that the world might see that he was truly sent by God, his Father. You must be, he told us, one flock and one shepherd.

And yet, most Christians are not the least concerned that their churches refuse to take seriously that command of Jesus. In fact, some of them consider priests and parishioners dedicated to ecumenism as traitors to that old-time religion.

Pope John and Pope Paul have taught nothing more forcefully in their words and actions than the commitment of the Roman Catholic Church to Christian unity. Vatican Council II summed it all up in its magnificent *Decree on Ecumenism* for Catholics everywhere. So ecumenism is no fad found among a few far-out priests, nuns, and fellow travelers corrupting the loyal laity. It is an essential part of our belief and life as informed and responsible Roman Catholics.

There is no better time to realize this fact than during the annual Week of Prayer for Christian Unity, January 18-25. Sponsored by the Protestant and Orthodox National Council of Churches and by the National Council of Catholic Bishops, this week is to be devoted to prayer and study of the teaching of Jesus about the unity of his Church. Pope Paul has gone across the world to pray and confer with Protestant and Orthodox leaders, and they have come to him in Rome. This past week he announced with the Archbishop of Canterbury that the Roman Catholic and the Anglican Churches have now come to full basic agreement on the teaching of Jesus on the holy Eucharist. Similar studies have been proceeding with the Lutheran Church. Beautiful things are happening!

And yet, we still have Catholics, including a few priests, now and then warning darkly that the Catholic Church "is becoming too Protestant." Recently in an open-forum session, a shocked listener fearfully asked, "What are we coming to — one Church?"

Centuries and centuries have longed to see the things that we see and have not seen them. We are just beginning to glimpse the dawn of a grand and glorious day for the whole Church of Jesus. No one can stop that sun of Christian unity from rising steadily on our horizon now — thank the Lord.

Despite the mess we Christians have made of it all these years, it is still his Church.

(Mobile, January 14, 1972)

A Real Happening

It struck me right in the middle of the meeting last Friday night. This was really a happening. I thought I should tell you about it.

It began on Friday evening at the Visitation Monastery in Mobile. After prayer for the light of the Holy Spirit, a clergy spokesman from seven Christian churches presented his denominational belief in the sacrament of the holy Eucharist. Each did so by comparing his faith with that expressed in the *Agreed Statement on Eucharistic Doctrine,* which was the joint publication several years ago of representative Catholic and Anglican theologians. In that document, substantial agreement had been reached. The question last week was, "Do the other major Christian churches also agree?"

Amazing Grace: What struck me in each speaker was their growing realization of the centrality of the holy Eucharist and the deep faith in the unique presence of Jesus Christ in the sacrament. The fact of the Lord's presence was emphasized repeatedly, although the manner in which he is present was considered a mystery, which could not be explained. Again and again, I was amazed by the emphatically professed faith in the Lord's Real Presence in the Eucharist. All the Protestant speakers mentioned that this trend has been discernible in recent years in their churches.

On Saturday morning, the conference went deeper into the same subject. The session ended with a question about the possibility of intercommunion among us in the foreseeable future. Since we have not yet arrived at the essential unity of faith required for intercommunion, it was with yearning for that day that all gathered in the monastery chapel to pray with Saint Paul that someday we all might become one body, all who partake of the one bread. We parted remembering the prayer of Jesus at the Last Supper "that they all may be one in order that the world may know that thou hast sent me." It was a real happening, a beautiful experience.

(Mobile, November 5, 1976)

*John L. May
with his sisters,
Margaret (left)
and Jeanette
(right).*

*John L. May
as subdeacon,
1946.*

*With his sisters and brothers-in-law following his installation
as Archbishop of St. Louis; March 25, 1980.
(From left): Lee and Margaret Cordell, the Archbishop,
Jeanette and John Kliejunas.*

Archbishop May ordains his former Vicar General in Mobile
as his successor in the See, raised to the rank of archdiocese,
on November 16, 1980. With him are the Bishops Raymond W. Lessard
of Savannah and William B. Friend of Shreveport.

CHURCH
AND
STATE

*"The President
[Ronald Reagan]
could not have been
more affable.
On almost every
subject, he took a
definite part in the
conversation and
seemed informed.
The time passed very
quickly and the
President seemed
reluctant to leave"
(page 329).*

*During a campaign stop in St. Louis in late September 1988 then
Vice President George Bush requested a meeting with the Archbishop.*

Shortly after coming to St. Louis, the Archbishop achieved every golfer's dream: a hole-in-one.

"Recently, I was featured in these pages holding a baby at our Catholic Charities adoption office. By return mail, I received a note from an amused parishioner who reported, 'At the end of Christmas Mass, the priest announced that he would read a letter from Archbishop May. At the sound of your name, every baby began weeping and wailing to match any mention in the Bible. This screaming continued, without pause, until its abrupt stop at the end of your letter.' (I just wonder who was pinching those babies.)"
(St. Louis, January 18, 1991)

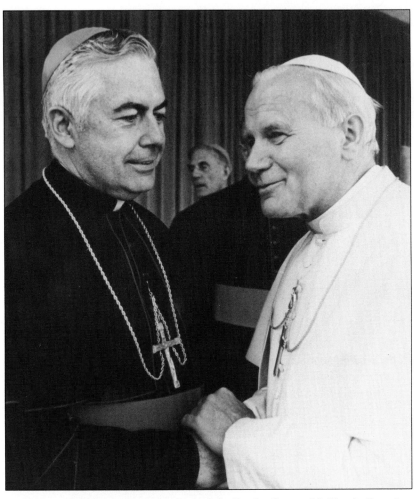

*On the eve of the 1987 visit of Pope John Paul II (here with May in Rome)
to the United States, the Archbishop wrote his priests:
"You are either with this Pope or against him" (page 189).*

"In the mysterious plan of God, Jews and Christians are inextricably linked for all time" (page 163). *The Archbishop is shown speaking at Temple Israel in Creve Coeur, St. Louis County.*

"The newly elected Russian Orthodox Patriarch Alexy received us very formally in his impressive headquarters at the Danilov Monastery" (page 334). Flanking the Patriarch are Cardinal Joseph Bernardin of Chicago (left) and Archbishop May.

In the fullness of years: 1990.

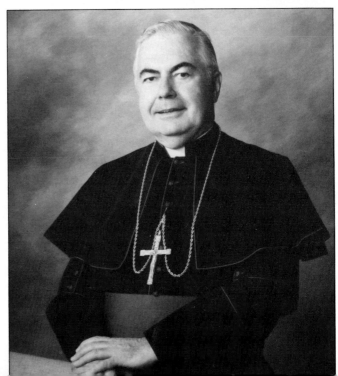

Q In mixed marriages, why are not the Protestant spouses of Catholics permitted to receive holy Communion with their partners? Pope John XXIII would probably have permitted it.

A Sharing in holy Communion is a sign of unity in faith, the supreme sign. It is what we are working toward in the ecumenical movement. When people just receive together without agreement about what they believe about the Eucharist and the Church, they are sailing under false pretenses. The various Christian denominations are not yet united. We have no right to give the impression that we are by shared holy Communion.

Pope John did not grant any such permission. Pope Paul VI permitted other Christians to receive holy Communion in an emergency situation under clearly stipulated conditions. Such a situation rarely occurs in our country.

We all need to work toward Christian unity so we can someday be one at the Lord's Supper.

(Mobile, March 14, 1980)

Did you know? There is no season when we are more ecumenical than when we are singing Christmas carols. "Adeste Fidelis" and "Silent Night" are by Catholics; "O Little Town of Bethlehem" and "Oh, Come to My Heart" are by Episcopalians; "It Came Upon a Midnight Clear" was written by a Unitarian; "Joyful, Joyful We Adore Thee" by a Presbyterian; "Away in the Manger" by a Lutheran; "While Shepherds Watched Their Flock" by a man named Tate from Dublin, Ireland, with music by Handel from Prussia; and finally "Hark the Herald Angels Sing" by Wesley, a Methodist, with music by Mendelssohn, a German Protestant of Jewish ancestry.

(St. Louis, December 12, 1980)

The Pope and Luther

This Pope is really something, isn't he? Sometimes the liberal press characterizes him as a reactionary because of his theological stands on marriage, clerical celibacy, religious life, and so forth. At other times he is painted by the conservative press as a radical socialist because of his teaching on the rights of labor, free enterprise, and the capitalist system.

The same is true in ecumenism. Some feel he is dragging his heels. Others are shocked by his dramatic moves for Christian unity. Such was the case this past week when John Paul II released a remarkably warm recognition of Martin Luther and then participated in a Lutheran ceremony in a Protestant church in Rome itself. Just a week earlier, a Catholic conservative newspaper denounced and derided Archbishop John Whealon of Hartford for a similar gesture during this five-hundredth remembrance of Luther's birth. We all need to learn from the Pope. We need to read his words about Luther. We need to review our history.

For a Catholic in 1983 to speak or write on Martin Luther is a special challenge. He or she must try to be objective and balanced. It will be necessary to say some bad and some good things about the Catholic Church in the sixteenth century. And it will be necessary to say some bad and some good things about Martin Luther. The truth, if presented in an understanding way, should prove offensive to neither Lutherans nor Catholics.

It is consoling to know that even Lutherans cringe at some of the words of their Father Martin. But for too long Luther has been presented in Catholic circles as only a foul mouth, a psychopath, as one who was said to sin boldly, who rejected the Epistle of James, and married a nun. For too long, Luther has been presented to Catholics as something like a Billy Sunday who needed to have his mouth washed out with soap. Luther has not been presented to Catholics for what he was: a Catholic, a Christian loyal to the Church, to her creeds, and to her sacraments. His magnificent religious virtues need to be appreciated by all. Luther had Catholic theology, perception, imagination, and a sense of humor. He had a lifelong devotion to Mary, the Mother of Jesus, and to the *Magnificat.*

He preached that no one would ever take private confession away from him, for he personally knew its benefits. (I wish Luther could preach about confession and Mary to our Catholic people of this generation.)

It is impossible to understand Martin Luther without knowing something of the times and the Church from which he came. Most people then were uneducated, illiterate, and superstitious. Most people lived and died where they were born and never traveled more than a few miles away from home. The memory of the Black Death was still strong, and illness was commonplace.

As the sixteenth century dawned, all Christians in Europe were, generally speaking, Catholics under the pope. But in the Catholic Church there was much decadence. At the heart of the decadence was money. The pope was head of the government of the papal states and needed an army, government officials, and so forth. In those times, a strong papal state meant that kings and commoners paid more attention to the pope. We can afford to be critical of such an approach to religion, but we are of the twentieth century.

In the decadence, the pope in Rome was the central malfunction. Popes of that time were usually more political than religious, overly concerned about money and power, given to nepotism and luxury. This infection spread to many ecclesiastics — cardinals, bishops, aristocratic cathedral chapters, ignorant and venal parish priests. There was an unholy union of money and bishops and state.

From the religious viewpoint, these were terrible times. There were repeated calls for reforming or cleaning up the situation "from the head down to the members." But every attempt to change ended in failure. The need for financial support was unending, and this was the only system that people knew.

But it would be wrong to picture the Catholic Church of the sixteenth century as totally corrupt. In that Church were many holy and sincere cardinals, bishops, priests, and laity. There was much sincere and solid religion. The number of saints from the sixteenth century was surprising. It was "the best of times, the worst of times."

And at that time, at the end of the fifteenth century, in November 1483, Martin Luther was born in Germany.

(St. Louis, November 18, 1983)

"First to Hear the Word of God"

Next week, on April 13, Pope John Paul II will visit Rome's main synagogue for an interfaith prayer service. Some Jewish and Catholic leaders believe that his action may well "start a new era" in Jewish-Catholic relations. We need to unite our prayers with our Holy Father next week.

Last week, Catholics all over the world heard in more than a hundred languages, as part of the Church's public prayer on Good Friday, the invitation:

> Let us pray for the Jewish people, the first to hear the Word of God, that they may continue to grow in the love of his name and in faithfulness to his covenant.

Good Friday is a beautiful day for us Catholics. For thousands of our Jewish sisters and brothers, especially for those who grew up in Europe before World War II, Good Friday is not beautiful. A recent incident in England can help us to see why.

In early March, Cardinal Hume of Westminster invested as a papal knight of Saint Gregory the Great, a leader of the Jewish community in England, Sir Sigmund Sternberg, in recognition of his services to Catholic-Jewish understanding. After the ceremony, Sir Sigmund called the changes that had made his honor possible "a miracle." He recalled as a small boy in Hungary going home in tears from school after being threatened that all Jews would be punished for killing Jesus Christ. There are Jews in our own community with similar recollections. They would testify that on no day of the year were the threats from their Christian and Catholic neighbors as menacing as on Good Friday.

This centuries'-old history of anti-Semitism is still too little known to Catholics. Without it, we cannot possibly understand the declaration of the Second Vatican Council in 1965:

> Even though the Jewish authorities and those who followed their lead pressed for the death of Christ, neither all Jews indiscriminately at that time, nor Jews today, can be charged with the crimes committed during his passion. It is true that the Church is the new people of God, yet the Jews should not be spoken of as rejected or accursed as if this followed from holy Scripture.
>
> *(Declaration on the Relation of the Church to Non-Christian Religions, #4)*

In the same document, the Council condemned anti-Semitism explicitly:

> The Church reproves every form of persecution against whomsoever it may be directed. Remembering, then, her common heritage with the Jews and moved not by any political consideration, but solely by the religious motivation of Christian charity, she deplores all hatreds, persecutions, displays of anti-Semitism leveled at any time or from any source against the Jews.

A Common Heritage: The Council recalled the teaching of the apostle Paul, a Jew like Jesus, and most of the first Christians that "the Jews remain very dear to God for the sake of the patriarchs, since God does not take back the gifts he bestowed or the choice he made" (the Council's paraphrase of Romans 11:28-29).

The "common heritage with the Jews" mentioned by the Council includes the whole of the Jewish Scriptures, which we call the Old Testament. The Church's public prayer bears, even today, the marks of its origin in the Jewish liturgy of the synagogue and of the Jerusalem Temple, destroyed by Roman pagans in A.D. 70. The Divine Office, prayed daily by all Catholic clergy and many religious orders, consists largely of the psalms of David. The Mass cannot be fully understood apart from the Jewish Passover meal in which it originated. The celebrant's prayer at the offering of bread and wine ("Blessed are you, Lord, God of all creation...") is based on the table blessing still used today by devout Jews the world over.

The oldest eucharistic prayer of the Western Church (the Roman Canon, now called Eucharistic Prayer No. 1) calls the Jewish Patriarch Abraham, "our father in faith." On September 6, 1938, when the dark clouds of anti-Semitism were already gathering over Hitler's Third Reich, Pope Pius XI mentioned this prayer to a group of Belgian pilgrims who had just presented him with an ancient and valuable missal: "Whenever I read the words, 'The sacrifice of Abraham, our faith in faith,' I cannot help being deeply moved. Mark well, we call Abraham our Patriarch, our ancestor. Anti-Semitism is irreconcilable with this lofty thought, the noble reality which this prayer expresses." And, with tears in his eyes, the Pope concluded: "Anti-Semitism is inadmissible; spiritually, we are the Semites" (cited from Pinchas E. Lapide, *The Last Three Popes and the Jews,* London and New York, 1967, page 114).

Inextricably Linked: In the mysterious plan of God, Jews and Christians are inextricably linked for all time. It was surely a desire to express this connection that moved our Holy Father, Pope John II, to announce his intention of visiting a Roman synagogue on April 13, between Easter and Passover. With our Jewish friends we await this visit, and the Pope's words, with keen anticipation.

In preparation we would do well to recall some statements in the catechism of the Council of Trent (1566). This said that the guilt for Christ's Crucifixion is "more enormous in us than in the Jews, since according to the testimony of the apostle (Paul): '...if they had known it, they would never have crucified the Lord of glory' " (1 Corinthians 2:8). Whereas we, on the contrary, professing to know him yet denying him by our actions, seem in some sort to lay violent hands on him.

Vatican Council II reaffirmed this teaching (too often neglected, with tragic consequences for Christians as well as Jews), when it said:

> The Church always held and continues to hold that Christ out of infinite love freely underwent suffering and death because of the sins of all men, so that all might attain salvation.

The final working out of the destiny common to Jews and Christians is a mystery hidden in the design of the God who has told us, through the Jewish prophet Isaiah: "My thoughts are not your thoughts, and your ways are not my ways" (55:8). The Church's prayer for our Jewish brothers and sisters on Good Friday respects this mystery:

> Almighty and eternal God, long ago you gave your promise to Abraham and his posterity. Listen to your Church as we pray that the people you first made your own may arrive at the fullness of redemption. We ask this through Christ our Lord. Amen.

May this Easter and Passover season bring to all of us, Jews and Christians alike, the assurance that our common Lord is truly "Emmanuel: God-with-us."

(St. Louis, April 4, 1986)

– ◆ –

Reykjavik and Assisi

What really happened in Iceland? Was the recent meeting of President Reagan and General Secretary Mikhail Gorbachev a hopeful move toward world peace or a spiteful step toward a wider arms race into space itself? Despite all the subsequent analysis of what happened in Reykjavik, we really do not know — at least for now. The whole world watches and waits — with its heart in its mouth.

Assisi: Pope John Paul has chosen this time of expectation and apprehension for his own move.

On Monday, October 27, twenty-seven leaders from every major religion in the world — Catholic, Orthodox, Protestant, Anglican, Jewish, Moslem, Buddhist, Hindu, Shinto, the traditional religions of Africa and other continents — will meet in Assisi, the town of Saint Francis, to pray for peace.

It will be the first time in history that every religious tradition has joined to pray for a common goal.

Pope John Paul II, who initiated the event, has named it "Assisi '86." He will greet participants in St. Francis' Church, and then each delegation will go to a separate place for two hours of prayer. After that, all will meet in the Basilica of St. Francis for a joint service.

Participants will fast throughout the day and then conclude the day's activities with a common meal in the Franciscan dining room, hosted by the Pope.

Assisi '86 has caught the world's imagination, but will it make any real difference in international politics?

Most people consider prayer useful in solving personal problems, but not something that has any real political value. They feel that the real action on world peace would be talks like those between President Reagan and Soviet leader Gorbachev.

Pope John Paul sees things differently. Prayer, he said, is "a very potent weapon." It is "a key, capable of unlocking even the most ingrained situations of hate."

It is significant that the meeting take place in Assisi, the city of Saint Francis. Saint Francis, a thirteenth-century mystic and religious reformer, advocated a life of strict poverty and deep respect for all of creation. He has been an inspiration in the spiritual lives of many, whatever their religious background, and thus provides a powerful witness to the cause of peace and understanding.

We commend Pope John Paul for making this opportunity possible. In these weeks after the summit in Iceland, we are painfully reminded that it takes more than political negotiations to bring about peace. Who's to say prayer can't end the arms race? How can we be so sure the way we're doing things now is the only way? Why don't we think prayer makes any difference?

It's becoming clearer every day that without a spiritual base, none of our problems have solutions. That's what Saint Francis tried to tell us some seven hundred years ago, but now nuclear weapons are forcing us to listen.

(St. Louis, October 24, 1986)

— ◆ —

A New Martyr

As Catholics, we belong to a worldwide family of faith, which now numbers some 887 million people. It is good from time to time to raise our eyes from our local concerns to those of the Church elsewhere. May 1, when this column appears, is a good opportunity to do so. On that day, our Holy Father, Pope John Paul II, will declare the German Jew, Edith Stein, "blessed." From today we may publicly invoke her prayers and pray that she will one day be declared a saint.

Called by God

Edith Stein was born on October 12, 1891, the last of eleven children of a devout Jewish family in Breslau, Germany. It was Yom Kippur, one of the two holiest days in the Jewish calendar. (The other is Passover.) A year and a half later, Edith's father died, leaving her mother to rear the large family and manage their lumber business.

Like many young people today, Edith Stein abandoned her faith as a university student and declared herself an atheist. She joined a socialist women's group and agitated for women's liberation. Though she rejected religion, she studied philosophy for answers to ultimate questions: the meaning of life, suffering, and death. In 1917, at the age of twenty-five, she earned her Ph.D. with the celebrated Jewish philosophy professor Edmund Husserl. Three decades later, Husserl's writings would influence a young Polish priest named Karol Wojtyla, the present pope.

That same year, Edith Stein had an experience that was to change her life. She visited the young widow of a friend killed in the First World War — dreading the meeting since she did not know what to say. To her astonishment, she found the widow not crushed by bereavement but drawing inner strength from her faith in the crucified and risen Christ. "It was my first encounter with the power of the cross," Edith Stein would write later. "In that moment, my atheism collapsed."

Four more years were to pass, however, before Edith Stein received the full gift of faith. In the summer of 1921, she discovered the autobiography of the Spanish Carmelite, Saint Teresa of Jesus. She read it through in a single night and declared the next morning, "That is the truth." On New Year's Day, 1922, she received Catholic baptism, taking the name Teresa.

United With Her People: Edith Stein's conversion was such a bitter blow to her devout Jewish mother that on the advice of two Catholic priests, Edith put aside the hope of becoming a Carmelite nun and devoted herself to a teaching career. During the next decade, she became well known in academic circles as a candidate for a prestigious professorship. This prospect vanished in 1933, however, when Hitler became Germany's chancellor and enacted laws excluding Jews from public life. On October 15, 1933, the Feast of Saint Teresa of Jesus, she entered the Cologne Carmel as Sister Teresia Benedicta of the Cross. Her eighty-four-year-old mother was crushed.

Following the mother's death four years later (on September 14, 1936, the Feast of the Holy Cross), Edith, remembering the heavenly vision of a "huge crowd which no one could count, from every race, people, and tongue" (Revelation 7:9), wrote: "I am confident that my mother has found a merciful judge and is even now my most faithful advocate, to help me toward my goal."

Despite Hitler's violent anti-Semitism, few people in Germany foresaw the coming tragedy. Even many German Jews thought that their well-known patriotism and public service would avert the worst. Edith Stein never shared this optimism. Already in 1933, she wrote: "God has again laid his heavy hand on his people, whose fate is also mine." During a holy hour in the Cologne Carmel she prayed that she might bear the cross on behalf of her fellow Jews. "At the end of the hour," she wrote later, "I knew in my heart that my prayer had been heard. But I did not know what my cross would be."

On October 21, 1938, she wrote: "I am confident that God has accepted my life on behalf of all Jews. I think continually of Queen Esther (in the Old Testament), who was taken from her people to stand on their behalf before the king." Not three weeks later, on November 8-9, 1938, came the terrible "Kristallnacht" ("night of crystal"), when Nazi thugs smashed Jewish shopwindows and burned synagogues all over Germany. At the news, Edith Stein "was paralyzed with pain." At year-end, to avoid danger for her fellow Carmelites and herself, she was sent to a Dutch Carmel at Echt in Holland.

Auschwitz: There she was joined by her sister, Rosa, who had also become a Carmelite. They remained unharmed through the German invasion of neutral Holland in May 1940 and the subsequent deportation of Jews to a then still uncertain fate "in the East."

On July 11, 1942, the Dutch Catholic bishops joined Protestant leaders in a private telegram protesting against these deportations. The Reichskommisar for Holland, Seyss-Inquart, responded with a promise that baptized Jews would be spared. Not satisfied, the Catholic bishops publicized the exchange in a pastoral letter on behalf of *all* Jews which was read in every Catholic church in the Netherlands on Sunday, July 26, 1942. Seyss-Inquart was furious. The very next day, he ordered the immediate arrest and deportation "this week" of all Catholic Jews. Three days later, he stated that this measure was a response to the Catholic bishops who, "unlike their Protestant colleagues, interfered publicly in a matter that was outside their competence."

Dutch Jews who were members of Protestant churches were spared for the time being. Some three hundred Catholic Jews were arrested, including fifteen members of religious orders. When two SS officers came to the Carmel at Echt to arrest the Steins, Edith said to Rosa: "Come, we're going for our people." A few days later, amid the horrors of the detention camp at Westerbork, Edith Stein told a Dutch official named Wielek: "I never knew that human beings could behave in this fashion or that my sisters and brothers would have to suffer so much." On August 7, 1942, Edith Stein, with hundreds of others, started the two-day rail journey to Auschwitz in Poland, crammed like animals into sealed cattle cars. Upon arrival, they were sent straight to the gas chambers. The date: August 9, 1942.

The Holy Father has granted the joint request of the German and Polish Bishops that Edith Stein be enrolled in the Church's official list of martyrs — the title given her spontaneously from the time of her death by those who had known her in the last years. Her simple memorial tablet in the Cologne Carmel bears the inscription: "She died as a martyr for her people and her faith."

With deep sorrow for the horrors Edith Stein and her people suffered at the hands of those who were embittered enemies of Jews and Christians alike — and yet with the joy of our resurrection faith, we invoke the prayers of the Church's newest martyr:

- For all young people who have lost faith in God and see no meaning or purpose in life;
- "For the Jewish people, the first to hear the Word of God, that they may continue to grow in the love of his name and in faithfulness to his covenant" (Liturgy of Good Friday);

- For ourselves, that walking in the way of the cross, we, like her,
  may find it the way of happiness and peace;

Let us pray to the Lord.

(St. Louis, May 1, 1987)

Lutherans in Our Cathedral

It was my intention to announce to you that the new Evangelical Lutheran Church in America would celebrate its birth in their first solemn liturgy in our cathedral, but another local paper beat me to it. It will not occur until November 22, so I was a bit surprised to have them break the news. Perhaps some background on all this will help.

Merger: In January 1988, one church body to be known as the Evangelical Lutheran Church in America will come into being officially. It is being created from three church bodies that were formerly independent. There are forty-seven congregations in the St. Louis area that will be part of this one new church body. We thank God for this step toward the day when we will be "one body, one spirit, in Christ." We pray, too, that this one step will be one of many prompted by the Holy Spirit, so that the prayer of Jesus at the Last Supper will be realized: "That all may be one."

When representatives of those who are involved in this church reconciliation began to meet to plan their celebration of their new unity in Christ, they wrote to me asking if it might be possible for them to gather in our cathedral for this occasion. Among other reasons that they cited for their request, one stands out. The Evangelical Lutheran Church in America is committed to seeking further unity with all brothers and sisters in Christ. Furthermore, they were seeking an appropriate setting with adequate seating capacity. They hoped to avoid a convention hall or sports arena.

We have agreed to extend the hospitality of our cathedral to the congregations of the Evangelical Lutheran Church in America in the St. Louis area for their celebration of unity and thanksgiving on the Feast of Christ the King, Sunday, November 22, 1987. The newly elected bishop of their church will preside at their eucharistic celebration and preach on that occasion. I plan to be present as a gesture of goodwill to give a word of welcome and congratulations.

Example: In coming to this decision, I was mindful of the commitment to Christian ecumenism in the teaching of Vatican Council II. More recently, the example of our Holy Father was persuasive — especially in his approaches to Lutherans in his sermon in their church in Rome and during his two visits to Germany. In our country, very fruitful Catholic-Lutheran theological dialogues have been going on over recent years, thanks to our Bishops' Conference. The new emphasis on Eucharist in Lutheran worship has been noted in this dialogue, and it is something we greet with joy.

This is not the first time for a gathering like this in our cathedral. The United Church of Christ gathered in our cathedral some years ago for a worship service. More recently, the Methodist Church in Washington, D.C., gathered in the National Shrine of the Immaculate Conception for a eucharistic celebration and the ordination of deacons for service in their church. Years ago in Springfield, Illinois, Bishop McNicholas hosted the installation liturgy of the new Episcopal bishop in Immaculate Conception Cathedral there. So this is really nothing so new or controversial.

Someone has said that this is a nice gesture, but four hundred years too late. We may be latecomers in ecumenism, but I hope we can make up for lost time.

(St. Louis, June 12, 1987)

– ◆ –

Last Sunday's first liturgy of the newly united Evangelical Lutheran Church in America was celebrated by our neighbors here in our cathedral. It was beautiful, and I was glad to welcome these Christian people to our mother church.

The ceremony was glorious, the capacity congregation was overawed by our cathedral, and we were able to practice hospitality as Saint Paul directs us to do. Through the history of our archdiocese, there were many times when Catholic congregations were offered use of Protestant churches, especially in emergencies and special occasions. This is a beautiful old St. Louis tradition, and I am happy to continue it. Our Holy Father has shown special concern for Lutherans both in Rome and especially during his visit to Germany. The Catholic bishops of our country have done the same in our ongoing dialogues with Lutherans ever since Vatican Council II.

I was very proud of our Catholic hospitality shown by so many of you last Sunday. That was the real story, but a few counter-demonstrators were given the headline in the daily press. Allegedly, a group of local dissident

170

traditionalist Catholics not in union with the Pope were aided and abetted by some activists from Chicago who had unjustly tabbed these Lutherans as "pro-abortion." The Chicagoans were politely admitted to the cathedral but later had to be just as politely escorted out when they insisted on praying the rosary out loud just as our guests began their liturgy. Ah, Chicago!

(St. Louis, November 27, 1987)

Our Neighbors

This past week our Jewish neighbors have observed their high holy days. This sacred time in their year began on September 9, Rosh Hashanah, and it continued until September 18, Yom Kippur. It is a time of memory, repentance, and resolution for another year. It is a time, I am sure, when many of our neighbors ponder and pray over the overpowering mystery in Jewish history — the Holocaust.

The Holocaust is a mind-numbing event. Our brains are not conditioned to absorb death on such a gigantic scale. We can weep over the death of a loved one; we are stunned by the sudden annihilation of a family. But what human mind can cope with the deliberate execution of six million people? Even more astonishing, perhaps, a remnant of this ancient people survived in Europe to carry on a history that reaches back to the patriarchs, and many of the survivors are refugees today, fleeing Eastern Europe and the Soviet Union to join their own people in freedom.

The history of the Jewish people is stained by tragedy: enslavement, exile, the destruction of their beloved Temple; still they survived and preserved their identity. The holy Scriptures show a people who were profoundly convinced of God's presence to them, again and again reaching into the shadows of death to summon them to new life.

I once asked a rabbi how his people's faith could have survived the horror of the Holocaust. He pointed to the state of Israel. Out of their darkest moment, new hope had been born. Trusting in God's redemptive presence, remembering his faithfulness to them, they offer a lesson to the world.

Each of us writes our own autobiography in the days and weeks of our lives; inevitably, it is a record of triumph and failure, of laughter and tears. Our history, however, takes on tone and perspective only if we are men and women of faith, only if we believe in God's redemptive presence in our lives. There are no depths of failure, disappointment, even tragedy, that he has not enveloped with his Spirit, promising to transform them into moments of salvation. He asks only our trust. Yet it is his heaviest demand.

A French poet once wrote of the difficulty we experience in trusting God. He imagines the Lord standing at the bedside of a man who tosses and turns in his search for sleep.

> My poor friend, you worry about so many things.
> I see your cheeks stained with tears.
> I hear your heart pounding as you look to tomorrow.
> If only you could trust me...
> I ask you for faith, and you give it readily.
> I ask you to love, and you do so generously.
> Only one thing you refuse me — your trust.
> My dear friend, I am with you.
> Sleep now and I will watch.

And We: Something else comes to mind when we think of the Church today, the people of God on pilgrimage to the Promised Land, as we often portray it.

Our ancestors, poor immigrants, built the enormous infrastructure of the Church in the United States. They had little but their dreams, but they erected the hospitals, orphanages, parishes, and schools that stretched across the land. Their sons and daughters by the thousands were the priests and religious who staffed them.

Our own record is somewhat dimmer. In the past twenty-five years, we have closed so many schools and opened so few. Our inner-city parishes are withering, our teachers are underpaid, and the thinning ranks of our priests, Brothers, and nuns have not been reinforced. Yet we Catholics are not the poor immigrants of generations back. We are the most numerous, the best educated, the most affluent Christian body in the United States. How do we explain it?

The "prophets of doom" among us, as Pope John XXIII called them, proclaim the approaching end of it all. But good Pope John, remembering the words of Jesus, "I am with you all days, even to the end of the world," proclaimed something else — trust, the message of that French poet above.

They tell the story of a crowded, exhausting day in the life of the Pope: nothing seemed to go right despite his hard work all day. Worries of all kinds assailed his spirit at the end of that day. As John finished brushing his teeth, he simply said, "Lord, it's your Church — take care of it. I'm going to bed."

(St. Louis, September 20, 1991)

- 11 -
ROME AND
ITS BISHOP

Just as in the gospel, the Lord so disposing, Saint Peter and the other apostles constitute one apostolic college, so the Roman pontiff, the successor of Peter, and the bishops, the successors of the apostles, are joined together.... But the college or body of bishops has no authority unless it is understood together with the Roman pontiff, the successor of Peter as its head.

(Constitution on the Church, 22)

Who Is the Pope? This coming visitor to our shores — who is he? Why the big fuss?

For the answer to that question, we need to go back to that scene in the Gospel of Matthew (16:13-18) when Simon, son of John, spoke before all the apostles in professing his belief that Jesus was the Messiah, the Son of God. Jesus answered that this faith was a gift from God the Father, and he then changed Simon's name to Peter, which means rock, and he said, "On this rock I will build my church — I will give you the keys of the kingdom of heaven; what you bind on earth will be bound in heaven, what you loose on earth will be loosed in heaven."

Even though Peter was a coward in denying Jesus the night before Calvary, Jesus never abandoned Peter. After his Resurrection, he again challenged Peter, and upon assurance of Peter's love and loyalty, Jesus, the Good Shepherd, said, "Feed my lambs, feed my sheep" (John 21:15-19).

Through the rest of the Bible, we see Peter speaking for the apostles especially from the day of Pentecost. The Lord made decisions for the infant Church by revealing them to Peter. Although he was still fearful and hesitating at times, Peter was still the acknowledged leader who strengthened the rest as Jesus said he would. Peter went to Antioch and finally to Rome, where he was martyred for the Faith in the year 67.

Peter's Successor: What Peter did in the early Church, as we read in the Bible, the pope does today. When he emerged last year from Saint Peter's Basilica (built over the tomb of Peter), Karol Wojtyla was not just a brilliant Polish churchman. He was now the two hundred sixty-fourth successor of Peter, the Vicar of Christ, the visible sign of unity for Catholics all over the world.

Like Peter, this man may have his faults. But he has the promise of Jesus, as did Peter, "I have prayed for you that your faith may not fail." He will make decisions for the whole Church under the guidance of the Holy Spirit as did Peter. He will strengthen his brothers in the Faith.

The pope is Christ's own will for his Church, that it might truly be one, holy, catholic, and apostolic. We therefore receive the pope in faith and joy as the gift of Christ. That is why there is all the fuss when he comes.

And that is why we should prepare spiritually for the visit of our Holy Father. We can do it in this way:

1. *Prayer:* The intention of the Pope's fruitful visit here should be part of the prayer of the faithful in every Mass. A daily rosary in every parish church, in every family, by every individual Catholic, should be added.

2. *Penance:* A special penance service in every parish and extra times for confession should be provided. All Catholics should be invited to reconciliation with the Lord in this beautiful sacrament. In Poland and Ireland, all Catholics were urged to abstain from all alcoholic beverage as penance also.

3. *Charity:* Offerings can be made toward the hurricane sufferers or for the Propagation of the Faith, the world missions of our Holy Father.

The Pope's visit can be a great "teachable moment" for us all, a time of special grace from the Lord. Prepare the way.

(Mobile, September 28, 1979)

"Shepherd I"

That was the name painted on the side of the TWA plane assigned to fly Pope John Paul II on his recent pastoral visit to our country. Perhaps TWA was just trying to be cute, but I believe they could not have chosen a more apt title for their plane and its celebrated passenger. In his crowded first year as successor of Peter, our Holy Father has truly become pastor to the world, the first and foremost shepherd of all the Lord's flock.

Jesus said that the good shepherd must know his sheep, and they must come to know him. Pope John Paul is obviously determined to know all the people of the world. Already he had probably been seen and heard by more people than any pope in history. All the world's media have done a superb job in making him known. I would like to give you some personal impressions.

Bishop-elect Friend[1] and I went to Chicago last Thursday afternoon. Bright and early on Friday morning, we were on our way across the city to Quigley Seminary, where we were scheduled to meet the Holy Father with all the American Bishops at 10 a.m. We began with a prayer service in the chapel, then went to the auditorium for the actual meeting (meanwhile the Pope spoke to the handicapped people of the Chicago area, who were gathered on the front lawn with their families). Following the meeting, we all had a very pleasant lunch with the Pope in the gymnasium. Immediately thereafter, we left by bus for downtown Chicago, where we concelebrated the Papal Mass for the congregation of well over a million people. Friday evening I watched on TV as the Pope continued his sixteen-hour day with more appearances to various groups in Chicago. I was tired just watching.

Saturday morning we flew to Washington, D.C., to attend the reception President and Mrs. Carter gave for the Pope at the White House, after which

---

1 Auxiliary of Shreveport-Alexandria, Louisiana; from 1982 Ordinary.

we returned to Mobile Saturday evening. It was quite a forty-eight-hour experience.

What Were My Thoughts? Once again, I am amazed at how God works in the history of his Church. In the final days of Pope Paul VI, the world's writers were prophesying less and less attention to the Pope, and then came the tragic death of the winsome, smiling John Paul I who had won the world's love in a month. Everything seemed to be going from bad to worse for the Catholic Church. There was a crisis of confidence indeed. A year later how all this has changed! I am convinced that Pope John Paul II is God's great gift to his Church just at this time. He is exactly what we need right now.

He Will Make Us One: We need to overcome our separations. With all our differences, there is still one Lord and one Faith. Pope John Paul will make that very clear in no uncertain terms. He will sound no uncertain trumpet. We will know exactly what we stand for as Catholics.

He Will Make Us Proud: You can see that everywhere in the crowds that pour out to be with him. They thrill to be his sons and daughters, and they sing out their joy with him in being members of the same vast Catholic family.

He Will Challenge Our Youth: Young people everywhere are captivated by the Holy Father. He obviously loves them in a special way. In Chicago, a twenty-year-old Notre Dame student jumped a fence to shake the Pope's hand and found himself in the clutches of the police, who were leading him away for questioning and possible arrest. The Pope saw all this, called the police, and talked a moment with the frightened youth. He ended up giving the young man a big bear hug and release from the police. I would bet that the number of seminarians will rise dramatically in the next few years, and young people all over the world will have a new outlook on their Faith.

"Pope of Promise": That is what *Newsweek* called him in its cover story last week. That is how I would sum up these few thoughts also. People of every faith are yearning for a leader, for inspiration at this time. A Methodist man and his wife on our plane traveled from Houston to Washington and back last Saturday just to see the Pope. People everywhere — on the street,

in the airport — asked us if we had seen him. So many were not Catholic, but all spontaneously expressed their admiration for him, their hope in him, and what he can mean for all men in the years ahead. He is truly the Pope of Promise. Let us pray for our Holy Father, John Paul. *Sto lat! Sto lat!*

(Mobile, October 12, 1979)

— ♦ —

Clarification

Just a few days back in the daily papers, I learned that Archbishop Marcel Lefebvre will be visiting our city soon. Allegedly, he will be dedicating a chapel in a converted school building. I believe it is necessary for me to make the following statement.

Some years ago Pope Paul VI was forced to suspend this French prelate from his episcopal functions. The Pope's action was taken only after years of fruitless effort to reconcile the Archbishop to the official teaching of the Catholic Church. Pope John Paul II has made similar efforts in a series of personal meetings with Archbishop Lefebvre. The suspension remains in effect, even though both Popes have mercifully not excommunicated this aging Archbishop who has caused so much misunderstanding in the Catholic Church.

Let no one tell you that the issue is the Latin Mass. As I mentioned recently in this column, Mass may be offered in Latin wherever it will be pastorally helpful. The issue is simply the authority of the Pope. Archbishop Lefebvre will not accept it.

Accordingly, no Catholic may support in any way this tragic movement headed by Archbishop Lefebvre. I regret very much his coming to St. Louis because of the disunity he represents. I call upon all Catholics at this time to reaffirm our loyalty and allegiance to our Holy Father, Pope John Paul II, by ignoring this visit and this chapel. Let us show all who would come to this archdiocese to divide us that we stand strong with the Pope as one flock and one shepherd.

(St. Louis, May 16, 1980)

— ♦ —

Q Will it be all right for me to attend the Tridentine Mass that is being offered at Holy Rosary Chapel in St. Louis?

A When I was asked that question this past week, I was quite surprised to learn that some of our people still do not understand that a representative of the "Lefebrve schism" has organized a group here against our Holy Father. It is especially tragic that they have now brought a discredited priest here to use the Mass, the symbol of Catholic unity, as a means to turn our people against the Holy Father and the one Catholic Church in union with him. Just recently, a second group has been formed in Farmington.

According to the canon law of the Catholic Church, no priest may come into a diocese to set up a church and preach without the permission of the local bishop. Every bishop is always happy to "grant the faculties of the diocese" to any priest in good standing on his request. In this case, the priest is not in good standing, and he has, of course, not been authorized by me in any way. There has been no evidence that he is a priest of any diocese or religious order in the United States. If he was ordained, as I suspect, in the "Lefebrve movement," then his ordination was illicit and contrary to the direct prohibition of Popes Paul VI and John Paul II.

Let no one tell you that the issue of this movement is the offering of a Tridentine Mass or a Mass in Latin. That is only a subterfuge to obscure the real issue. This group denies the authority of our Holy Father and all the bishops of the world assembled in ecumenical council to prescribe the liturgy of the Catholic Church. They have become more strident lately in writing nationally and locally against the Bishop of Kansas City and me. Accordingly, I must make the following statement:

If you are a Catholic, you stand for the authority of the Pope and full unity with him in faith. If you do not, you are not a Catholic. Accordingly, I formally disapprove and decry this movement in our archdiocese. Catholics of the archdiocese may not attend these chapels in good faith. I call upon everyone of you simply to ignore this attempt to separate our people from our Holy Father. This Archdiocese of St. Louis stands in full union and loyalty with our Holy Father, Pope John Paul II.

(St. Louis, October 3, 1980)

– ◆ –

Violence

Last week I sent this mailgram to Rome in your name: "Most Holy Father, Cardinal Carberry, and the whole Church of St. Louis join me in pledge of renewed loyalty and unceasing devotion. We are all praying for a speedy and complete recovery [from the assassination attempt in St. Peter's Square] of Your Holiness."

But we are not alone in those prayers, I assure you. Immediately after the tragic news from Rome, I was flooded with calls and letters from all over our community. The Jewish community in many messages assured me of prayers for the Pope in all Sabbath services. Methodist, Episcopal, and Presbyterian leaders promised the same. The Conference of Christians and Jews was represented at the cathedral Mass, and the graduation exercises at St. Louis Community College at Forest Park began with a prayer for the Pope. People all around the metropolitan area said the same thing to me and so many of our clergy. It was a beautiful outpouring of love for which I am most grateful.

You know, it may be that the Lord will bring much good out of this mad act of violence after all. People all over the world have been forced to face the issue of world violence as indicated in the superb editorial in the *St. Louis Post-Dispatch* last Sunday that said, "In St. Louis, within twenty-four hours of the attempted assassination in the Vatican, four men were shot to death. Last year thirty-one thousand Americans died as a result of accidents, suicides, or murders involving handguns." The editorial continued outlining the arms sales of the major nations — much of it to poor nations who have hardly enough to eat. And the ultimate belief in violence is, of course, reflected in the continued stockpiling of nuclear weapons by the major powers.

We live in a truly violent world. The madness of the attack on the Pope may help us to see our global insanity in the arms race. It may help us listen more to this Pope who constantly warns the world against its trust in violence. In Ireland in 1979, he said, "Violence is a lie, for it goes against the truth of our faith, the truth of our humanity....On my knees I beg you to turn away from the paths of violence. You may claim to seek justice. I, too, believe in justice and seek justice. But violence only delays the day of justice. Violence destroys the work of justice."

(St. Louis, May 22, 1981)

— ◆ —

Arrivederci Roma!

As you read this, I will (God willing) be over the Atlantic on my way to Rome for my quinquennial report to our Holy Father. Each diocesan bishop in the world must make this personal accounting of his stewardship to the Pope every five years, hence its name.

Written Data: The format of the accounting to be made is supplied by the appropriate Vatican offices and is quite exhaustive. There are two methods of reporting employed: analysis by the bishop and statistics of the whole archdiocese. Our archdiocesan departments have provided information on their work. All our individual parish reports were also summarized and included. Finally, the entire compilation was sent some weeks ago to the Sacred Congregation of Bishops, which shares appropriate information with other Vatican offices dealing with such specifics as liturgy, family life, education, vocations, and so forth. Finally, a digest of the entire report is prepared for the Holy Father.

Ad Limina: On arrival in Rome, each bishop makes his *ad limina* (to the threshold of the apostles) visit to the tombs of Saints Peter and Paul. These two apostles are the Fathers of the Church of Rome and the patrons of all bishops. We are instructed to pray at both tombs for the successor of Peter and for our brother bishops and all our people that we may follow in the footsteps of Paul in his "care of all the churches." It is most impressive to ponder there the long line of successors of the apostles who have done the same down the centuries.

Each bishop is also invited to consult Vatican officials during this time to discuss various sections of his report and sometimes to take up other archdiocesan concerns.

Meanwhile, definite time is given each bishop for his appointment with the Pope. The Pope interviews each of us individually in his study. He discusses the report and asks further questions and welcomes our questions of him. Every opportunity is given for a full, open discussion. Later when all the bishops of that week have been interviewed, the Holy Father receives us all in a body and gives a formal address. The next day he has us all together for an informal lunch and further discussion. There will be about twenty American Bishops in our group. The Holy Father does this year after year covering all the bishops of the world every five years.

Judging from the written data we have sent to Rome, I am confident that Pope John Paul will be pleased with what has been accomplished in the Archdiocese of St. Louis since the last report. I am pretty sure we will get a passing grade.

(St. Louis, September 23, 1983)

— ♦ —

My trip to Rome was great; everything worked out as planned. But the best part was the last part — coming back home. Lambert Field never looked so beautiful, despite the encircling gloom last Sunday night.

While in Rome, I read the October 10 *Newsweek* article, "The Pope vs. the U.S. Church." For the last year or more, I have noticed increasing efforts in some Catholic publications to paint the Pope and the American Bishops as antagonists. Such reports appeared invariably in the far left or far right Catholic press. So I guess it was inevitable that the idea would be reflected in a national secular newsmagazine.

Such alleged rifts among the successors of the apostles are familiar to any reader of Church history. (You might read about "Americanism" in the late nineteenth century.) Today I would rather just tell you what happened to one American Bishop last week on his regular five-year reporting visit to the Pope.

I saw Pope John Paul II personally four times last week. The first time was Monday morning, October 17. I walked over to St. Peter's from the North American College where I was staying. After a brief prayer at the tomb of Saint Peter, I went to the Pope's library for my appointment. The Swiss Guards and finally a priest secretary guided me on my way until the library door opened and the Pope welcomed me with a warm smile and a strong handshake, which prevented my kneeling to kiss the ring of the Fisherman. Instead, he took me by the arm and seated me beside him at his big desk where a map of the U.S.A. was spread out.

With his finger on the juncture of the Missouri and Mississippi rivers, the Holy Father began reminiscing about his brief stop in St. Louis while he was Cardinal Archbishop of Crakow. He mentioned visiting Cardinal Carberry then and reviewed the location and history of the archdiocese. Then there were questions about the Church of St. Louis, especially the faith and prayer life of our laypeople. He was impressed by the number of clergy and religious men and women in our archdiocese and asked about our vocation picture. There were questions about our social-service work and urban problems. We discussed the needs for the immediate future, and the interview came to a conclusion with my congratulations in your name for the fifth anniversary of his election as Pope on October 16. I assured him of the love and loyalty of St. Louis, and he responded with a number of gifts as the photographer came in to snap pictures. It was a genial, informal, and most enjoyable visit that passed all too quickly. His last words as I reached the door were soft, with a squeeze on my arm: "Pray for the Pope!"

Two days later on Wednesday, I joined all the American Bishops and a small number of Canadian, English, Polish, and Italian Bishops as attendants to Pope John Paul at his weekly public audience. It was in the immense Piazza of St. Peter's, and I would guess there were at least seventy thousand people there under a bright Roman sun. I was surprised to see the Pope pass through the entire crowd in his open white Jeep — no bulletproof glass. He walked down the final aisle, touching people on both sides as he approached the platform in front where we were. It was a brief Bible service with a twenty-minute meditation by the Pope in Italian on the Book of Sirach. Various groups from all over the world were then recognized, and the Holy Father spoke briefly to each language group in French, English, German, Spanish, Portuguese, Polish, and Hungarian! Finally, we joined him in giving the final blessing, with a closing hymn to our Lady. Once again, he greeted each bishop personally and thanked us for being with him. He looked healthy and happy, smiling there in the noonday sun.

On Friday, two days later, the Pope invited fifteen American Bishops to join him for lunch and the remaining fifteen to have supper with him. I was in the second group and was seated directly across the table from him. The dining room was just large enough for the Polish Sister and Italian waiter to serve. There were a few artworks on the cream-colored walls and just a few flowers in the center of the white tablecloth. It was a bright, pleasant dining room.

It was Friday, so we had a salmon appetizer and then broiled bass with vegetables and salad. For dessert, there was a fruit tort and fresh grapes with a dry, white wine. I noticed that the Pope did not eat too much, but we all seemed to do pretty well.

After a brief toast to the Holy Father led by a senior bishop, our host inquired about our various consultative bodies, clergy councils, parish and diocesan councils, and so forth. He was interested in their election procedure and amused by accounts of spirited campaigning in true American fashion by some candidates. He commended the widespread consultation in the American Church and said it had also been most helpful to him as Archbishop of Crakow. The Pope then led into a discussion of our American universities and Catholic education to which he paid great tribute. Further discussion centered on population trends in the U.S.A., the ecumenical situation, and the beautiful tradition of faithful Catholic practice of our people. We asked him in turn about the progress of the Bishops' Synod, and he gave us an optimistic summary and prognosis of its work. The supper ended with the rousing Polish hymn for health and long life *Sto-lat, Sto-lat,* led by one of our Slavic Bishops whose Polish, the Pope noticed, was "a little rusty." So it ended with a laugh, and it was a most delightful, relaxing, and happy meal.

The following morning on Saturday, all thirty American Bishops who had made their report through the past week gathered for the formal group session or *allocutio* with the Pope. Philadelphia's Cardinal Krol spoke a word for us, and then the Holy Father delivered his twenty-five minute talk in English. It was a masterful theological summary of the unity in teaching and preaching necessary in the college of pope and bishops. He stressed our need for one another and our sharing in the official teaching office with the help of our theologians. Then there were the final personal farewells with each of us for the next five years when our next report will be due. His final words were of love and blessing for all back home. I left amazed at his endurance as I saw many other groups waiting to see him in adjoining rooms. I resolved not to complain again about crowded schedules around here.

Nowhere through the week did I sense any opposition to or criticism of our work or the life of the Catholic Church in the U.S.A. It was just the opposite. So I wouldn't worry about articles alleging division between the Pope and his brother bishops in our country. In unity, there is strength, and we have it. I saw it last week.

(St. Louis, October 28, 1983)

My week in Rome from Sunday, June 24, to Sunday, July 1, was busy but very satisfying. Starting that first Sunday night and continuing until the following Saturday at noon, it was a round of visits to all the offices of the Roman Curia. As officers of the National Conference of Catholic Bishops in our country, Bishop James Malone, the president, Monsignor Daniel Hoye, our general secretary, and I are making these regular visits to foster the closest possible communications between the American Bishops and the Holy See.

Until now, I had only once visited one curial office in Rome, so this was a basically new experience for me. It was a real education to see how these officers of the Holy See try to understand and serve the Church in all the varying situations across the face of the earth. It is a most difficult responsibility for them. In every instance, they were most gracious, and I believe we accomplished very much. On both sides, there was full commitment to continue the process in working together as closely as possible. Accordingly, the Church in our country is in ever closer unity with our Holy Father.

Papal Pranzo: Talking about Pope John Paul, he very graciously invited us to *pranzo* (lunch) in his personal apartment. The Holy Father had just finished his Wednesday general audience in St. Peter's Square with many thousands of pilgrims under a hot sun. After a couple hours of that, he still looked remarkably fresh as he welcomed us into his quarters with a smile and strong handshake. So he is obviously in good health.

At the table with the Pope were Cardinal Casaroli and Archbishop Martinez, both of the Vatican Secretariat of State, and we three Americans. (Again and again during lunch, I kept marveling at such an intimate meal with the Pope for seventy-five minutes — an amazing experience.) The food was Italian but cooked by Polish Sisters, a typical Roman lunch.

The Pope is a great listener. He gets the conversation started with a question or two and then listens with occasional reactions — a smile, a wink, a wave of a hand, and so forth. He began by mentioning his recent visit to Alaska and his meeting with President Reagan and then asked about the coming presidential election and our American political process. (Non-Americans are usually mystified by it all.) We tried to explain. One real stickler was "What is the difference between a Republican and a Democrat?"

After perhaps ten minutes of that, we reviewed the work of our visit — liturgy, the ongoing seminary study in America, the consultations with our religious men and women, our discussions at the various Vatican offices, and so forth. The Pope was most positive, encouraging, and grateful for our assurance of regular, frequent visits from now on. He clearly appreciated the extra efforts to keep the Church in our country closely in union with him — one flock and one shepherd. He sent his best to all of you.

Other Visits: Just before our lunch with Pope John Paul, we were received by the new Father General of the Society of Jesus, Very Reverend Hans Peter Kolvenbach, S.J. He was waiting at the door of the Jesuit Curia when we arrived, just down the street from St. Peter's. After our brief introduction, he said to me, "I know that you live across the alley from our Jesuit Provincial in St. Louis." So I knew that he is a typically informed Jesuit. We had a short but very fruitful discussion, especially on the Jesuit universities in our country.

I was also able to spend a good deal of time with Archbishop Paul Marcinkus who has been so vilified in media discussion of the Vatican bank problems and recently in the sensational book on the death of John Paul I. While I know little about international banking, I do see how hazardous it all is, especially these days. My impression is that the Archbishop was simply betrayed by bankers who are now either dead, in prison, or in exile. Perhaps he should have been less trusting, but I know that his personal integrity and devotion to the Church are beyond question. Through all these allegations, he has continued doing his usual competent job as he has done for nearly thirty-five years now in faithful service to the Holy See. We can be proud of this American in Rome!

(St. Louis, July 13, 1984)

– ◆ –

Solidarity

To many people today that word *solidarity* means Lech Walesa's labor union that the communist government in Poland is trying to suppress. That word has become a rallying cry in Poland expressing a total unity of the Polish people in their courageous battle for freedom in their own country.

It seems to me that we need solidarity in our Catholic community these days. Sadly, there is too much divisiveness among us coming from strident voices on both the Catholic right and left. We have our differences, but I am getting tired of the "prophets of doom" (John XXIII) among us who constantly focus on those disagreements and try to portray them as evidence of a "schismatic American Church."

Again and Again: These critics tell us that Catholics have lost trust in the bishops and that there is a widening chasm between the bishops and the laity.

From my observations — and I think I meet as many Catholics as any reporter — I fail to see evidence for that charge. Outside of certain highly vocal and critical folks in the archdiocese, I see the vast majority of our people at peace with their Church here, and proud of it. They know, as Catholics always do, that the clergy are human beings subject to many faults that afflict most mortals, but they love their Church. They support it in ever greater cooperation — note the growing Catholic population each year, the record response to our Archdiocesan Development Appeal, the increasing sacrifice for Catholic education, the participation in the RENEW program, and so forth. Does this look like the Church in tatters as portrayed by the negativists among us?

Then they say that on the national scene the American Bishops do not teach in agreement with our Holy Father, Pope John Paul II. As I have reported to you several times in this column, it has been my privilege to represent our National Conference of Catholic Bishops with our president, Bishop Malone, in Rome. We report twice each year to our Holy Father personally and to each of his offices in the Roman Curia. There is the closest unity evident in these regular visits. The Pope says so also. He also said very clearly to the Catholics in Switzerland recently what some people need to hear in our country, "It is not possible to be in unity with the pope unless you are in unity with your bishop whom the pope sends to you."

Divisiveness: Christ said: "By this shall men know that you are my disciples: that you love one another." He said that he was the vine — one vine, and we all are the branches. He said that there should be one flock and one shepherd. At the Last Supper, he prayed, "That all may be one, as you Father, are in me and I in you; I pray that they may be one in us." Paul told the Corinthians that just as many grains of wheat are made into one piece of bread, so we all, though many, are made into one bread, one Body of Christ. In the second eucharistic prayer, we say: "May all of us who share in the body and blood of Christ be brought together in unity by the Holy Spirit." Again and again at Mass we pray in one way or another that we may be "reconciled to the Father and to one another."

It seems to me that according to the teaching of Christ, unity is a concern that outranks all other concerns. Unity does not negate other concerns or make them irrelevant, but it is not subordinate to them. Unity is a concern that must be faced as one of primary importance.

Because we are human and limited and self-centered, the achievement of unity is difficult, but we should be working for it.

Some requisites, it seems to me, would be these:

1. Love for the Church, which lives in the Spirit of Christ, reaching out with ever new vitality and resources to every culture in every age.
2. Recognition that unity is not uniformity. Acceptance of pluralism where it is legitimate. Flexibility.
3. Humility, willingness to listen, willingness to consider other viewpoints.
4. Respect for persons.
5. Respect for the depth of truth, the fruitfulness, the perennial freshness of truth.
6. Respect for legitimate authority.
7. Respect for authentic professional competence.

O Lord, teach us to love the unity of your Church. Help us to be truly one flock and one shepherd in you. Amen.

(St. Louis, September 28, 1984)

I have been asked at times whether the various Vatican officers are concerned by the letters they receive from our country critical of the Church here. As I went from one curial office to another during my recent visit to Rome, I did not get that impression. From my own experience, such letters are usually returned to the local American Bishop for information and handling. That is, of course, where they should have gone in the first place.

I really believe that the curial offices know, as every bishop does, that satisfied people rarely write and dissatisfied folks often do. They know further that once all the facts are in, the situation often looks much different. Vatican officials have the whole world to serve, so it seems unfair that certain Americans swamp them with complaints that could be better handled at the local level. I have the same problem in receiving complaints that should be sent to the schools, cemeteries, charities, or first to the pastor or principal involved. I guess it will be forever thus. But recently there has been an organized effort to deluge Rome with this kind of mail. I get the impression that most Vatican representatives consider it all pretty judiciously and realize that this vigilante movement is not representative of most of our clergy and people. Every Catholic always has the right, of course, to write to Rome about anything, but the Holy See has to work through the local bishops all around the world. After all, the Pope has appointed them all and they report to him. Rome cannot begin to supervise every detail everywhere. We need to appreciate that.

(St. Louis, July 26, 1985)

Teachable Moment

The coming of the Pope is indeed such a moment. The media publicity will be something we could never provide. It is time to instruct our people on the role of the pope and his service in the Church. They need to know why they are Catholics, not just Christians, why we are called Roman Catholics.

You are either with this Pope or against him. Many voices in our land will speak out against him. We need to profess our loyalty and love for him — for his office primarily and for his person. He is the successor of Peter. *Ubi Petrus, ibi Ecclesia.*

You have received material to help you do so. I hope you will lead your people to use the prayer cards sent to them in their homes and in your churches. The coming of the Pope to our shores is a great grace. Let us not receive this grace in vain.

(*Notanda,* July 31, 1987)

Big Trip

This coming week will begin a once-in-a-lifetime experience for me. I will leave for Miami on September 9 to join Pope John Paul on his pastoral visit to our country through September 20.

Prophet? In May 1982 an American reporter posed a question to John Paul II on the return flight to Rome following the Pope's successful visit to Canterbury, where he and Anglican Archbishop Robert Runcie had prayed and renewed baptismal promises together at Canterbury Cathedral. Did the Pope agree, the reporter asked, with Archbishop Runcie and others, who had suggested the possibility of full reunion between the two churches by the year 2000?

John Paul hesitated briefly, smiled, then said in reply: "I share in the prophetic ministry of Christ, but I am not a prophet."

Not bad for an off-the-cuff answer to a surprise question, especially since it was given in English, said to be the Pope's fifth best language. But the answer probably didn't do the Pope justice. In some ways, he is the very epitome of a prophet, especially in the Old Testament sense of one who comforts the afflicted and afflicts the comfortable. In this latter role, he has pointed out more than once that a prophet is said to be a sign of contradiction speaking out against social and moral evils.

Such characteristics of the Pope have been apparent many times. At his Mass on the mall in Washington, D.C., in 1979, for example, he defended the indissolubility of marriage, rejected the ideology of contraception, condemned homosexual activity and sex outside of marriage, and called abortion an unspeakable crime.

He was equally tough on American Catholics at Yankee Stadium, telling them to cast aside their easy way of life and reach out to the poor throughout the world until it hurts. The Pope has never shunned issues of importance. In Africa, he has defended native cultures and the right of all persons to be free of all vestiges of colonialism. In France, he spoke of the role of the Church in a secularized state. In Brazil, he was eloquent on the needs of the poor. And in country after country, he has made dictators squirm while championing the rights of the oppressed. Even those who don't like him will usually concede John Paul this: he calls things as he sees them and lets the chips fall where they may.

Shepherd: By the time Pope John Paul reaches Miami on September 10 to start his nine-city, ten-day pastoral visit (some would say whirlwind tour) of the United States, he will have made nearly forty trips outside Italy since becoming pope in 1978. Why does he do it?

The Pope has given his own reasons for his pilgrimages — visits to "the sanctuaries of the people of God," as he calls them. He says he wants them to be occasions for deepening an awareness of Christ, for increasing a living, conscious and active faith, and for helping the people of God to become a servant Church for the whole world.

John Paul has pointed to what he regards as his mission — to draw people to a consciousness of Christ's presence — as the primary goal of his trips. "The more difficult the life of people, of families, of communities, and of the world become, the more necessary it is for them to become aware of

Christ the Good Shepherd, 'who lays down his life for his sheep,' " he has said.

If the journeys are opportunities for strengthening the faith of others, John Paul has said his own faith is strengthened by getting in touch with the people. Like Saint Paul, he says, "I love to see you that I might impart some spiritual gift to strengthen you, that is, that we may be mutually encouraged by each other's faith, both yours and mine."

Servant: Finally, the Pope regards his pilgrimages as a time for calling the people of God to be servant Church for the whole world, in the spirit of the Second Vatican Council. The mission of the Church is to serve the Father, Son, and Holy Spirit in their will to save all people and establish the kingdom of love, justice, and mercy.

That his pastoral visits are meant to implement the vision of the Second Vatican Council should surprise no one. Although it is largely overlooked, John Paul was one of the Council's principal architects. As Archbishop Karol Wojtyla of Crakow, he attended every session (1962-1965) and influenced and helped to write several major documents.

Because of the Second Vatican Council, in less than four years the Church, while holding fast to its dogmatic tradition, underwent more revolutionary changes in liturgy, in practice, and not least in attitude than in the previous two thousand years of its history. Archbishop Wojtyla, now Pope John Paul II, was a principal actor in that drama.

What has that to do with now? If the Church has grown, if it has become healthy and vibrant once again, this has not come about without drawbacks and problems. There are not a few persons in the Church who are confused about what it means to be a Catholic today, for there are many conflicting bids for their loyalty and attention. To put it in the starkest terms, for some the pace of change has been too fast, for others too slow. It is now John Paul's task, one for which he is uniquely suited by past experience as well as temperament, to draw together divergent elements within the Church. For, not withstanding the importance of the Pope's outreach to America at large, his dialogue with Jewish leaders in Miami or Protestant leaders in South Carolina, the visit is first and foremost a visit to the Catholic Church in America. He has much to say to the Church in this country, and American Catholics have much to say to him. Both have much to gain from a successful visit by this daring and dynamic leader.

(St. Louis, September 4, 1987)

The Pope's Visit

My brother bishops and friends: In this my first presidential address to you, I would like to concentrate on what will certainly be the major moment of my first year in office if not indeed my entire term: the second pastoral visit of our Holy Father, Pope John Paul II, to the United States.

We chose as the theme of this visit the words of another apostle, Paul, also a traveler, who wrote: "And to some his gift was that they should be apostles; to some, prophets; to some, evangelists; to some, pastors and teachers; so that the saints together make a unity in the work of service, building up the Body of Christ." In constructing this trip, we wanted the Holy Father to meet a cross-section of American Catholics who, in various ways but always in unity with us and with him, work together in building up the Body of Christ, strengthening the faith, and contributing to the community of faith.

Precisely because we are Americans who live our lives in an open and pluralistic society, we wanted the Holy Father to have an opportunity to listen to the longings of our heart for this Church which we love and serve, to hear of the joys and sometimes even the challenges of our ministries and apostolic service to the Church, to, if you will, touch the "heartbeat of America" in its Catholic experience. In the more significant and substantive encounters, many of our coworkers had an opportunity to speak to the Holy Father of their finest hopes and aspirations.

On several occasions, the Holy Father affirmed our confidence in the format and context for the trip. He expressed his appreciation for the candor and honesty with which even the occasional difficult issue was joined and time and again showed himself a good listener.

What did the Pope see and hear during his second pastoral visit? He saw a Church alive, dynamic and vibrant, and when the visit was over, Pope John Paul spoke of the "profound bond between American Catholicism and the universal Church."

From my perspective, the most wonderful moments were the times of prayer, specifically the liturgies he celebrated throughout the ten days he was with us. If there is one aspect of postconciliar American experience where we have grown, it is the liturgical renewal. For ten days in September, American Catholics joined the Holy Father from Miami to Detroit, in fields in Miami and Monterey, in New Orleans and San Antonio, in the great arenas of Los Angeles, Phoenix, San Francisco, and Detroit, in lifting their minds, hearts, and voices to the Almighty in that chorus of praise and thanksgiving which is the Eucharist. It may be that too much attention was given by commentators to the cost and design of altars and not enough to the faith of those great choirs of faithful who assembled with the successor of Peter to celebrate the Eucharist with that simple majesty which is the American liturgical experience. Pope John Paul II saw once again a church which is alive because of how it prays as Church.

Nor shall I soon forget the affirmation which he provided to those who work with us in the apostolates of education, healthcare, charities, and more especially, our brother priests, religious men and women, and deacons and lay ministers. From these encounters, I believe the Holy Father saw a Church also alive with generous women and men who, in different ways and through different institutional responses, work hard to build up the Body of Christ.

It was clear within three hours of his arrival in Miami that Pope John Paul II had come to strengthen his brothers when he lovingly affirmed and supported the ministry of our priests. In San Francisco, the Pope applauded the service of our devoted religious and laity, and in Detroit, in the first ever meeting with the permanent diaconate of any nation, issued a strong message of support for our permanent deacons.

I remember today the movie which the deacons had prepared to show the Holy Father the multifaceted nature of their ministerial service to the Church in this country. It had no soundtrack other than the music to the very popular hymn which we sing so often, "Here Am I, Lord." Spontaneously and quite unexpectedly, without the benefit of the words before them, the three thousand deacons and their wives started to sing that hymn. It was totally spontaneous, unrehearsed, and very much who we Catholics are in America! Here we are Lord, we come to do your will!

No one can rightly say that the Holy Father and this Church are not interested in pursuing better relations with our Christian and non-Christian brothers and sisters. Three times formally and on many other occasions throughout the trip when entering cathedrals, churches, meeting places, and so forth, Pope John Paul reached out to embrace our Protestant, Jewish and other non-Christian religious leaders. All had a chance to speak to him. He responded to them all, often moved by the love and unity which is already present and felt among us. I know that he was deeply touched in South Carolina to experience the peace and harmony in a pluralistic society of many denominations walking together under the one common banner: In

God We Trust. He said on his reception in predominantly Protestant Columbia, "This could never happen in Europe."

Pope John Paul had a special impact on the young men and women of our land who came into contact with him. We had seen it in Madison Square Garden in 1979 — this unique bonding between our Pope and our young — and we saw it again in 1987 in New Orleans and Los Angeles. There is something about the pope, this Pope, that can raise the sights and aspirations of our young people not only to their faith but to their future potential and their present dignity and worth.

I have some special memories of our time together, yours and mine, with the Holy Father in Los Angeles. He was with us for four and one-half hours and we prayed with him, dialogued with him, and dined with him. He moved among us, desirous of greeting us all, totally indifferent to any demands of his hectic schedule which might have militated against taking that extra time with us. He listened to four of us who had the unenviable task of speaking to him about important aspects of our pastoral ministry. At the conclusion of this meeting, the Holy Father affirmed in my hearing both the appropriateness and importance of this format. He genuinely enjoyed and appreciated our time together.

I know that the Holy Father saw the many faces and cultures which comprise American Catholicism. If anyone has any doubt about the Hispanic presence in our Church in this country, its love of this Church, and its practice of this faith, they should have been with us in September. There is no mistaking the Hispanic presence, and there can be no minimizing the Hispanic challenge. Certainly no black Catholic leader will soon forget that magical hour in New Orleans when the Pope embraced their hopes and aspirations and made them his own. The faces of American Catholics Pope John Paul II saw were also red and yellow as well as brown and black and white. He saw graphically how this Church has opened its arms to embrace our brothers and sisters in faith from many regions and many countries. America is beautiful precisely because America has welcomed the stranger. I was reminded of President John Kennedy's opening words in his talk to the Daughters of the American Revolution: "Fellow immigrants." There must have been moments of absolute amazement for the Holy Father during those ten days. I know that his Secretary of State was incredulous when I tried to explain Guido Sarducci in his Roman hat with his partner fully garbed in cardinal red conducting a press conference on the curb along the parade route in several cities.

The precision of schedule, transportation, security, and planning all moving smoothly along for those ten days were awesome — absolutely American. Cardinal Casaroli said that only the German army could perform as efficiently.

I have spoken of what the Holy Father saw. I would like to mention now what the Holy Father said after he had listened. I believe I can identify four dominant themes to be found in his speeches and homilies.

1. The Holy Father concentrated many times on the importance of family life, reaffirming the indissolubility of marriage and elevating conjugal and family love as a profound sign for our society.

2. He spoke often of the need for social justice, for solidarity with and respect for all life. The centrality of human dignity, of the intrinsic worth and value of all, was at the core of his teaching while he was with us.

3. He challenged us often to risk being countercultural. While applauding cultural diversity, he exhorted resistance to some predominant tendencies in our culture: namely, selfishness, sexual license and excess, neglect of the poor. He insisted on our full Catholic identities.

4. Time and again he emphasized the need for encouraging our young people to consider the priesthood and religious life. At the same time, he consistently developed a broader notion of vocation as a call to all the faithful to transform the world, to bring their unique gifts and talents to the whole community.

What happens now? The trip is over, the two years of planning ended at 8:57 p.m. in Detroit when Shepherd One departed Detroit for Canada and Rome. I would like to conclude with what I believe to be some long-lasting and enduring effects of the visit which will be of benefit to our ministry:

This latest dialogue with the Holy Father began in March during a planning session in Rome with several members of our conference. It continued during the papal visit in September and will be extended through the *ad limina* visits each of us will make next year to Rome. We need to continue to share with the Holy Father our experience as shepherds. It will be easier to do because he has been here once again. He knows us better.

Our formal dialogue will even go beyond the *ad limina* visits when we anticipate having an opportunity once again to send representatives to Rome to meet with the Pope to discuss at even greater length the challenges which we face as pastors of the Church.

No one should question the fidelity and authenticity of our life of worship. American Catholics are alive with the genuine prayer experience that marks our liturgical renewal.

All of us feel supported in our work as bishops as a result of the visit. We know, too, that the daily ministries and apostolic activities, which are so vital to the success of our work, have been strongly affirmed by Pope John Paul, and we know them to be on the right path.

After ten days of very close proximity to the Holy Father, I would be remiss if I did not mention the example of his personal prayer. No matter how tightly scheduled his days were, there were always plenty of moments for prayer and few opportunities were wasted.

Many negative predictions were made before the trip:

- The Pope was coming to scold us. He didn't.
- The Pope would be greeted by massive protests and demonstrations. He wasn't.
- The trip would be greeted by vast indifference. It wasn't. Witness the media coverage and the testimony of so many viewers and listeners.
- The talks given to the Pope would be irrelevant and insensitive. Nothing could be further from the truth.
- The trip would cost too much! The benefits which the local churches derived, and in which the entire Church in the United States also shared, proved the enduring value of this pastoral visit.

A national Catholic newspaper summed it all up after the papal visit:

This is not a Church in revolution. It is a faithful Catholic community, perhaps the strongest in the world. The itchy matters of ferment which make headlines do not touch most American Catholic lives. They are a people of a deep and rich faith, struggling to apply it in a highly secular culture. Their success in doing so has been nothing short of extraordinary.

This papal trip has already accomplished a vital task: It has convinced Catholics in America of the depth and unity of their faith. They will no longer accept either the prophets of gloom or the heady malcontents who claim to represent them.

(Our Sunday Visitor, October 11, 1987)

For ten days in September, we were affirmed in a unique way by the successor of Peter in our common work of service building up the Body of Christ. If we carry on what we have begun, the challenges, the joys, the happiness, of many moments of his visit to us, will have borne fruit a hundredfold.

(Origins 17 [1987] 417,419-21; slightly abridged)

– ◆ –

"Peace!"

That was our Lord's first greeting to his apostles on the first Easter Sunday. That is the greeting his followers give to one another before receiving him in holy Communion at every Mass. That should always be the wish we Catholics have for one another — and especially on Easter. So peace to you one and all on this feast of our Lord's Resurrection!

Again and Again: Before and after the recent meeting of our Holy Father, Pope John Paul, and his collaborators with the U.S. Archbishops in Rome, I described it as a peaceful meeting. We are all doing the same job, since we are all bishops teaching the same doctrine of the one Church. Since the Church is catholic, or universal, that one doctrine must be taught by bishops of many different nations, in many diverse cultures. In some of these national cultures, the Catholic faith fits in quite easily and naturally. In others, there is considerable resistance. The Pope proposed our meeting to help us all understand the situation in the U.S.A.

So we reviewed together the cultural context of teaching Catholic doctrine in the U.S.A. today. After the Pope's warm welcome and praise for the work of the Catholic Church in our country, it was my privilege to outline in ten minutes the American cultural context in which we work.[1] From then on, one topic after another was reviewed together — priests, seminaries, religious orders, liturgy, the laity, family, ecumenism, education, and so forth. It was four days of most interesting, friendly, and calm conversation. I enjoyed it immensely.

Then we came home to hear again and again that it was a battle royal between Rome and the American Bishops. That kind of "news" is really tiresome and irresponsible. The Pope and we U.S. Bishops are on the same team. We are in the same boat — the boat of Peter.

---

1 See pages 209-211.

Closeup: You have read much in these pages and elsewhere about this historic meeting. Maybe it might be more helpful to share some human interest. Because of my job with the Bishops' Conference, it was my privilege to sit next to the Pope on the platform throughout the meeting. It was an interesting experience.

The Pope attended every session except when he was tied up twice in another commitment. For four days, he sat there listening, not saying a word except for leading the prayers and giving opening and closing remarks. Hour after hour, he listened closely. I noticed he had a rosary in his hand much of the time. He reacted with a "hmm" now and then at certain points, and I was not always sure if it was in approval or disapproval! Twice he asked me a brief question of clarification, but that was all. The proceedings were all in Italian or English. I bet he would have liked a little Polish now and then. He is an intent listener — a good example for a bishop these days. He also helped me stay awake!

(St. Louis, March 24, 1989)

- 12 -
BISHOPS' CONFERENCE

An episcopal conference is a form of assembly in which the bishops of a certain country or region exercise their pastoral office jointly in order to enhance the Church's beneficial influence on all, especially by devising forms of the apostolate and apostolic methods suitably adapted to the circumstances of the times.

(Decree on the Pastoral Office of Bishops, #38)

"*To Jesus Through Meetings:*" Some wag said that was the theme of the Church these days. I hope that is where all those meetings lead, but there may be some skeptics around. Elsewhere in these pages there are accounts of the annual assembly of the National Conference of Catholic Bishops this past week in Washington, D.C. I just thought you might wonder what goes on behind the agenda.

Not that much, I am afraid. The schedule is so packed that there is little time for much socializing, which is regrettable when all two hundred fifty or so bishops are together for much of a week. And lately because of airfares, and so forth, the extra committee meetings are packed on the days before and after the general assembly and also during the lunch and dinner periods. Each day begins with concelebrated Mass, and the last full day ends with a beautiful liturgy of all the bishops in the National Shrine of the Immaculate Conception, followed by a buffet supper and reception with the delegate of the pope, Archbishop Pio Laghi. I usually try to get in a good walk every day around some of those Washington sights, lest Jack be a completely dull boy. So it is a full week but a most stimulating one as we review and plan the work of the Church for another year with all the bishops of the country. There are also clergy, religious, and lay observers at the general sessions with the staff people and all the media types, so it is quite colorful and interesting most of the time. And I always find it a real joy to get together with the other bishops. When I hear the problems faced by so many today, I always feel like kissing the ground at Lambert Field when I get back. That's the best part of the week — coming home.

(St. Louis, November 20, 1981)

— ♦ —

A funny thing happened to me last week on my way through the meeting of the National Conference of Catholic Bishops. As was duly noted in last week's Review, I am now vice president of the Conference. Needless to say, I am grateful to my brother bishops for their kindness to me, and I shall do my best to serve them well in this national work of the Church.

Recently, it has been open season on bishops both from the right and the left. Some days when you read the mail and certain publications, it seems that the American Bishops are nincompoops or charlatans or perhaps a combination of both. So it is really quite disappointing to attend a meeting of the Bishops' Conference and find the participants not at all that colorful. From my sixteen years of such meetings, I have found the bishops a hardworking, wise, and concerned group of clergy. I have always felt humble to be one of them.

(St. Louis, November 25, 1983)

— ♦ —

Bishops' Meeting in Zaire

Some time back I told you of my coming trip to Africa to represent our National Conference of Catholic Bishops at the seventh general assembly of the Pan-African Bishops Symposium (SECAM). I write this on my way home about six miles up on my way across the Atlantic in a Dutch KLM 747.

200

The actual meeting lasted a full week, from Sunday, July 15, to Sunday, July 22, in Kinshasa, the capital of Zaire, in south central Africa. Just a short distance south of the equator, Kinshasa was cooler and less humid in its annual "dry season" than St. Louis. We saw rain only twice during our stay.

Zaire is as large as the U.S.A. west of the Mississippi and has about thirty million people scattered through that vast area. (Ten percent live in and around Kinshasa.) Half of the population are Catholic because of the work of colonial missionaries when Zaire was the Belgian Congo and because of the continuing efforts of the native clergy today. This huge country has fertile land, plenty of water and rich mineral deposits, but it is still basically undeveloped. There is widespread poverty and much illiteracy with an inefficient and despotic government, but the potential is tremendous. Very appropriately then the theme of the Conference was "The Church and Human Development."

All the Bishops' Conferences of Africa were represented by about eighty delegates. Besides our three American observers, there were representatives from Europe, Canada, and Latin America. Almost all of the African Bishops (including five Cardinals) were black, along with their clergy staff members. So were the Sisters in authentic African garb, who provided hospitality in the Seminary of John XXIII where we were all housed.

Liturgy: The assembly began on Sunday in the Cathedral of Our Lady with a magnificent liturgy in the true Zairean style (we also attended a Wednesday night Mass in a huge typical neighborhood parish). Both were breathtaking in their adaptation of the Roman rite to the African musical and artistic culture. It is amazing to see our same Mass in a total African expression — a perfect example of what Vatican Council II taught in its *Decree on the Sacred Liturgy.*

The music in native instruments was overpowering with exultant singing by several thousand people packed into a huge church. There were processions at the entrance, gospel, offertory, Communion, and exit — all done in tasteful and majestic dance with flags, banners, clouds of incense, and so forth. The laity, including women, took full part. The preaching in the Lingala native language with periodic assent and cheers from the people had their full attention. All received holy Communion very devoutly and showed awesome, silent reverence in their thanksgiving and at the elevation. It was a thrill for me to be part of this huge throng at prayer. As I felt last January in Bolivia, it seems that the people of the Third World are accomplishing much more beautifully than we what Vatican Council II called for in adaptation of the one universal Catholic liturgy to the separate cultures of the local churches. We have much to learn from them.[1]

Meeting: The rest of the meeting was equally thorough and progressive. It was my privilege to come to know these remarkable bishops from all over the African continent. Many were born of pagan families (one still bore the tribal scars on his face), but all are superbly educated, energetic bishops today. They were preparing to issue a pastoral letter on development, which will probably get as much attention in Africa as our American Bishops' pastoral letter on the arms race did here. I was increasingly edified by these friendly brother bishops who face difficulties that would prostrate most of us in our country. Governmental opposition in most of these emerging nations, grinding poverty, illiteracy, corruption and inefficiency, tribal divisions, scores of different native languages in every country, unbelievably poor transportation and communication — these are just some of their problems. And yet they push on in the peace and hope of Christ. The African people are responding, vocations are increasing, and native clergy and religious are now in full leadership. It is a beautiful thing to see the "Coming of the Third Church," as one European Catholic missiologist has termed it.

Undoubtedly, the Church in Africa will be one of the greatest in the universal Catholic community. Our Holy Father has said so many times, and there are now fourteen African Cardinals. It was a thrill for me to see it all, just a glimpse of the beautiful things to come.

All the same, I am glad to be back and to see that all went better than ever at the Catholic Center during my absence — thanks to all our staff here. It is always good for my humility.

(St. Louis, August 3, 1984)

NCCB

With all the talk lately about the Catholic Bishops' pastoral letter on the U.S. economy, I thought you might like to hear a bit about the group that issued that letter. Some columnists portray the American Bishops as senile

---

1 See pages 337-338.

bunglers, others say they are detached philosophers, and some warn against their sly manipulation of our country. Maybe it would help to peek in at the recent meeting of the NCCB — National Conference of Catholic Bishops.

Paper: Going to this meeting seems like setting out to climb the Himalayas — the mountains are of paper. This year's agenda consisted of three books (8½-by-11-inch format) totaling 491 pages. There was a separate booklet full of marvelous legalese on the Equal Rights Amendment. And four days before the meeting began we received the fifty-thousand-word first draft of the proposed letter on the economy.

Many people see their chance in the fact that most of the bishops in the United States are gathered in one place for a few days. Thus, the mountain of paper grows with invitations to promotional receptions, to rooms where vestments and clerical clothing are sold, to rooms where groups of lobbyists are gathered, to special events arranged for the bishops. Individuals who have learned of items on the agenda leave messages to share their wisdom — and plead their cause.

Maybe I should get two seats on the plane, one for me and one for the papers. I should have begun lifting weights months back in order to carry all the papers — even after carefully sorting them out before departure. The real problem, of course, is not that of lifting or transporting all the pages but of reading them, of really being prepared for the discussions of the meeting.

Pastoral Letter: This year the item that attracted greatest public attention was the draft of the letter on the U.S. economy. The rules of the conference require that a document of this kind should have been in the hands of the bishops at least two months before the meeting. An exception was made in order not to make the draft public just before the presidential election and expose it to the charge of having some political or partisan intent.

Atmosphere: Washington was cool, sometimes dreary and rainy, sometimes with a little sunshine at midday. The trees were mostly bare of leaves, with some survivors in rusty fall colors.

In a way, the weather outside is really not that important. Because of the beautifully prepared concelebrated morning Masses (with homily) and the daylong NCCB meetings and evening meetings or special events, it is difficult to find the time to get outside. In fact, toward the end of the meeting I begin to feel like I'm in jail. Usually, however, I try to get a quick turn around the block after lunch — the block is like a track, with bishops stepping briskly to catch a breath of fresh air.

After the afternoon session ending at five or a little later, I try to take a little longer walk in the gathering dusk, passing the glittering shops on Columbia Road and enjoying the feel of life in the crowds of people heading home from work, hurrying along the street, disappearing down the entrance to the subway.

Somewhere in the hotel there is always a small room that has been made into a chapel of the Blessed Sacrament. During breaktimes, there are always some bishops there. It is a place of silence, small and out of the way. But it explains the whole meeting.

Purpose: The NCCB is not a kind of super-church. Each diocese is under the care and direction of its own bishop. The conference has no authority over the individual bishop. It exists to enable the bishops as a group to address issues and to take actions which the individual cannot do alone or at least not as well. It also enables us to address as a group issues and subjects that are of importance for the whole country and not just one diocese. It also helps us to maintain unity in such matters as doctrine and liturgy. There is wide diversity in the Church, and we don't need uniformity. But we do need unity in essentials.

I find our annual meetings very exciting. I assure you that we rarely pass a motion to take a particular action without a lot of study and a lot of debate. Some proposals, of course, are debated more than others. The debates can become very intense at times. The bishops are always polite in how they express themselves, but they certainly disagree at times, and they can get into very lively debates.

Although our days are filled with meetings, there are opportunities for little visits and conversations with individual bishops. It's very affirming to share experiences with them. We all have similar challenges, responsibilities, and problems. I personally find it a great help to hear other bishops' experiences and to share my own.

Our meetings are all business, but we do have opportunities to share some laughs together. We need that. As a group, bishops are generally cheerful men. They are also well-informed and usually very articulate. That's what makes our meetings so interesting and so enjoyable for me.

Each bishop is keenly aware of the very heavy responsibility he has for the flock of Christ. He knows how serious are his duties to teach sound doctrine and to lead God's people in the ways of the gospel. And he knows how accountable to God he must be.

So please pray for us every day that God will give us the strength, the wisdom, and the courage to be truly good shepherds.

(St. Louis, November 30, 1984)

Delightful Days...

Almost a month ago, the Catholic Bishops of the United States gathered at St. John's Abbey in Collegeville, Minnesota, for an eight-day meeting. This convocation was partially a time for prayer in common, partially a time to reflect on a single subject, namely vocations, and finally a time to be with one another to exchange ideas and experiences.

The spiritual director for the meeting was Cardinal Carlo Maria Martini, S.J., the Archbishop of Milan. The Cardinal is a Scripture scholar, formerly a teacher and rector at the Biblical Institute in Rome, and still later, rector of the Gregorian University in Rome. As the Archbishop of Milan, one of the largest archdioceses in the world, he is the successor of Saint Ambrose and Saint Charles Borromeo and Giovanni Montini (Pope Paul VI).

The first day of the gathering was a day of recollection during which Cardinal Martini gave a series of conferences. All of the liturgies were beautifully arranged and conducted. On the first day, with Cardinal Martini acting as the principal concelebrant, all of the bishops concelebrated in the Ambrosian rite, a special order of the Mass used only in Milan and going back all the way to Saint Ambrose in the fourth century. On each of the subsequent days, the principal concelebrant for the eucharistic liturgy was a different bishop who also preached the homily at this Mass. (My turn was on June 11.)

Besides the eucharistic liturgy, each day the bishops recited the Liturgy of the Hours together, both morning and evening prayer. During morning prayer, Cardinal Martini gave an extended homily each day. Evening prayer was celebrated by a different bishop who preached a homily. Each day, therefore, we heard three homilies, four on Sunday and more on the day of recollection. (So we know, too, what it is to listen in the pews!)

There was plenty of time for relaxation and for conversation among the bishops, especially at mealtimes. The Benedictine Fathers and Brothers who operate St. John's were most gracious hosts. The grounds are spacious and well kept, and we had two afternoons free for outdoor sports. There were also some excellent movies in the evenings (with free popcorn, too).

The Abbey Church, built nearly thirty years ago, is still strikingly modern and is internationally famous. On June 14 the bishops concelebrated there in the Maronite rite with Bishop Francis Zayek, a Maronite bishop, as principal celebrant. The Mass was a memorial to the Blessed Virgin, under the title of Mary of the Seeds, and reflected the deep devotion of the Maronite people to the Blessed Virgin. The opening prayer read:

> O Christ God, Word from the Father, like rain you fell on the Virgin's field, and like a perfect grain of wheat you appeared where no sowers scattered seed. Make us worthy to praise you by recalling the memory of your Mother, who knew the planting and rejoiced at the harvest. We shall praise you, Father, Son, and Holy Spirit, now and forever. Amen.

The homeland of the Maronite rite is Lebanon and Syria. Later many bishops commented on the cruel contrast between the sensitive, tender, poetic language of the liturgy and the chaos and violence and war that in our time afflict Lebanon and Syria. We said with particular emphasis the prayer that is part of the Rite of Peace:

> O Father, you are the infinite Peace and undivided Love. In your great goodness, you created man; through the life-giving coming of your Son, you filled the earth with peace. The angels praise you and say, "Glory to God in the highest and on earth, peace and goodwill."...Make us worthy to give one another a greeting of peace that we may share your heavenly gift.

(St. Louis, July 11, 1986)

— ◆ —

Presidential address to the National Council of Catholic Bishops in November 1988.

My brother bishops and my brothers and sisters all:

The concept of the ad limina, the periodic visit to Rome of each residential bishop to consult on the state of his diocese, dates back to the fourth century. This year we bishops received several vivid reminders that these visits are much more than merely an administrative procedure. They are both the instrument and vital expression of the catholicity of the Church, of the unity of the college of bishops embodied in the person of the successor of Peter.

Pope John Paul II has given the visits a radically new stimulus, taken a personal interest in discussing pastoral problems and offering guidance in his doctrinal and pastoral discourses.

After reviewing at length the many ways in which the Pope had affirmed the work of the American Bishops, Archbishop May continued:

We can be pleased about what the Pope has said about our past. What is even more significant and deeply reassuring is that he has indicated we are moving in the right direction. We have both the right and the duty to remember that the Pope praised *The Challenge of Peace* and *Economic Justice for All* not as interesting relics of our past but as living organisms within a community that has the power to transform lives and structures, something in which he has more than a passing interest.

Our people need to hear that the work we have begun on "social issues" — whether on nuclear policy, human rights or advocacy for the unborn, the poor and the homeless — will continue. This is required by our role as bishops, teachers, and pastors in the Church in the United States. Catholics in America have long since passed the time in which we must prove ourselves to this country that we love. Now is the time to translate our teaching into action, to build a more just nation and a more peaceful world.

The Church, with her God-given mission, serves the whole person and has a unique call to serve the spiritual needs of humanity. Our people also need to hear of our absolute determination to deepen our prayer life and theirs, to restore the sacrament of reconciliation, to teach sound doctrine, to do all of the things to which our Holy Father has asked us to recommit ourselves with the same priestly fervor we experienced on the day of our ordination.

As we come together in our nation's capital this week, it is appropriate to offer our congratulations and best wishes to the newly elected president of the United States. The bishops as well as all Catholics have always stood ready to serve their country, and they do so now as much as ever. But our voices will not be heard only in praise and appreciation. We will stand with the Holy Father in denouncing injustices and actions that foster disrespect for human life, from abortion to the death penalty; in opposing policies that undermine human dignity, from poverty to the arms race; and in standing up for human rights, from Eastern Europe to South Africa. Such a counter-cultural stand sometimes involves a message that is unpopular with fellow citizens and with the government itself. No one seeks confrontation, but the Church cannot be true to its mission if we fail to live up to our responsibility to defend the human person.

Parenthetically, yet within the context of papal statements and the coordinate actions of the Church in the United States, I want to discuss briefly our response to the initial working draft on episcopal conferences. This has been portrayed by the news media as if it signaled some sort of struggle with the Holy See. With all due respect for the creative imaginations of certain writers, this is simply false. The simple fact of the matter is that Cardinal Gantin requested all the bishops of the world to take a critical look at this draft so that they might eventually send their judgments to the Holy See. For a year now, we have been hard at work on that directive, appointing as a task force to supervise this labor some of our most distinguished members, the past presidents of the conference. There has been widespread consultation with theologians and canonists; scholarly monographs and articles have been composed precisely for this purpose; the task force requested specific committees of the conference for their evaluation. During the June meeting at Collegeville, I spent a major section of my address in the analysis of some parts of this proposed working paper, and the entire body of bishops discussed it in small groups and reported to the general session. I doubt if any other national conference has responded more fully to the request of the Holy See.

That the conclusion of this evaluative process was to ask for a new working paper should shock no one. Anyone who remembers the last Council can cite any number of speeches by great figures in the Church whose evaluation of a proposed scheme was parallel to ours. The entire body of bishops will discuss the judgment of its task force, but there is one thing that I wish to stress here: that in this index of directives, there has been no action by the body this year that is more profoundly obediential and respectful than the work on this document. The task given to the bishops by the Holy See was one of critical evaluation. That is always a somewhat thankless office. That the Conference accepted this mandate and responded in a painstakingly scholarly and objective fashion reflects great credit both upon the Conference and for the overriding concern for truth within the Church itself.

More than two years have passed since the Conference of Bishops requested a special meeting in which we might share with the Holy Father our thoughts about the pastoral needs and challenges facing the Church in this country. That meeting will take place in the spring of 1989, which, fittingly enough, is the year of the two hundredth anniversary of the establishment of the Catholic hierarchy in the United States. I ask you to reflect upon the potential significance of this meeting, to share your thoughts concerning the subjects we might discuss, and to pray that this will be yet another occasion in which God's blessings are made manifest to the church in the United States through the person of Pope John Paul II.

(*Origins* 18 [1988] pages 381, 383-6)

On March 8, 1989, Archbishop May, speaking as president of the National Conference of Catholic Bishops in the U.S.A., opened the meeting of the American Archbishops with the Pope and Roman Curia with the following statement.

Most Holy Father, you have favored us with words of welcome, with words of encouragement, with words of advice — and we are grateful. We have come many miles from our own dioceses, yet we feel that we are home. Home is where family dwells, where love lives — and we feel that here. You are our father in Jesus Christ, and we have a keen sense of your love for each of us.

In September 1987, you graced our shores with your presence and our spirits with your words. Throughout the past year, when we came to Rome for our *ad limina* visits, we felt the warmth of your hospitality, the strength of your support. Now you have blessed us again by inviting us here to talk with you and with your Curia collaborators as a summation of your visit to us and of our own visits to you.

We come, thirty-three metropolitan bishops representing almost four hundred Roman Catholic Bishops of the United States and over fifty-three million Catholics who people our land. Several weeks ago, you wrote to us bishops, announcing that our teaching role in evangelization would be the theme of these conversations. That theme struck us as welcome and wise. It is rooted, of course, in the word for gospel, and that word was the title of a popular musical play in America some years back. It called us to see Jesus more clearly, love him more dearly, follow him more nearly, day by day. To help people do that is our work of evangelization both for those who share our faith and for those who are unchurched.

No one knows more about spreading the gospel than you do, Holy Father. In your work here in Rome and in your missionary journeys around the world, you have carried the Good News of Jesus in a courageous and loving way. We are here to learn from you. But we are also here to speak to you as you have invited us to do. We are your brother bishops, linked with you in the love of the Lord. And so we want to share — with you and with your fellow servants here in Rome — what we are seeing and hearing as we walk the streets of our land.

May I speak, then, of the cultural context in which we live and work? There are several elements of that ambiance that impact our work directly, and I will list them before I explain.

The United States is pluralistic; it enjoys total religious liberty; organized religion abounds in America; there is full freedom of thought; and the spirit of democracy runs strong. Perhaps it might help if I comment briefly on each of these factors.

First, the pluralism. On the same street in America, you may have living side by side, a black Baptist family with roots in Africa; a Cambodian couple who fled Indochina with their Buddhist faith intact; a Jewish family who came to escape discrimination in the Soviet Union; Polish and Latin American refugees seeking a home in the local Catholic parish. That street, for all of its bewildering diversity, is the typical strength of America. Our coins tell of the American experiment — *E pluribus unum* — to fashion one nation from many diverse people. It is an experiment that has been working well for more that two centuries.

One of our original ideas is freedom of religion. Our traditional principle of separation of church and state means that there can be no established religion in our land. Yet while no particular religion enjoys a preference, religion itself is favored. Our sessions of Congress begin with a prayer; public officials take office with an oath made to God; our coins proclaim that "in God we trust"; and our courts exist to safeguard religion, not to inhibit it.

Organized religion is strong in our country, with most Americans claiming membership in a formal religious body. Churches and temples of every faith across America are built by the freewill efforts of their people, along with religious institutions of education and charity of every kind. The most recent figures show that fifty-two percent of U.S. Catholics have shared in the celebration of Mass during the last week.

In the United States, there is widespread ecumenical and interfaith cooperation. Your Holiness has often spoken with joy about your meetings in America during 1987 with Protestant and Orthodox officials in Columbia, South Carolina, with Jewish leaders in Miami, and with representatives of non-Christian religions in Los Angeles.

The communications media wield tremendous influence in our country. There is total freedom of thought in public educational and cultural media, and any form of censorship is abhorred. While the sources of information are rich indeed, there are often materialistic, secularistic, and hedonistic values widely disseminated among our people in some of our media.

Perhaps most significant of all, the spirit of democracy courses through America and influences our lives. Authoritarianism is suspect in any area of learning or culture. Individual freedom is prized supremely. Religious doctrine and moral teaching are widely judged by these criteria. Therefore, to assert that there is a Church teaching with authority, binding and loosing for eternity is truly a sign of contradiction to many Americans who consider the divine right of bishops as outmoded as the divine right of kings. Accordingly, bishops live and work constantly in this atmosphere.

In these days, Holy Father, we ponder together the challenge of teaching the universal and ageless truth of the Roman Catholic Church in the above-mentioned cultural context of the United States. We value this opportunity. We are here with open minds and open hearts, here to listen and to explain, here to seek wisdom and strength in the presence of the Lord, who has sent us all to preach the Good News to all the nations.

(*Origins* 18 [1989] page 680)

– ◆ –

Presidential address to the special meeting of the National Conference of Catholic Bishops at Seton Hall University, New Jersey, on June 16, 1989.

Since we last met, one event — more than any other — has occupied the time of many of us and the interest of all of us: the March meeting of the U.S. Cardinals and Archbishops with our Holy Father, Pope John Paul, and the cardinals of the Vatican Curia, a meeting which had the somewhat ponderous theme, "Evangelization in the Culture and Society of the United States and the Bishop as Teacher of Faith."

There were ten topics related to the general theme. On each of these topics, the format was the same — two presentations (one by a Curial representative and then the other by one of our members), followed by more than an hour of open discussion. During those discussions, I am told by people who count such things, the U.S. Archbishops made some ninety interventions, while the Curial cardinals made nine or ten. The Holy Father, who was present for nearly every session, simply made brief introductory and closing addresses. He said he wanted to listen and learn.

I believe that it would be pointless for me to try to summarize in a few minutes a discussion which originally consumed nearly twenty hours.

My own conviction is that the ultimate value of this meeting goes beyond anything specific that was said. It has to do more with "bridge-building," with understanding, with unity. Before the meeting began and during its early stages, the media notion, by and large, was that the meeting was focused on "dissent," on "differences," on "confrontation." But as the texts of the presentations became available and as we began to speak with the press about what went on within the Old Synod Hall, a perceptible difference developed in the coverage. By the meeting's end, the media had caught what all of us participants felt was the true flavor: "Meeting with Vatican soothes U.S. Archbishops," *The New York Times* reported; "Vatican conferees profess harmony on U.S. issues," said *The Washington Post; The Boston Sunday Globe* headlined its wrap-up story, "U.S. Bishops upbeat, Vatican officials pleased after gathering"; "Bishops encouraged by Vatican meeting" was the headline of the *Chicago Sun Times;* and the *Minneapolis Star Tribune* reported, "U.S. Bishops back from Vatican say meeting improved communication."

The media "got it right." I believe that the bridge between Rome and the United States is stronger than it has been in recent memory; this has happened because of several factors — the Pope's trip to these shores in 1987, our own *ad limina* visits last year and, most recently, this March meeting at the Vatican. I believe that I speak for all the archbishops when I say that we felt that we were listened to and that we learned. We had the opportunity to "tell our stories," to share our experiences of living and working in America. Equally important, we had the chance to listen — to hear the views of the Curial cardinals, who come from all five continents and whose concerns must revolve not simply around a single nation but around the globe and the eight hundred fifty million Catholics who people it.

Clearly, there were and are some differences in perspective. It would be a startling thing in a room of some sixty people if that were not so. But whatever differences there are have to do with approach and not with doctrine. All of us in that room were clearly on the same team, and our opponents were common ones: exaggerated individualism, secularism, moral relativism, consumerism.

The format of the meeting was an excellent one: the prepared presentations as a point of departure and then open-ended discussion for generous periods of time. Never before did we have the benefit of that — a large group of us engaging in extended discussion with Vatican leaders about the Church in the United States. The idea was so good, in fact, that it should not surprise me if this were to become a standard format for meetings between the Vatican and the hierarchies of many countries. It gave us (the U.S. Archbishops) a chance to explain some of the uniqueness and the glory of our nation: the pluralism of ideas and cultures, the freedom of expression, the democratic spirit which values the opinion of each individual. It gave us the chance to brainstorm with our confreres at the Vatican how best the Church can function in such a society, how a Church whose values are deep and eternal can speak to a culture which is sometimes shallow and ephemeral, how a Church which values discipline and authority can relate to a milieu which accepts ideas on their intrinsic merit and not on anyone's fiat.

The focus of our meetings was by no means limited to problems. Pride had a place too. We U.S. Archbishops are tremendously proud of our nation and proud of our Catholic people here. It was gratifying for us to learn how much Rome shares that pride. Over and over again, both in the formal presentations and in the discussions, there was evident the high regard which the Pope and the Curia have for the Church in the United States — for the zeal and fidelity of our priests and religious, for the committed and growing involvement of the laity in the work of the Church, for the way in which we bishops have engaged the great moral issues of our day in our pastoral letters. It was, more than anything else, a time of affirmation for us — a week in which we felt proud to be Roman Catholics, proud to be Americans, and happy to be involved in fashioning a faithful blend of those two traditions.

And how, it might be asked, do those days in Rome relate to our work this week here at Seton Hall? I would answer that we are here to do what Rome asks us to do: to be evangelizers and to be teachers. It is a ministry which we exercise each day — individually in our own dioceses and in a collective way when we speak as a conference.

It is part of our common mission as Christians to speak up for the God-given dignity of all people, especially for those who are most vulnerable. It is something that our Church has been doing for a long, long time. A little history wouldn't hurt here: in 1919, for example, in a statement on "social reconstruction," American Bishops spoke in favor of child labor laws, of unemployment insurance, of social security benefits, of equal pay for women — notions which seem tame now but which were fairly radical in that day.

When we bishops say today that every single person counts and must be treated with justice and compassion, we believe we are acting as teachers.

In these very weeks, the U.S. Supreme Court is deciding the fate of a million and a half children whose lives are snuffed out each year within the wombs of their mothers. *Time* magazine on May 1 phrased the question well: their article was headlined "Whose Life Is It?" We would say to the Supreme Court what we say to this nation: "Do not forget the child. The child has a life of its own."

When someone asks why the Church and the bishops involve themselves in social issues such as these — peace and justice, rights of the unborn, help for the poor — we say that we have no choice. Jesus said, in Matthew's Gospel, that the final standard on which we're going to be judged for eternity is what we did for the poor, the hungry, the homeless, the weak, the vulnerable in our society.

The challenge, of course, is that the issues change, and new concerns come constantly rolling toward us over the horizon. We have to listen carefully to be sure that we are hearing people's questions, sensing their concerns. Our principles remain the same, but new issues come year after year. And that is why bishops get involved in so many things.

Nor is our agenda this week limited to questions of public policy. Pastoral and theological issues will occupy us. We will spend, for example, a considerable amount of time discussing and, I hope, approving a document on "Doctrinal Responsibilities." We believe that most Catholics are involved in a quiet struggle, not to solve theological disputes but to bring gospel values to their families and their work. Yet theological ferment does have a relevance to the ordinary Catholic because it can lead to religious enrichment or to religious confusion. The Pope himself, speaking to our bishops from New York State last October, framed the question. He spoke of the Church's responsibility to foster "a legitimate pluralism in theology," but noted that pluralism is limited by the unity of the faith we share and by "the Church's authentic magisterium." So our document tries to present guidelines to assist the bishops and theologians to work together to deepen the Church's understanding of herself and to prevent confusion.

Evangelization also will draw our attention today and tomorrow: how the pastoral plans for black Catholics and for Hispanics can be implemented, how the core content of the Church's message can best be translated and transmitted in particular cultural settings.

For all of our discussion, the most important thing we'll do here at Seton Hall may well come on Sunday — when, with the help of Cardinal Danneels, we will make a day of recollection. As for every Catholic, as for every person, so for each of us: We need to draw nearer to the Lord, to make his love ever more genuine in our lives, lest the words of Ralph Waldo Emerson apply to us when he said, "What you are stands over you the while and thunders so, I cannot hear what you are saying."

(Origins 19 [1989] pages 126-8)

Our Country and Our Church

On August 15, 1790, Father John Carroll, S.J., was consecrated as Bishop of Baltimore, the first shepherd of the struggling, scattered Roman Catholic community in the infant republic of the United States of America. As we look forward to July 4, our annual celebration of our nation's birthday, the American Bishops are completing a national convocation at Santa Clara University in California. More than two hundred bishops from across the country came together not to transact business as the National Conference of Catholic Bishops this time, but rather as brothers conferring and praying together for a week, pondering their role as teachers of the Faith. Their speaker in the scheduled conferences was the celebrated Archbishop of Brussels, in Belgium, Godfried Danneels, surely one of the leading thinkers in today's Church.

History: Someone has said that those who do not learn the lessons of history are condemned to repeat its mistakes. So for just a few paragraphs, it might be helpful today for us to do a brief historical review.

When Pope Pius VI named John Carroll as the first bishop of the United States two hundred years ago, it meant that the Church in our country had come of age.

Quite likely, neither the Holy Father nor John Carroll imagined the marvelous and nearly miraculous growth that would occur in the fledging Catholic community on these shores.

The history of the Church in this nation since that day — a combination of joys and struggles — has been a proud one.

In contrast to the handful of parishes and several thousand Catholics in these states in 1790, we look now at a Catholic mural painted wide across America — 55 million Catholics, 19 thousand parishes, 232 Catholic colleges and universities, 9,633 elementary and secondary schools, 650 hospitals, 206 clinics and dispensaries, 667 nursing homes, and 239 child-welfare centers.

In rural settings and on city corners, in villages and in suburbs, Catholic churches and the institutions they have spawned serve as centers of prayer and worship, of education and of Christian service.

I mentioned these facts and figures at the regular general meeting of the National Conference of Catholic Bishops last November as I ended my three-year term as president of the Bishops' Conference.

My term showed me the spirit of togetherness that is displayed when the bishops work in concert with one another.

The story of episcopal collegiality in our country is nothing new. It began in November of 1810 when John Carroll met for two weeks in Baltimore with the bishops of the newly created Dioceses of Boston, Philadelphia, and Bardstown, Kentucky, to discuss joint concerns and policies. From that day until this, their cooperation has been genuine and productive.

Bishop Carroll — while never waffling on matters of faith — felt that the manner of presenting Catholicism in the United States had to be adapted to a land that had been founded on principles of religious liberty and democracy.

Where the issue is policy, not doctrine, we are committed to working things out by discussion and consensus. The genius of the American way is that everyone's voice is heard — and, where possible, accommodated.

Today: The Catholic Church is a strong force in this country in the struggle for human dignity. While speaking out to protect the unborn child, it also reaches out to help the woman who often must face agonizing situations alone, sometimes with the father of the child having long since fled the scene. Every woman in America should know that the Catholic Church is willing to care both for her and for the baby she is carrying.

The Church also reaches out to refugees from other nations — helping twenty-six thousand a year — farmworkers seeking protection from pesticides, the homeless in need of housing, the terminally ill hospital patients, and to many others. It gratifies me greatly that the Bishops' Conference has been such an integral part of these efforts.

Rome: The Church in the United States today has a close, personal bond with the Church in Rome.

Two hundred years ago Catholics in this land made substantial sacrifices to maintain their union with Rome. Early colonists referred to Catholicism snidely as the "Romish religion." It was a time when the colonies had just shaken off foreign domination, and anyone with external links was viewed with suspicion. John Carroll, in fact, was appointed to assuage just such fears — he was a man whose patriotic credentials were impeccable, whose loyalty to the revolution was unquestioned, but who also was fearless in defense of Catholic values and rights.

The Church, under Bishop Carroll's leadership, had twin loyalties — one to a tradition of democracy and liberty and the other to a faith and moral teaching that transcended the borders of our nation. That link to Rome, that channel of spiritual vitality, was central to Catholic life in Carroll's day, and it is, indeed, in our own.

As we pause to celebrate once again this July 4 all the blessings of America, we prepare to receive Archbishop Agostino Cacciavillan, the newly appointed pro-nuncio to the United States. He is, of course, the personal representative of Pope John Paul to the Church in our country and ambassador of the Holy See to the United States. His appointment reminds us of the close working relationship between Church and state in our blessed land in keeping with our American principle of separation of Church and state. The older I get, the more convinced I am that of all Catholic communities across the face of the earth, we American Catholics are most blessed. The Church in our country has enjoyed unique liberty through these two hundred years. Accordingly, it has enriched this nation beyond all others in teaching its values and implementing them in the many institutions of education, healthcare, and social service mentioned above.

Our country and our Church — they have been good for each other. Amen and Alleluia on July 4, 1990!

(St. Louis, June 29, 1990)

- 13 -
MORAL
ISSUES

Proclaim the message, press it home on all occasions, convenient or inconvenient, use argument, reproof, and appeal, with all the patience that the work of teaching requires.

(2 Timothy 4:2)

Questions of personal and social morality, in the broadest sense, have been a recurrent theme in the Archbishop's writings. Taken together, they could easily fill an entire volume. The selections below are representative, not inclusive.

It was last Friday night that I met him walking along Conti Street near the cathedral. As I passed him, I said "Hello" and he replied with a grin.

A minute later, around the corner, he called to me. He had turned around and followed. He just wanted to talk, he said. Not a Catholic, about twenty-two, he was at least half-drunk.

We had quite a talk. (Suppose we call him Jim.) He had a job now that he was back from service in Vietnam. But Jim was out of touch with his folks. "They were always putting me down." Most of the time he was lonely. He was on his way to a cocktail lounge.

Jim said he would be back "one of these days" because he wanted to talk more when his mind was clear. He admitted that his life was unhappy and felt that no one cared about him. He insisted that he was old enough to get drunk.

How many "Jims" are there in this diocese? How many will be confirmed alcoholics before they are thirty? Lots of us are horrified by the abuse of drugs by our youth today — and rightly so. But lots of us are also indifferent to the most abused drug of all: alcohol.

And I do mean us Catholics of whom one of our poets wrote some years back: "Catholic men are deep in the wine. Wherever I go, I find it so. *Benedicamus Domino!*"

Catholic theology does not forbid moderate use of alcoholic beverages, and we do not believe the Bible does either. At the same time, we should be aware that total abstinence is an old Catholic ideal too, and not some weird Protestant aberration. In fact, we might say that in our society it is an ideal whose time has come.

Just recently a federal study on "Alcohol and Health" appeared. The consequences of alcoholism in our country are frightful: shattered health in millions of people, half of the highway fatalities and injuries, one third of all the annual arrests, broken families, and so forth.

Many a Catholic complains that the Church got soft in not insisting on Friday and Lenten abstinence from meat. At the same time, it may never occur to the same man (or woman) that the abstinence he might better practice would be in the matter of alcohol. The Church has asked us to search our own consciences for the best penance we should practice. Catholics, both individuals and some of our organizations, might well do so. What does our use of alcohol say to our young people? What does it say to our neighbors? What does it say to Jim, the fellow I met near the cathedral?

I hope Jim comes back. We could talk about this latest government study. But I know he won't care. He'll figure it will never happen to him. Jim doesn't need new information. He needs the old news, the good news that someone does care about him. He needs to know that his life does have meaning. He needs to know Jesus Christ.

(Mobile, October 20, 1972)

Teen Pregnancy and Abortion

Despite their differences, most Americans seem to agree that abortion is not desirable in itself. They often say it is an unattractive but necessary solution to problems. High on the list of such problems is teenage pregnancy, which is reaching epidemic proportions in our country. What can be done to reduce teenage pregnancies?

The answer seems obvious to pragmatic minds. Pregnancies are prevented by contraception. If we increase contraceptive information and services for teenagers, we shall be well on the way to cutting down on the number of pregnancies and so reducing the need for teenage abortions.

As I see it, there is good reason to doubt that more and better contraceptive information and services will make major inroads in the number of teenage pregnancies. We already live — and have lived for many years — in a contraceptive culture; one, that is, in which contraception is taken for granted. Contraceptive information is widely disseminated and readily available. So are contraceptives. If sexually active teenagers do not practice contraception, it is not because they lack opportunity.

But, the counterargument goes, we haven't been getting through to them. Despite our best efforts, teenagers in increasing numbers are getting pregnant. What to do? Obviously, more of the same.

So now the push is on for massive contraceptive indoctrination of the nation's teenage population — through the schools and through television and radio advertising (if the rules and customs of the broadcasting industry can be breached). Thus, the twin problems of teenage pregnancy and teenage abortion will be solved.

Perhaps. But it does not seem very likely. More contraceptive indoctrination of teenagers seems at least as likely (more likely, I would say) to have the same result that the contraceptive indoctrination of recent decades has had: it will motivate them to precocious sexual activity but by no means to the practice of contraception (especially in this day of free and easy abortion), in which case the "solution" will merely have made the problem worse.

Is There an Alternative?

I believe there is one, but I do not think it is easy. It certainly does not have the attractive but delusory simplicity of more and better contraception.

It amounts to turning things around and, instead of telling teenagers that they can have sex without consequences, telling them the truth: there is no such thing as sex without consequences, whether these be emotional, physical, social — or all three.

It amounts, in other words, to telling them early what they need to know anyway. Sex is not merely for fun or for the expression of transitory affection. It is an enriching and serious business between mature people who are emotionally, socially, and even economically able to accept the consequences, of which pregnancy is hardly the only one.

I agree that more education of teenagers — indoctrination, if you will — is needed. But I believe it should be education in such things as family values, a healthy and integrated acceptance of sexuality, stability in marital relationships, a sense of obligation toward other persons, and willingness to accept the consequences of one's actions. In other words, it should seek to help them grow up as sexually mature adults.

There is no reason to think more and better contraception will do this. This approach is a formula for shortchanging young people, truncating the development of their emotional — and, yes, their sexual — lives. It is a cheap solution that will not work and, if it did work, would not meet the real developmental needs of teenagers searching for their sexual identity.

What I am suggesting, admittedly in the most general terms, is a very large order. It would not be easy at any time. It is particularly difficult at a time when the fruits of our contraceptive culture, bitter as they are, are widely accepted as staple fare. So much so that today's proposed solution to the conspicuous failure of more-and-better contraception is — more and better contraception.

Abortion is a very serious problem. But from a certain perspective, it is only the tip of the iceberg, beneath which lie some very strange ideas about sex and sexual responsibility.

There is growing realization abroad that we are in trouble in the whole area of sex and marriage. Thinking people are concerned all over this country. They are trying to find solutions to our present cultural malaise. If we look for the answers in what we have been trying these recent years, what has aggravated rather than solved all these problems — will not our last state be even worse than the first?

(Mobile, February 17, 1978)

— ◆ —

221

Is There Sin Anymore?

There certainly is. To deny sin would be to deny one of the most basic truths in the Bible as well as in our everyday experience. As long as we believe that God is our Father and that we all are brothers and sisters through Jesus, then there will be the realization of sin. We are free to accept or reject God and his truth. We need only to look about us. We cannot deny the evil all around us. When we deny that God cares about all this, then the idea of sin wavers or disappears.

Q Is there really such a thing as mortal sin?

A There certainly is. We must remember that sin either hurts or kills our friendship with God. A mortal sin means that we have deliberately chosen to turn away from God or to direct our life in a way opposed to his will. It amounts to a "divorce from God."

We have a wonderful gift from God: freedom. We are free to say "Yes" to God, which is to love him, or to say "No," which is to reject him. Complete rejection is what we call mortal sin.

This complete turning away from God doesn't seem to happen often in the lives of most Catholics. Does this mean that scarcely any of our actions are gravely wrong?

We would hope so. But occasional hurts may occur between a husband and wife. They may not seem serious. But such offenses can tend to become habits. To ignore such tensions or hurts can lead to a growing and grave strain on married love and sometimes to the death of that relationship. We see that happening all around us. The same can happen to our love of God.

Unfortunately, our emotions and weaknesses sometimes blind us so that we don't read the signs in our own lives. We need to be more honest with ourselves.

Q May I decide for myself what is right and wrong?

A Today the Church puts much emphasis on personal responsibility and mature witness to the truth. In the area of conscience, some have erroneously taken this to mean that "everyone decides for himself; it is right if I think it is right; it is wrong if I think it is wrong." But our Christian life is not simply a matter of "God and me." As Catholic Christians, we are members of a community of faith, the Church of Jesus Christ.

It is true, when all is said and done, that we must follow our own conscience. But it should always be a well-informed conscience that respects the teaching authority of the Church and listens to its voice. To refuse to listen to the Church in moral matters is to cease to be a Catholic. The teaching of the Catholic Church on right and wrong is clear. Jesus said to his Church, "Who hears you, hears me. Who rejects you, rejects me." And he said to Peter, the first pope, "I will give you the keys of the kingdom of heaven. What you bind on earth will be bound in heaven. What you loose on earth will be loosed in heaven."

Q But if I don't have any mortal sins, why should I go to confession?

A Strictly speaking, the obligation to confess our sins applies only when we are aware that we have turned away from God in grave sin. But if we were to receive the sacrament of penance only then, we would miss so much. (We only *have* to receive communion once a year during Easter time, but we know that is not enough.) A regular approach to this sacrament of penance gives us the opportunity:

1. to meet Christ, who continues to heal us in this sacrament by his grace and strength;
2. to read the signs of any weakening in our relationship with the Lord;
3. to make a fresh start, for the Christian's life is one of constant conversion;
4. to acknowledge our dependence on God, and our own weakness;
5. to obtain spiritual counsel and encouragement.

Q How often should I go to confession?

A Whenever we need a change of heart! In practice this means

1. the sacrament of penance is necessary when we have completely turned away from God by mortal sin;
2. it is very helpful at certain times, which invites us to make a

fresh start in our relationship with God and neighbor — in Advent and Lent or at times of decision in our lives;

3. it is advisable on a regular basis, for example, as each season begins — four times a year; or for others — every other month or once a month.

(St. Louis, February 26, 1982)

— ◆ —

"Happy Hours?"

I must express a serious concern. I have been surprised to see "happy hours" so long and so prevalent all over this archdiocese. They are sometimes over an hour and often become truly embarrassing. This seems to be a pattern in some rectories, at parish gatherings, at other Catholic events — almost everywhere. Frankly, I have been disappointed and disturbed by this cavalier attitude toward alcohol among us people of God. Maybe I was in the Bible Belt too long, but I would ask us all to examine our consciences in this regard. Much of our modern culture in this regard is pagan in my judgment. What about the prevailing practice in the household of the faith?

(Notanda, March 10, 1982)

— ◆ —

Reappraisal

It has been fourteen years since the promulgation of Pope Paul's encyclical *Humanae Vitae,* a document that shook up Catholics and many others around the world. They had been primed to expect the Holy Father's acceptance of the practice of contraception. Instead, the Pope reaffirmed the traditional Catholic doctrine that contraception is intrinsically immoral. At the same time, he called upon physicians and scientists to develop new methods of natural-family planning and encouraged married Catholics in the challenge of living their holy vocation in today's world.

Dreams: Proponents of contraception had often taught that any kind of sexual abstinence was detrimental to the psychological and physical health of normal individuals, that anything standing in the way of spontaneous sex militated against marital happiness. They argued further that children who are wanted and planned are more loved, better adjusted, and consequently destined to be a superior class of adult citizens. Proponents of the use of the pill, the IUD, and all the barrier and chemical contraceptives were eloquent in attesting to the improvement in health of women freed from childbearing and consequently ready for careers in significant areas of public life. The contribution of women to the betterment of the world scene was hailed as the great promise we could all expect.

The Awakening: Developments of recent years have brought a sobering reaction to the sanguine expectations of those who have rejected or who have failed to consider with discernment the message of *Humanae Vitae.* Side effects of contraceptives have continued to be a problem. Medical journals are concentrating more and more on epidemic veneral disease. The sexual revolution, unleashed to a great extent by the contraceptive mentality, has left us some unwanted progeny indeed.

And what of the wanted child, the loved child it promised? He has become a somewhat shadowy little creature in the face of staggering statistics of teenage pregnancy, abortion, child abuse, disturbed and abandoned children. The Bible asks, "Can a woman forsake her child?" What has happened makes every thinking person wonder, "Where have all the wanted children gone?"

Advocates of free and easy contraception predicted improved marital relations everywhere. Instead, these past years have seen a skyrocketing divorce rate, rampant infidelity, the denial of basic values in matrimony, and a radical refusal on the part of many young people to commit themselves to a lasting marriage agreement. Temporary cohabitation has not just been tolerated; it has been idealized.

At the time the pill was first introduced, the Planned Parenthood people stressed that abortion should not be considered part of their program. Today, in the case of the surprise pregnancy, Planned Parenthood, our state boards of health, and our courts ratify the pragmatic solution — abortion, even at an advanced stage of development, even by the most abhorrent methods, even at the risk of serious physical or psychological effects on the aborting mother.

The delivery rooms and nurseries of American hospitals are often the scene of heroic measures to save a life, such as the round-the-clock skilled care for the critical newborn child. In contrast, abortion clinics, be they ever so aseptic, tastefully decorated, equipped with piped-in comforting music, are the places where human bodies are torn apart or, if delivered half-alive, are left to die, unprotected, without a whiff of oxygen or even a warm blanket.

With the advent of the contraceptive pill, marital self-restraint was declared obsolete. The spontaneity of the sex act was assured — but so was safe adultery. Wives have turned against husbands, husbands against wives, because the holy, life-giving aspect of the marriage act has been obliterated, and partners saw themselves as sex objects, a fact that strikes at the deepest, subconscious realities of the personality.

To bypass the adverse effects of the pill and still to leave the road wide open to sex as you please, sterilizing operations have been performed increasingly, notably vasectomies in men, with other side effects.

And now children are given the pill. Clinics are at a loss to know what to do about the ever younger children who request contraceptive services. It has become standard practice to honor their requests without parental consent and later to do the same with abortion.

Humanae Vitae warned of some of these tragic consequences but never even dared to predict what has really happened. It would have seemed incredible.

A New Look: It seems that the time has come to take a second look at the whole problem of America's contraceptive mentality and to reread with discernment Pope Paul's *Humanae Vitae.* In the light of what has transpired since its promulgation, whole new insights are revealed that at the time of its appearance were so obscure that the encyclical was headlined as a document coming out of the Dark Ages. Nature has a way of teaching its inevitable law much better than documentation, and it has the further power of imposing sanctions. While obviously there are many causes of the erosion of marriage and family life in our society, the widespread contraceptive mentality of Americans is clearly a principal factor. Pope John Paul has confirmed the teaching of the Church on this issue and has called for a rethinking, a reliving of holy matrimony in his own encyclical, *Familiaris Consortio.*

The time has come for Catholic people to regain a Catholic conscience in marriage and family life. That is why we have our policy of marriage preparation and our programs of natural-family planning in our archdiocese.

We hope to do more in fulfillment of the Pope's call for positive support to Catholics in their need for safe and sane family planning in keeping with

Catholic doctrine on the holiness of marriage and the family today. More and more young people are committing themselves to holy matrimony and parenthood. The pendulum is beginning to swing back again. Thanks be to God.

(St. Louis, September 10, 1982)

A Sick Play

There have been a number of plays lately about Catholic life, along with movies like *Monsignor* and soap operas, *Saturday Night Live,* and so forth. Some are nostalgic spoofs like *Do Patent Leather Shoes Reflect Up?* and others are thoughtful probes of Catholic belief like *Mass Appeal.* A few are tasteless like Monsignor Guido Sarducci's latest stint. But none can compare with *Sister Mary Ignatius Explains It All to You.* It is a vile diatribe against all things Catholic.

From beginning to end, this play caricatures and ridicules every doctrine in the catechism and every Catholic value. For instance, this is Sister Mary Ignatius describing her family: "I had twenty-six brothers and sisters. From my family, five became priests, seven became nuns, three became brothers, and the rest of them were institutionalized. My mother was also institutionalized shortly after she started thinking my father was Satan. Some days when we were little, we'd come home and not be able to find our mother, and we'd pray to Saint Anthony to help us find her. Then when we'd find her with her head in the oven, we would pray to Saint Jude to make her sane again." Sister Mary Ignatius shoots two of her former pupils dead in the last scene, but it still is one dull play, and I read every word of it.

The Theatre Project Company, a member of the Arts and Education Council of Greater St. Louis, with funding from the National Endowment for the Arts and the Missouri Arts Council, has chosen to bring this play to St. Louis next January. St. Louis Catholics are asked to contribute to this effort by their tax-deductible contributions, in addition to paying their taxes for its support.

This decision was made in freedom of expression, which we respect. But we also reserve our right to express ourselves on this project of our own theater company. The more than half million Catholics in this area can do so most emphatically by our total absence at the box office. I believe that thousands of our neighbors of every faith will do the same. Would you attend a racist minstrel show or an anti-Semitic spoof of the Holocaust? I'm afraid our Theatre Project Company has really laid one big egg this time.

(St. Louis, November 12, 1982)

– ◆ –

"Bless Me, Father"

"Whatever happened to sin?" That question was asked by the famous psychiatrist, Carl Menninger, in his book by the same name. Actually, sin is alive and well — as your daily newspaper will attest. But sometimes it goes by new names.

Times come and go, but the teaching of Jesus goes on forever. His word is as modern as last night's TV special and really does not depend on the ratings. It was here for our grandparents and will be around for the grandchildren. "Heaven and earth will pass away, but my word will not pass away," Jesus said.

In these last days of Advent, it is time for us all to make a good confession. Every parish will provide a communal penance service and extra opportunities for this sacrament of reconciliation, this sacrament of our Lord's peace. To prepare to receive the mercy of Jesus, we all need to ponder our lives in an honest examination of conscience. The word of Jesus in his Sermon on the Mount (Matthew 5:1-12) provides a simple examination of conscience for today's Catholic. Here it is:

Blessed are the poor in spirit. Have I accepted the teaching of the advertising and commercial world that "more is better," that "things" will make me and my family happy? Do I buy "things" for my children instead of spending time with them? Do I practice personal self-denial in any aspect of life: food, drink, use of energy, recreation? Am I wasteful? Do I envy the rich?

Blessed are the gentle. Has anger, rudeness, "me-firstness," become a way of life for me in dealing with strangers, friends, family? Do I bully my children, spouse, or employees? Do I practice the violence of ignoring those closest to me or being too busy to listen to other people?

Blessed are those who mourn. Have I fostered a sensitivity for the hungry, the sick, the elderly, for victims of crime or circumstance? Have I shared my time and possessions? Have I taught my children that we are only

228

stewards of this creation, that everything we have is a gift we do not deserve and cannot just keep for ourselves?

Blessed are those who hunger and thirst after justice. Am I willing to modify my stereotypes and to sacrifice my comfort in order that a more just world can come about? Do I, as a worker, give an honest day's work for a day's wages? Do I, as an employer, give an honest day's wages for a day's work? Do I pay my just taxes? Do I use my vote to help elect a government that is just, which respects life and assures freedom? Do I serve jury duty when it is my turn? Have I tried to use my purchasing power in patronizing businesses that benefit the common good?

Blessed are the merciful. Do I gossip? Have I been the one to pass along a story that puts another in a bad light? Do I enjoy my grudges and refuse to let go of them? Do I try to believe the best of others and of myself, despite the failings of both? Can I forgive myself for not being all that I had hoped I might be by this time in my life?

Blessed are the pure of heart. Do I love chastely, without using another person for my own pleasure, prestige, or gain? Am I faithful to my marriage commitment? Do I refuse to support the pornographic exploitation of other people in print, film, and music? Have I realized and taught my children that love, sex, and lust are not synonymous words, that people are to be reverenced, and that violence has no part of love? Am I "single-hearted" in my commitment to live in the Lord?

Blessed are those who are persecuted in the cause of right. Have I taken a stand against abortion, divorce, teenage or extramarital sex? Have I tolerated my children engaging in dangerous and illicit behavior with drugs and alcohol or even given bad example by my own drinking? Have I let my children know what and why I believe, even though they choose to act contrary to those beliefs? Have I done my best to support values that build up and develop our community?

The entire discourse in Matthew, Chapters 5, 6, and 7, contains a range of moral values. Jesus cautions against worrying, loving money, fostering lustful thoughts, and showing off our goodness. He urges us to be generous, forgiving, humble, and full of faith. Using the gospel as a guide to behavior, we may begin to see our sinfulness and perhaps, after that, to turn from the darkness to walk as children of the light.

(St. Louis, December 17, 1982)

Smoking

Recently, I happened to read what the surgeon general of the United States, Dr. C. Everett Koop, had to say about smoking. Some years ago, I met Dr. Koop when we appeared together on a pro-life panel in Montgomery, Alabama. A Protestant and a pediatrician, this physician impressed me as true professionals always do. He was obviously learned in his field and yet carefully modest in expressing personal opinions. That is why I was struck by his statement on smoking.

Dr. Koop, who says that he has now given up his pipe, calls smoking "the most important health issue of our time."

Millions, perhaps, who are still undecided about "giving up something for Lent" might take a hint, even a shove, from the surgeon general's report. There's little real sacrifice, though, in giving up a practice that may lead to something more devastating than a hole in a sweater or a burn mark on a table.

The modern emphasis is on doing something positive and constructive to express a richer sense of Lent. The denial of the self, a self that can be a bit pushy at any time of the year, is still a part of all this. But today's idea is to accomplish something for others as well as for the self during this season of penance.

More power to those who break off their enslavement to cigarettes, cigars, and pipes for forty days. They spare themselves, their relatives, and their associates.

Special congratulations to those, whether inspired by the Lord or the surgeon general, who use this time to gain permanent freedom from an expensive habit that may tragically undermine their health.

Catholics who do not smoke are usually tolerant of those who do. That's good. It is fine to encourage those who want to shed the burden of smoking, but it is not so fine to apply the abrasive behavior of the fanatic. The common smoker may be a nuisance in a crowded room, but the common scold is no better. Maybe that's why the American colonists used to dunk common scolds in the village pond, a treatment apparently not accorded to smokers.

But then, the colonists did not know that smoking will cause about fifty thousand U.S. cancer deaths this year, that smokers who quit reduce the risk considerably, that smoke inhaled by nonsmokers may be a serious health problem, or that cancer death rates are related to the number of cigarettes smoked.

Best wishes for a successful conclusion of your Lenten commitment, whatever it may be. And I hope that many of you have cut out the tobacco weed for Lent and for good.

(St. Louis, March 11, 1983)

Coincidence?

In recent years there has been a flood of pornography let loose upon America. We have been told to be more tolerant of what appears on our movie and television screens. It all seems very sophisticated and chic.

During these same years, there have been frightful epidemics of venereal disease, brutal rapes, and child molestation, not to mention "kinky sex," today's euphemism for all kinds of perversion. Is there a connection between that first paragraph and this one? Or is it all just a coincidence? Suppose we consider some clichés often heard whenever this discussion heats up.

You can't legislate morality. Every law legislates morality. Private morals are private; public morals are the business of the entire community. Commercial obscenity is public business. It is public morality that obscenity laws are designed to safeguard, not private morality.

I'd rather see people make love than make violence. There is no love in pornography. It is totally loveless, debasing women, children, and humanity generally. Ordinarily, violence is inherent in pornography.

War, poverty, hunger, and violence are obscene, not sex. Of course, sex is not obscene. It is the design and creation of God. It is the debasing abuse of sex that is obscene.

If you don't like porn films and books, you don't have to look at them. Right, but they still pollute the environment in which we are trying to raise children.

The United States Supreme Court has said that what you do in the privacy of your home is your own business, but it is against the law for anyone to sell or exhibit obscenity in public.

Freedom of expression is protected by the First Amendment. It most certainly is. But the Supreme Court has said that obscenity is not protected by the First Amendment any more than libel or slander are. Obscenity is not a First Amendment issue. It is a crime, and ninety percent of the traffic in hard-core pornography in this country is controlled by organized crime.

Obscenity is a "victimless crime." There is no such thing as a "victimless" crime. Try telling that to the rape victim or the children used in child pornography.

That is why there are laws against pornography as detrimental to the public health, morals, and welfare.

If you'd let pornography flow freely, people would get bored and the problem would take care of itself. Research shows that heavy users of pornography do not get bored. They do go deeper and deeper into more and more bizarre forms of it.

Denmark is a good example. The Danes legalized pornography, and then underworld infiltration of the porno industry, gangland violence, and tie-ins with traffic in narcotics forced Copenhagen police to close down most of the smut dens.

How do you define obscenity? The Supreme Court has defined obscenity as materials that "taken as a whole appeal to the prurient interest of sex, which portray sexual conduct in a patently offensive way and which, taken as a whole, do not have serious literary, artistic, political, or scientific value."

The porno industry is growing, so the American people must want it or simply don't care. Certainly, there are some who want it, and obviously there are some who don't care. But all surveys show that the majority do care. But they are confused and discouraged in the face of a highly organized industry and the loud prophets of false freedom.

One of the major factors in the growth of the pornography traffic is the lack of vigorous enforcement of obscenity laws, particularly at the federal level.

Why bother enforcing the law? The porno places keep operating. Continuous, vigorous enforcement of the law is the answer. It can be done. For example, Atlanta, Jacksonville, and Cincinnati are clean cities because of vigorous, continuous enforcement of the law. Experts say that with aggressive enforcement of federal law, the back of the porno industry would be broken in eighteen months.

So much for the law. As Catholics, we respect the pronouncement of our courts, but even more, we need to hear what the Lord says about all this. Speaking to children, Jesus put it this way in Matthew 18:6-7:

...it would be better for anyone who leads astray one of these little ones who believe in me, to be drowned by a millstone around his neck, in the depths of the sea. What terrible things will come on the world through scandal! It is inevitable that scandal should occur. Nonetheless, woe to that man through whom scandal comes.

(St. Louis, June 3, 1983)

Second Thoughts

Some time back *Newsweek* carried an essay by Anne Taylor Fleming. A most thoughtful young lady, Ms. Fleming tells of how her generation of American women has been brainwashed into opting for no babies in the interest of a career, independence, women's rights, population zero, world stability, and so forth. She explains that she bought the whole package.

But now, as the years pass, she is beginning to wonder whether "we might enter middle age alone — perhaps divorced or widowed — childless, womb-tight, and woebegone." Something to think about.

Ms. Taylor then goes on to a most astute analysis of the American contraceptive mentality of recent years. She points out that once sex and parenthood are put in separate compartments, the woman becomes basically a sex object, with resulting unhappiness and insecurity of both husband and wife. She confesses her worried confusion:

> When the women's movement was in first bloom a few years ago, women, in their first exhilaration, could not resist gloating a bit over male sexual insecurities. But now the movement is in its revisionist stage and men and women seem to want to be tender with one another again and to honor each other's needs, old and new. In that spirit, many of the women I know long to tumble easily and hopefully into pregnancy, like their mothers and grandmothers before them, with no agony aforethought, long to pledge allegiance with their wombs to the men they love. But they can't. They're stuck in a holding pattern. So am I....

In her feminine and feminist approach, Anne Taylor Fleming has come, I believe, to the same insight expressed in more formal terms by the late Pope Paul in his encyclical Humanae Vitae. She has expressed it touchingly for so many women across America who must also be wondering how the new sexual freedom has now come to lock them up tight into lonely middle age.

(St. Louis, June 17, 1983)

— ◆ —

1984

Last week there was no longer any doubt that George Orwell's *1984* has indeed dawned in population control. We have all read about Red China's "one-child-family" policy, but two television documentaries *(60 Minutes* and *Nova)* let us see and hear the real people caught up in the overall plan.

There was "Big Sister," a frightful coordinator of the network of women at the neighborhood level who report any second pregnancy, and even an unsanctioned first one. There were the two mothers who dared fight for a second child, the first hunted down in a distant city after fleeing to save her child and the second harrassed over months to accept an abortion or suffer economic and social ostracism. Compulsory abortion and sterilization are the solution to such problem parents.

The absolute regimentation by the all-powerful state that stared out of the eyes of reproductive engineers and those engineered was horrifying. Orwell himself might have been fantasizing when he conjured up *1984,* but he underestimated man's potential for inhumanity to man. The Chinese have put his pale literary speculation into shocking, living color.

There was another voice that also mentioned a slippery slope looming ahead in this regard. Back in the sixties, Pope Paul VI warned at the end of his *Humanae Vitae* encyclical where free and easy contraception could lead. There were smiles all around then. Today facing our epidemics of veneral disease, juvenile pregnancy, contraceptive abortion, infanticide, and family disintegration, fewer are smiling. It has come in less than twenty years — in 1984.

The American reporters and commentators in the above-mentioned documentaries on China's new family policy were clinically objective. There were few references to civil rights, family rights, cultural tradition, or personal freedom. There was mention of the population pressures and a certain recognition of the Chinese efficiency and dedication in facing such alternatives. Some of us may have wondered why Pope John Paul made such a big point of his November 24 Charter of Family Rights. His twelve principles proclaiming the individual and family rights of every human person may receive even less attention that the *Humanae Vitae* encyclical of his predecessor. The pace of genetic engineering is speeding up. Last week showed that the Pope spoke up none too soon. He knows it is already here — in 1984.

(St. Louis, February 24, 1984)

– ◆ –

Tomorrow's Mothers?

This Sunday, Mother's Day, we might all do some serious thinking. Our own mothers, living or dead, will be first in our thoughts, of course. And most probably they will be beautiful thoughts of love and gratitude for so much. Certainly, one of life's greatest gifts is a good mother. The older we are, the more we see the profound truth of that fact.

All of this makes many thinking people wonder about the next generation of mothers. Teenage girls today are being bombarded with jaded views of marriage, motherhood, and family life. Accordingly, it is more necessary than ever that the Catholic Church stand faithful to the moral teaching of Jesus Christ on the issues of love and marriage. At the same time, it is more important than ever that Catholic parents and young people know exactly what the Catholic Church teaches in the name of Jesus Christ in this regard.

Some years ago, our late Holy Father, Pope Paul, approved a *Declaration on Sexual Ethics.* Pope John Paul has reiterated and emphasized the same teaching. This document speaks clearly. Its message is what the future mothers and fathers of this nation need, and we are all charged with the responsibility of seeing that they hear it. Here are its main points.

1. Sexual morals come from God's plan in creating human nature and his revelation of Jesus Christ. They are, therefore, not determined by local, transitory, human opinions, or by majority vote. These moral principles are basic to human dignity and happiness and are therefore universal and lasting.
2. The first of these principles is that sexual relations have honest meaning and moral purpose only in a true marriage. Therefore, premarital sexual intercourse is devoid of its real meaning of

full and lasting giving of oneself to the beloved. No binding commitment is made, and the act becomes a dishonest charade. This is true even in the case of an engaged couple. Read the words of Jesus about God's plan for marriage (Matthew 19:4-6) and Saint Paul's beautiful description of Christian marriage (Ephesians 5:25-33). The Church does not condemn sexuality. She embraces, exalts, and blesses it. Read also Ephesians 5:3-8 and 1 Corinthians 6:15-20.

3. Homosexuality is a sad abnormality. Some people slip into this practice and can be cured of it. They must, therefore, use every means to overcome this problem. Others may be constitutionally incurable, and they deserve the concern and ministry of the Church in their suffering. Their human and civil rights must be safeguarded, and they deserve the sympathetic consideration given to all people in need. But homosexual conduct may not be defended as justifiable and acceptable in the sight of God. The Catholic Church therefore does not accept this position so much in vogue today that "gay is good."

4. The practice of masturbation is not just a morally indifferent, socially acceptable expression of self-discovery as some people would say today. Consequently, the sexual education of young people should not indicate that there is no sin involved in such acts. A sympathetic confessor will know how to guide struggling people between scrupulosity on one hand and laxity on the other in this regard.

5. Chastity is possible and necessary in this day and age. Perhaps, as never before, it is the sign of a follower of Christ. The Catholic Church is committed to celibacy for her priests, marital fidelity, and parenthood for her married members, and Christian self-control or chastity in every vocation in life. This Catholic doctrine and discipline flows from the life and teaching of Jesus. Chastity is God's plan for the happiness of each individual and for all of society. If we are Catholics, it must also be ours. If so, we will have happy and beautiful mothers in the years ahead.

(St. Louis, May 10, 1985)

— ♦ —

Happily Ever After?

Do children still read or listen to stories that end with the marriage of the hero and heroine and the statement: "And so they lived happily ever after"? Or am I betraying my age as a member of the pretelevision age?

Even on television, however, the fairy-tale ending seems to be alive and well. It is the basis of numerous commercials. "Buy our product or service," the ads tell us, "and you'll live happily ever after." Often this message is linked with romantic love and marriage. This involves two false ideas that do immense harm.

The first is the notion that "everyone should be married, and if you're not, there is something wrong with you." This idea is false. What every one of us needs for happiness and fulfillment is love. It need not be married love, however. All too many people are pressured into marriage by the constantly repeated question (spoken or implied): "When are you going to get married?" A marriage entered into for that reason is in trouble from the start.

To all who have not yet found a partner, or who have made a conscientious decision to forego marriage temporarily or permanently, I say, "Hold your head high. The single life, lived in a spirit of generosity, is a good life." I can back up that statement with my own experience.

The romantic idea that after the wedding, husband and wife "live happily ever after" is harmful in another way. It encourages unrealistic expectations. Nothing really worth having is cheap. Show me a married couple who have achieved deep happiness in their life together, and I will show you two people who have sacrificed for what they have. People in love gladly sacrifice for each other. How many marriages break up, with untold suffering for the spouses, their children, and other relatives, because the sacrifices the couple made for each other during courtship cease after the wedding? One partner, or both, starts taking the other for granted.

Springtime, when "a young man's fancy lightly turns to thoughts of love" and weddings abound, is a good time to think about this subject. One sacrifice we ask of engaged couples today is adequate preparation. The statistics about marital breakup are alarming. There is roughly one divorce in our country today for every two marriages. Sadly, there is no evidence that the divorce rate for Catholics is lower. Statistically, therefore, there is only a fifty-fifty chance that a given couple will fulfill the vow they exchanged on their wedding day: to live together as husband and wife "until death do us part."

Some time back, preparation for marriage all too often consisted of the priest asking the couple some questions and filling out a form with some friendly conversation in between. The number of broken marriages has made that relaxed approach impossible. Just four years ago, the Catholic Dioceses of Missouri adopted a Common Marriage Preparation Policy that states:

> Preparation for marriage is preparation for the one experience in life on which our happiness most deeply depends.

The policy requires that couples "be willing to take an active part" in their preparation for marriage. It also says: "The date of their wedding shall be set only after they have completed the assessment process." This involves in-depth interviews with the priest who is to witness and bless the marriage. He will normally require that the couple attend a series of Pre-Cana Conferences led by a married couple, clergy, and other professionals or an Engaged Encounter weekend or parish conferences with himself and local married couples.

When one partner is not a Catholic, the policy requires "special sessions to acquaint or update the couple's understanding of Catholic beliefs and practices." It also recommends "that the Catholic party become acquainted with the religious tradition of his or her future spouse." It suggests "cooperative effort of the clergy of both faith communities, when requested."

What about second marriages? For Catholics, these are of two kinds: the marriage of a widow or widower and marriage following an annulment. An annulment is a declaration by the diocesan tribunal, following a careful investigation, that a previous union suffered from a crucial defect (an "impediment"), which prevented its being a true marriage in the eyes of God and the Church. The legitimacy of children is unaffected by an annulment. Since the couple were never validly married, they are free to marry.

People often assume that older or more experienced couples do not need much preparation. This presumption is wrong. Any marriage is an entirely new marriage for this couple. If the previous marriage was good, there may be unrealistic expectations with regard to the new partner. If it was bad, there can be defensiveness and hurt. Also, the divorce rate is higher for second marriages. If marriage is contracted within two years of the death or divorce of the first spouse, the divorce rate is eighty percent.

Why so much red tape? Our aim in all this is not to lay unnecessary burdens on anyone. We want to lift the terrible burden of unhappy marriages and the long drawn-out suffering of broken marriages. Our policy is a helping policy, not a hindering one. It has one goal only — to help couples establish good and stable marriages.

To all engaged couples and newlyweds, I offer my heartiest congratulations. Remember: It takes three to get married: you, your partner — and the Lord. Without his help, which you must seek daily in prayer and at least weekly at Sunday Mass, you can never fulfill the promise you exchanged before the altar:

> I promise to be true to you in good times and in bad, in sick- ness and in health. I will love and honor you all the days of my life.

I also make my own promise: to pray for you in the words of the Church's wedding blessing:

> Lord, may they praise you when they are happy and turn to you in their sorrows. May they be glad that you help them in their work, and know that you are with them in their need. May they reach old age in the company of their friends, and come at last to the kingdom of heaven. Amen.

(St. Louis, May 9, 1986)

Moral Education

Nine-year-old Jimmy was caught shoplifting. "Didn't you know it was wrong to steal?" he was asked. "Uh-huh," the boy said softly. "Then why did you do it?" The youngster just lowered his eyes. He was released to his parents with a warning.

If the boy had been nineteen instead of nine, the outcome of the case would have been quite different. Why? Jimmy had an intellectual awareness that theft was wrong. He did not have an appreciative knowledge of that fact. At nineteen, he would have been presumed to have both. The distinction between these two types of knowledge is important because it underpins all effective moral education.

Very often we act as though moral values are taught simply by communicating knowledge, so children are taught to memorize "Thou shalt not kill, lie, or steal." The technique is effective in communicating data (intellectual knowledge); it is less effective in transferring values.

How do parent and teachers communicate not only the knowledge of values but the values themselves? The first step is to be sure that they possess the values in question. For example, if we want our children to go to Mass on Sunday, we would do well to ask ourselves: Why do I go to Mass? Is it out of habit, or am I responding to the invitation of the Lord, who gave his life for me? Do I pay lip service to justice, charity, and compassion, or do I truly cherish these values? Until I live truthfulness and honesty, I may be able to define them, but I don't own them; and I will find it difficult, if not impossible, to teach them.

(St. Louis, March 20, 1987)

– ♦ –

The Tube

The average American, I am told, spends twenty-six hours a week watching television. If time is any measure of importance, television-watching must be among the most significant experiences of Americans, young and old. Our children spend more time in front of the tube than they do in school.

There is not very much that can be done to change so massive a behavioral pattern. Perhaps, however, we can change the way we and our children watch television. In our *Directory on Religious Education,* the American Bishops urged parents and other religious educators to "foster a critical understanding of this medium" (#262). In other words, we ought to encourage children to develop the ability to appraise the positive as well as the negative aspect of programs they watch.

Alan Alda of *M*A*S*H** fame once wrote: "The unspoken assumptions of a show are what mold an audience." Frontal attacks on Christianity are not so frequent. What we should alert ourselves and our children to are the unspoken and unquestioned assumptions that are taken for granted on TV: What is the role of men and women? Is honesty assumed to be important? Is marital fidelity a value? What does the program assume about sex, marriage, and the family? How are older people portrayed? Is religion part of anyone's life? Is violence acceptable for good guys?

Homegrown Critics

I don't imply that we must sit down before the tube armed with answers to all these questions. What is important is that we raise the questions for ourselves and our kids, that we attempt to probe the values that underpin the programs we are watching. Do we watch TV with our children and raise questions about what we see on that tube?

We would do well, I believe, to cast the same critical glance at the television commercials. In what does happiness consist in the world of the TV commercial? Is consumerism, and the acquisition of more and more, a key to the "good life"? What does the "instant relief" promised by the drug advertisements say about the mystery of Christian suffering? To what conscious and unconscious motives do commercials appeal? Commercials are not harmless appendages stapled to a program. They are often the tail wagging the dog.

Television is undoubtedly the most powerful sales medium ever developed by the human race. As Christians, we owe it to ourselves and our children to take a close look at the philosophy of life hawked by the tube that commands so many of our waking hours. We need to chew and analyze what we see, not just gulp it down whole.

(St. Louis, May 29, 1987)

Homosexuality

The AIDS tragedy and the Gay Rights Movement have propelled homosexuality into the headlines in recent years. At the risk of generating more heat than light, I will attempt a few observations.

First, it is worth noting that the Bible condemns homosexuality whenever it mentions it (for example, Leviticus 18:22 and Romans 1:27). This has been the stance of the Church since the time of Saint Paul; it is a position that has been reiterated in recent years, most recently by the Vatican statement *On the Pastoral Care of Homosexual Persons.*

The reasoning behind the Church's position is its Christian view of sexuality as a life-giving, love-giving activity. In other words, sexual acts are not merely an expression of love but a very special expression. They imitate the creative love of God, since they allow us to bring into being other people like ourselves. Homosexuality is, in principle, incapable of this life-giving function; and so it seriously depreciates the full Christian meaning of the sexual act.

Cure?

Because of this view of sexuality, the Church has always called on the homosexual person to "switch" to heterosexual behavior. The insistence is not unrealistic when we realize that all human beings stand somewhere along a homosexual-heterosexual continuum. At one end of the continuum, we find the exclusively heterosexual person; at the other end, the exclusively homosexual person. The closer the psychic needs of a person lie to the heterosexual end of the continuum, the easier it is to heed the Church's plea.

But what can be said for one whose total sexual orientation is homosexual? Here, a "switch," while theoretically possible, may realistically be out of reach. Traditionally, Catholic theologians have said that in this case, the homosexual must abstain from sexual activity. For physical, psychological, and other reasons, many other people also are in this situation. They need extra grace and pastoral care from the Church.

One principle that is beyond all dispute is that every human being is of inestimable worth. In a recent pastoral statement, Cardinal Bernardin of Chicago reminded his people that the life of all persons, whatever their sexual orientation, is sacred; and their dignity must be respected. In holding to this principle we follow the example of Christ himself. This must be our approach to homosexual people.

(St. Louis, May 29, 1987)

— ◆ —

Seldom Sin?

Just recently, I listened to a distraught father who was bewailing the moral dissolution of his daughter. "What is happening to our world?" he

asked. "No one seems to know any more what is right and wrong —
including clergy." I could share his feelings.

Sin? Describing the Reverend Doctor Harcourt, poetess Phyllis McGinley
said:

> Tall, young, urbane, he marshals out the younger crowd....
> And in the pulpit eloquently speaks on diverse matters with both wit
> and clarity: art, education, God, the early Greeks, psychiatry, vestry
> repairs that shortly must begin, all things but sin.
> He seldom mentions sin.

In reaction to the former overemphasis on sin, the last decades have
stressed a strange sort of Christian liberalism. It would have us believe that
a God without wrath brought men and women without sin into a kingdom
without judgment through the ministrations of a Christ without a cross.

And so now the thoroughly modern Christian, like the Pharisee of old,
stands in front of church and prays: "I thank thee, Lord, that my psychiatrist
has told me there is no such thing as guilt and that sin is a myth...."

Psychiatrist Carl Menninger admits that he once hailed the disappearance
of sin; he changed his mind. "Evil surrounds us," he says. "But when
everything is permitted, when no one is responsible, no one is guilty, no
moral questions are asked, we sink into despairing helplessness."

Confession: Jesus summoned us all to repent, lest we perish (Luke 13:3).
It wasn't that Jesus did not like sinners. They were his favorite people. The
gospels make one thing clear: Jesus did not spend a lot of time with reputable
people; he hung out with the hoodlum element of society. Of all the charges
made against him, only one was true: he ate with publicans and sinners and
frequented their houses.

When they first met, Peter warned him: "Depart from me, O Lord, for I
am a sinner." Jesus replied: "Leave your nets and follow me." He then went
on to search out Matthew, who was no ordinary sinner but a notorious
racketeer. The good news of his Incarnation was first announced to a Virgin,
but the risen Christ appeared first to Mary, a former shady lady.

The only people with whom Jesus was ever harsh were the scribes and
Pharisees who meticulously observed the law. "Woe to you hypocrites,
brood of vipers, whitened sepulchers full of dead men's bones."

The problem Jesus saw was not sin. *It was the denial of sin.* Christianity has little meaning for "good and righteous people," those without sin. The Good News that we have a Savior is senseless for those who have no need of salvation. "I have come," said Jesus, "to call sinners, to seek what was lost."

Reflecting on Adam's sin, the Church mysteriously sings at the Easter Vigil, "O happy sin, O fortunate sin that merits for us so great a redeemer."

When did you make your last confession?

(St. Louis, August 3, 1990)

- 14 -
PRO-LIFE

God, the Lord of life, has entrusted to human beings the noble mission of safeguarding life.... Life must be protected with the utmost care from the moment of conception: abortion and infanticide are abominable crimes.

(Decree on the Church in the Modern World, #51)

On no subject has Archbishop May written more, or more often, than on abortion. He has always espoused the "consistent ethic of life," being concerned not only with the killing of the unborn but of the aged (through euthanasia) and criminals (through capital punishment). He has been outspoken in calling for generous compassion for the weak, the powerless, and the persecuted, wherever they are found.

Despite the repeated and clear statements of Pope Paul VI and the American Bishops, I have been asked to state clearly where I stand on abortion.

My teaching is the same as that of the Pope and other bishops: abortion is a heinous crime against innocent human life. Any Catholic directly responsible for the crime of abortion is automatically excommunicated according to the traditional law of the Church. Changes in state law do not affect Catholic doctrine in this matter.

(Mobile, March 5, 1971)

Two weeks ago, I felt an obligation to speak in defense of innocent, defenseless children who died at My Lai at the hands of a trigger-happy American soldier. *[See pages 289-290.]*

Today I feel the same obligation to speak in defense of innocent, defenseless human beings dying in Alabama at the hands of skilled, calm surgeons.

The issue is the same — thou shalt not kill. I am speaking this week about abortion. Recently, there have been meetings around this state on behalf of liberalized abortion. In this opening discussion, I would like to make the Catholic position clear.

Abortion should be prohibited by law. As Americans, we believe that all men are endowed by their Creator with certain inalienable rights. The first is the right to life. It is the state's duty to protect that right — especially for those who are most helpless to protect themselves. This we believe as Christians, as Jews, as Americans — as civilized human beings.

There are people who would deny that the unborn are truly human beings. But what are the genetic, scientific facts? All the evidence indicates a biological *continuum* from conception to birth and adulthood. The fetus is not merely a potential human being but rather a human being with potential. All it needs is time.

And what are the legal facts? Our courts have increasingly regarded the unborn as persons with many rights — to life, property, inheritance, and so forth. Proposals for abortion on demand are not an advance but a retrogression in the history of human rights.

But even if, despite the scientific and legal facts, there were some doubt about the presence of human life in the womb, should not such a doubt be resolved in favor of life? Certainly, many women face acute personal and social problems in pregnancy. Can our society with all its accomplishments offer such women no positive answers? Is our solution after all these centuries just a more antiseptic and anesthetic technique of killing the life within her — the life that we piously say is made after the image and likeness of God?

(Mobile, April 23, 1971)

— ◆ —

Words, words. There are so many of them in an election year. Lately, it seems that there have been certain phrases that sound so respectable but really mean something else down deep. These euphemisms have been tripping from the tongues of many in high places lately.

Many people think America is losing its soul, its drive for justice and protection for the weak, the poor, the helpless. Our moral ideals seem to be rotting away beneath a veneer of proper phrases. Here are a few typical slogans and what they really seem to be saying underneath.

- Termination of pregnancy should be permitted by the Church. (The Church should agree to the killing of babies in their mothers' wombs.)
- Termination of pregnancy should be legalized for psychological reasons. (Mothers should be permitted to kill their unborn children if they *feel* like it.)
- Women should have power over their own bodies. (They should have the power of life and death over the bodies of their unborn children.)
- Only wanted children should be born. (Unless a second car or a boat is wanted more.)
- We need governmental action to stimulate family planning and the quality of life. (The government needs to crack down on big families and all those babies who pollute our environment.)
- There should be a right for people to die with dignity. (It should be legal for us to kill incurable patients quietly and painlessly.)
- We must return to the neighborhood schools. (Let's get back to segregated schools in our segregated neighborhoods.)
- There should be equal educational opportunity for children in local schools. (There should be separate but equal schools.)
- We need to get back to freedom of choice in schools. (We need to get back to a majority free to choose its own schools and a minority without the freedom to choose the same schools.)
- Black people must have their own schools in their own community. (Some black people are just as segregationist as some whites.)
- We have to plug the welfare drain and build up our national defense. (More of our taxes have to go for bombs and less for babies.)

Someone has said you can tell how civilized a country is by how it provides for its weakest and neediest members. A civilization founded on the Jewish-Christian reverence for life should have a very clear priority of values. Jesus said he came that people might have life and have it to the full.

These final days of Lent might be a good time to examine our consciences. Are we mouthing some of the proper phrases mentioned above? If so, what do we mean by them — down deep?

(Mobile, March 24, 1972)

– ◆ –

Remember *Zorba the Greek?* In the course of that movie, there was an exuberant song and dance — a Toast to Life. The theme was a celebration of life and the realization that despite poverty and trouble, life was a precious gift of God.

Some years ago, Pope Paul wrote his famous letter, *Humanae Vitae*, a carefully reasoned statement on the inviolability of human life and the sacredness of sex and marriage in our time. Many people, and even some Catholics, thought the Pope was a bit behind the brave new world developing all around us then.

Today very thoughtful people are taking a second look. Here is what they see.

- Murders and crimes of violence against human life are skyrocketing.
- In some hospitals there is an admission now that abnormal newly born infants are often allowed to die, lest they be a burden on their families and society.
- "Abortion factories" have sprung up all over this country as a result of the Supreme Court's infamous decision permitting abortion on demand.
- In one year more unborn babies are killed by abortion than all the men killed in American wars since 1776.
- Euthanasia is being pushed especially in our neighboring state of Florida and almost everywhere across our country.
- The suicide rate in the United States is climbing fast, and there is a drive to permit people legally to end their lives because they have a "right to do what they want with their bodies."
- Almost invariably in recent years, the defendants in "mercy killing" cases have been declared innocent in American courts.
- There is an epidemic of venereal disease, rape, and divorce all over this country.
- Etc., etc., etc.

The quality of life, the right to privacy, emotional health, and almost every conceivable reason are alleged to justify snuffing out a human life — unborn, aged, abnormal, sick — but always innocent and defenseless. In Nuremberg, Germany, one of the Nazi defendants said when faced with undeniable holocaust in which millions of Jews were murdered, "I never thought it would come to this." The judge said, "It was inevitable — once you killed the first innocent, defenseless person."

Respect Life!

For the third successive year in all Catholic churches of the U.S.A., we are launching the Respect Life Program on Sunday, October 6. Every parish is to focus its attention these coming weeks on the rights and the needs of dependent and defenseless people in our society — especially the unborn, the mentally retarded, the physically abnormal, and the aging. We are also asked to study and pray over the pressing issues of prisons, healthcare systems, gun control, and poverty in our own immediate area.

For example, how many parishes are making any effort to visit regularly the many lonely, forgotten old people in the nursing homes in our neighborhoods? Do we realize what it could mean for an old man or a woman to have one person who came regularly to visit — one person who thought about him or her — one person who cared enough to come? There are many patients in many nursing homes or institutions who do not have one human being who cares that much.

In every age, Catholics are called to stand up strong for some teaching of the Lord Jesus Christ. In our time, in our country — it is *respect for life.*

(Mobile, October 6, 1974)

O Tempora, O Mores

That classical Latin expression is difficult to translate. But roughly it means, "O the times we live in; the conduct of our people!" I often recall that phrase these days when I read the following:

- In the last few weeks, one girl has died and another is in a terminal coma following abortions at a famous clinic in Atlanta specializing in safe, legal abortions.
- A *third* abortion clinic is preparing to open in Mobile. Recently, an eyewitness at a Mobile clinic described the "procedure" there — systematic mass killing of the unborn.
- Last year a Chicago newspaper exposed the abortion business there — a highly lucrative disgrace to the medical profession.
- Medical journals more and more are publishing studies revealing complications in pregnancies following an abortion — more spontaneous fetal deaths, smaller infants, more prematurity, labor and delivery complications. They also point out the high incidence of permanent sterility following abortion.
- The same publications have been noting a link between early, frequent sexual activity and cervical cancer. The daily papers continue to report today's epidemic in venereal disease, especially among teenagers. More than a million American teenage girls become pregnant each year, and one third of them have an abortion.
- In New Jersey, the state legislature nearly passed a law lowering the age of consent in sexual relations to thirteen. In Florida, the state legislature passed an ordinance requiring amoral sex instructions for all public-school children down to the fifth grade.
- Planned Parenthood continues to push for more dissemination of full contraceptive information for younger and younger children, often without parental knowledge or permission.
- Recently, the California Medical Association's journal said of doctors making abortion decisions: "One may anticipate further development of these roles, as the problem of birth control and birth selection are extended inevitably to death selection and death control whether by the individual or society." The president of Planned Parenthood serves on the board of directors of the Euthanasia Education Council.
- A euthanasian argued in the *Atlantic Monthly* that if the life of a mongoloid can be "ended prenatally (by abortion), why should it not be ended neonatally (shortly after birth)"? The author argues that a retarded child is not a baby but only "a reproductive failure."

On and on it goes. Day by day as I hear such things, I also recall the sorrowful prophecy of Pope Paul VI in his letter *Humanae Vitae* in 1968. The Pope warned that the "contraceptive mentality" would inevitably lead to abortion on demand, family breakdown, and dehumanized sexual mores. Many "experts," including some Catholics, laughed at the "poor old Pope" then. They are not laughing anymore.

(Mobile, July 7, 1979)

None of the Archbishop's pro-life writings evoked greater resonance than three articles originally published in the St. Louis Review *August 29 through September 12, 1980. They were reprinted in* Catholic Mind *for March 1981 and in the* St. Louis Review *October 23 through November 6, 1987.*

The Medical Facts

Well over a million abortions are now performed in this country every year. On the average that is one every thirty seconds, hour upon hour, day in and day out. Pro-abortionists claim that the unborn are only "potential life," or "mere tissue," a part of the mother's body that can be cut out like the appendix. Medical science shows such statements to be biological nonsense.

At fertilization, there are regularly present forty-six chromosomes that determine sex, skin pigmentation, facial structure, body height, and numerous other personal characteristics. As late as 1961, when Planned Parenthood was still condemning abortion as "barbaric" and as being, along with infanticide, "the killing of babies," Dr. Alan Guttmacher, Planned Parenthood president, wrote about life's beginning: "Fertilization has taken place; a baby has been conceived."

Four weeks after conception, a regular heartbeat can be detected. After five weeks, there is a face that begins to look human; scientists speak no longer of an "embryo" but of a "fetus." By the seventh week, there is a functionally complete cardiac system — at a time before many women even seek a pregnancy test. By the twelfth week, what Dr. Guttmacher decided in 1968 was "merely a group of cells that do not differ materially from other cells" can kick its legs, turn its feet, curl and fan its toes, move its thumbs, make a fist, bend its wrists, turn its head, squint, frown, open its mouth, suck its thumb, swallow fluid, and make inhaling and exhaling motions.

The mother does not experience these movements within her womb until sixteen or seventeen weeks. However, this age-old rule of thumb for life's beginning ("quickening") is insignificant for modern biology, which knows that human life is present in the womb from conception on.

Under the law of our country, as interpreted by the Supreme Court in 1973, it is now legal to destroy this human life for any reason at all, at any time right up to birth. The means regularly used (tearing limb from limb by scraping or suction, drowning or scaling in poisonous fluids) cause the tiny victims pain that, in the case of abortions after the third month of pregnancy, may extend over several hours. After five months, an operation called a "hysterotomy" is often done. This is medically indistinguishable from a Caesarean delivery, except that the survival of the preterm baby is not desired. Withholding the ordinary treatment now routine for premature infants at birth ensures that the aborted baby will choke to death, suffocate, or die from exposure.

Killing methods as cruel as these are forbidden by law in every animal slaughterhouse in the country. The same laws (and often the same individuals) that go to extraordinary lengths to protect snail darters, burnish louseworts, and peregrine falcons (endangered animal species), consider this cruel mass slaughter of the unborn a sign of human progress and of women's liberation.

How did we come to this point? In part, through the clever use of language that disguises what is happening. This concerted effort at linguistic camouflage begins with the use of the word *fetus*. This is a scientific term, quite appropriate in a medical textbook. But even doctors thoroughly familiar with the technical language of their profession abandon it in the consulting room, as new mothers know. Listening through his stethoscope to the new heartbeat in the womb of the expectant mother, her physician tells her: "Your baby is coming along nicely." Only when she has decided she does not want the baby, does it become a "fetus," an impersonal "it" to be disposed of at will.

People do not hesitate to say they are going to have their tonsils or appendix cut out. But to refer to having your fetus cut out is still offensive. Abortionists speak, therefore, of the "procedure" or "terminating a pregnancy," of "evacuating the results of conception," and of what they remove as "fetal wastage." A 1976 medical research paper on improved poisons for late-term abortions spoke of "improving delivery to the target organs" and of minimizing the side effects to "the patient." Until legalized abortion, the physician's care embraced two patients: mother and unborn child. Now, at the mother's request, her doctor cares for her alone and kills her child.

Is it any wonder that an early leader in the movement to legalize abortion, Dr. Bernard N. Nathanson, reports that as recently as 1970 "a majority of the nation's physicians opposed a change in the laws" that prohibited the killing of the unborn? Though many doctors have since bowed to the winds of change, and a few earn enormous incomes from abortions, the ancient adherence of physicians to their traditional role as the protector of life from conception on remains strong. How delighted I am each year to see the list of over seven hundred physicians, of all faiths and none, who annually on January 22, the anniversary of the Supreme Court legalization of abortion, publish a full-page ad in our local newspaper citing the 1948 Declaration of Geneva from the World Medical Association: "I will maintain the utmost respect for human life, from the time of conception; even under threat, I will not use my medical knowledge contrary to the laws of humanity."

This ad also asks: "Did you know that

- "the Supreme Court abortion decision allows abortions during the entire nine months of pregnancy — from conception right up to birth?"
- "your teenage daughter needs your written consent to have her ears pierced, but an abortionist can perform life-endangering procedures upon her without your consent and even without your knowledge?"

To the courageous physicians who pay for this ad, I would like to put a question of my own. Do you know that already the chances of your children being admitted to medical school are greatly decreased if, like you, they uphold the right to life of the unborn? A 1979 government survey of 122 of the 126 medical schools in this country revealed that 40 percent now question applicants about their views on abortion. It is not difficult to imagine the screams of civil libertarians if such questions had been asked ten years ago, when the struggle to liberalize abortion laws was still in doubt. The silence of these zealous defenders of the rights of conscience in today's changed situation is deafening.

To those who want to go more deeply into the medical evidence, I recommend a book by a doctor who spearheaded the effort to legalize U.S. abortion laws but who has since changed much of his position because of what has happened: Bernard N. Nathanson, M.D., *Aborting America* (Doubleday: New York, 1979).

– ◆ –

Pro-Choice?

Defenders of legalized abortion claim to be "pro-choice" — admittedly a catchy label. Who likes to be against choice? But not all freedom to choose is good. Before the passage of recent civil rights legislation, many owners of motels and restaurants claimed a right to choose their customers. They chose to exclude Blacks. Any other policy, they argued, would be bad for business. This argument, once legally accepted, is now rejected as contrary to basic human rights.

There are many other legal limitations on choice, even in the private sphere, which are generally accepted, also by pro-abortionists. You cannot choose to keep your children out of school, practice surgery without a license, or refuse to support the child you have conceived. We all recognize that human rights need to be protected. But then free-choice people go on to say that an unborn baby's right to life should be ignored by the law while his mother's "right" to kill him must be established by law. Curious indeed.

Parallel

There is a chilling parallel to the "pro-choice" argument for abortion in the dispute over slavery, which divided our people in the 1850s as the abortion controversy divides us today. Slaveholders then argued something like this:

> If you think slavery is wrong, then nobody is forcing you to be a slave owner. But don't try to impose your morality on others.

Substitute abortion for slavery and you have the same argument used by pro-abortionists today. But the similarities between slavery and abortion go further.

- Slaveholders argued that "a man has a right to do what he wants with his property." Pro-abortionists today claim that a woman has a right to do what she wants with her body. In both cases, language is used to conceal that human lives are at stake. Slaveholders talked of "property." Pro-abortionists today talk about the "fetus," "the results of conception," and so forth.
- Slaveholders argued that slavery was actually "merciful," since it fed and housed black people who were unable and ill-equipped to cope with the real world. Today we are told that abortion too is "merciful"; it prevents the birth of "unwanted children" destined to be abused. (Actually, statistics show that child abuse has risen steadily since abortion was legalized.) In our country, no child need be unwanted; the demand for adoptable children usually exceeds the supply.
- A decision of the Supreme Court vindicated the rights of slaveholders. In the *Dred Scott* case (here in St. Louis in 1857), the court declared that the authors of the Constitution regarded Blacks as "beings of an inferior order...and so far inferior that they had no rights which the white man was bound to respect." Hence no Black had a right to be protected by federal law as a person in the full sense of the term. In *Roe* v. *Wade* (1973), our same Supreme Court declared that unborn children, up to then the subject of innumerable legal provisions and protections, were not persons in the full sense and therefore could not enjoy the protection of the Fourteenth Amendment, which had been adopted in 1868 precisely to correct the *Dred Scott* decision.

Pro-abortionists are understandably indignant to be compared with slaveholders. Of course, the analogy is not perfect, since history never repeats itself exactly. But the comparison is apt nonetheless. Slaveholders from George Washington to Robert E. Lee were models of social responsibility. They were not conscious of doing wrong. On the contrary, they regarded themselves, and were regarded by others, as upholders of justice and virtue. Pro-abortionists occupy a similar position in society today. They are prominent in our courts, in the media, on the boards of our great foundations and elite universities. They work tirelessly for enlightened causes of all kinds. They falsely charge pro-lifers with being "anti-choice fanatics" who try to impose their unenlightened morality on society as a whole. The virtuous and respectable leaders of society in the 1850s brought precisely the same charge against the abolitionists who worked to end slavery.

One Issue?

Closely connected with this charge of intolerant fanaticism is another. Pro-lifers today, like abolitionists in the last century, are pilloried as "one-issue voters." In every election year, we must expect to hear this charge often. How much is it worth?

Actually, one-issue voting has been highly respectable, even encouraged, among those who condemn it in the case of pro-lifers. One-issue voting was an important factor in ending the Vietnam War and in pushing the Equal Rights Amendment. What chance would even the best political candidate have today if he or she opposed just one such key issue as aid to Israel, equal opportunity for women and minorities, or the core demands of the public-school lobby? All kinds of interest groups in our society use a single issue as a litmus test to disqualify candidates from consideration. By what reason is this right denied to those who defend the right to life?

Single-issue voting can, of course, be contemptible when a myopic position on that issue is cited to qualify candidates for office without regard to their views on related matters. A candidate who is pro-life with regard to the unborn only but lacks all compassion toward other suffering members of society (abused children and women, the handicapped, racial minorities, homosexuals, prisoners), has no more right to our votes than the candidate who supports Israel but is clearly unconcerned in other areas of foreign policy. Pro-life candidates worthy of the name should be motivated by a consistent ethic of respect for all life.

For those who wish information in depth on the legal, social, and historical aspects of this complex question, I recommend a book by a distinguished legal scholar at the Law School of the University of California at Berkeley: Judge John T. Noonan, Jr., *A Private Choice: Abortion in America in the Seventies* (Free Press-Macmillan: New York, 1979).

— ◆ —

Catholic Conspiracy?

"Catholics are always trying to impose their anti-abortion rules on us all in our free country." That is the charge of proabortionists. What about it?

Dr. Bernard N. Nathanson, an early medical leader in the drive to legalize abortion in this country, tells how Catholic Bishops were deliberately selected as targets for the pro-abortionists' attack. At the 1969 planning session, Nathanson's fellow crusader, Lawrence Lader, explained: "Every revolution has to have its villain." When Nathanson asked if Catholics were to be cast in this role, he was told:

> Not just all Catholics. That's too large a group....We have to convince liberal Catholics to join us...[as] valuable showpieces....No, it's got to be the Catholic hierarchy. That's a small enough group to come down on and anonymous enough so that no names ever have to be mentioned, but everybody will have a fairly good idea whom we are talking about.
> (Nathanson, *Aborting America,* pages 55ff)

In 1978, the National Abortion Rights Action League (NARAL) asked in a huge mass mailing, "Who finances the anti-abortion movement?" It answered this question by listing only the contributions of Catholic dioceses to the right-to-life cause. (They were really quite low.)

All Faiths

The charge that the pro-life movement is a Catholic conspiracy is a deliberate falsehood. To claim that it is directed by Catholic bishops is ludicrous. Today's pro-life movement is a broadly based citizens' campaign, one of the fastest growing grass-roots movements in the nation. I only wish Catholic support for this cause were greater than it is. But I thank God for the millions of Americans, of all faiths and none, whose civic conscience moves them to support this cause.

Here are a few examples.

- Prominent non-Catholics in the pro-life movement, or active in promoting it politically, include Professor George H. Williams of Harvard Divinity School, a Unitarian minister; Dr. Mildred Jefferson, a black female surgeon and a Methodist; Dr. Marjory Mecklenburg, also a Methodist; Senator Harold Hughes, an ordained Methodist minister; and our own Senator Danforth, a priest in the Episcopal Church.

- The Southern Baptist Convention, meeting here in St. Louis in June of this year, condemned abortion and called for a constitutional amendment to protect the unborn. The position of the Lutheran Church Missouri Synod is similar, and so is that of many Evangelical churches.

- The Union of Orthodox Jewish congregations of America considers abortion a "crime" under the Noachidic code, that part of the biblical law held to apply to all humankind, not just Jews. These Orthodox Jews have vehemently condemned public funding of abortion and compared silence about abortion to the complacency in Nazi Germany toward the persecution and killing of Jews.

- The Mormon Church since 1974 has called abortion "one of the most revolting and sinful practices in this day."

- Paul Ramsey, a Methodist professor of religion at Princeton University, has stated that every good argument for abortion is a good argument for infanticide and has urged reinstatement of legal protection for the unborn.

- Dr. C. Everett Koop (a United Presbyterian), surgeon general of the United States, told his colleagues in reference to current practice in the country's great university teaching hospitals: "You all know that infanticide is being practiced right now in this country...."

- Dr. Bernard N. Nathanson, already cited several times, is a Jewish gynecologist who, as director of the world's largest abortion clinic, presided over seventy-five thousand abortions. Though critical of what he regards as the "specious arguments" of some pro-lifers, he is now firmly opposed to abortion. At his appearance before the eighth annual Right to Life Convention in California, Dr. Nathanson declared that "the anti-abortion conviction is no more a religious position than the civil rights issue. I am an atheist."

The Record

Anti-abortion state laws struck down by the Supreme Court in January 22, 1973, were passed by legislatures with scant Catholic representation or none. In the late nineteenth century, militant feminists supported these state laws, arguing that abortion was often imposed on women by men anxious to avoid their responsibility for children they had fathered. A "Physicians' Crusade" led by the American Medical Association also supported these laws. Between 1967 and 1972, most state legislatures considered changing their abortion laws, but only nineteen did so. None ever approached the position decreed by the Supreme Court in 1973. The Court's opinion is based upon historical and biological misinformation. Its legal arguments have been challenged by many of the best legal scholars in the land. Supreme Court Justice Sandra Day O'Connor has said that the *Roe* v. *Wade* decision of 1973 is on a collision course with itself.

Consequences

This disastrous decision has besmirched our politics, altered the physician's role since pagan antiquity as the guardian and preserver of unborn life, prepared the way for euthanasia, and undermined the integrity of society's basic unit — the family.

- The "raw judicial power" (Justice Byron R. White) that deprived unborn children of legal protection, as it had excluded blacks from this protection a century earlier, is a threat to us all. What group may be next if this power is unquestioned?
- Legal abortion has deprived pregnant poor women of aid for their unborn children by pressuring them to abort their babies.
- Legal abortion has divided our people on a question never before in serious dispute: who should live and who should die. It has set Protestant against Catholic, secularist against believer, daughter against parents, wife against husband, mother against her unborn child. Pro-life leaders are not responsible for this division of our society, as is sometimes charged; but their pro-abortionist opponents are, who have abandoned the laws and traditions of our country as they were understood for almost two centuries — until January 22, 1973.

259

- Legal abortion has encouraged the coercion of conscience. Tax-payers have been compelled to pay for the killing of the unborn. Hospitals have been pressured to join the killing, and those who refuse are threatened with liability for damages. Public officials have been harassed, as in the case of a former mayor of St. Louis.

Reflecting on these dismal facts, and on the annual death toll from abortion now well in excess of one million, Judge John T. Noonan writes: "There must be a limit to a liberty so mistaken in its foundations, so far-reaching in its malignant consequences, and so deadly in its exercise" (*A Private Choice,* page 192).

Will the Supreme Court reassess and reverse its course? That is one of the most agonizing questions in our nation for the days ahead.

– ◆ –

"Know the Truth..."

Choice. We pride ourselves on our freedom to make choices. We choose whether and whom we marry. To become an automobile mechanic, a lawyer, a nurse, or a poet. We choose where to live and elect representatives we believe will best represent our views.

But there are limits to the choices we can make. Because we value the earth's resources, we cannot choose to pollute the waters or destroy the forests. Because we value human life, we may not choose to drive at excessive speeds or under the influence of drugs or alcohol. Nor can we choose to take the life of our elderly father suffering from Alzeheimer's disease, no matter how imperfect he may judge his life.

Recently, our society has been bombarded by the media, direct mail, and advertising campaigns with demands for the right of "choice." We are told that "a woman has the right to choose" an abortion. But the discussion stops there, at the level of slogans and clichés.

Simply a Matter of Choice? From the moment he or she is conceived, the child in the womb is human. A human being, nothing more, nothing less, with the same inherent right to live that all human beings possess. There is little difference between a child of six months in the womb and a child six months after birth — just size, maturity, and habitat. Both are dependent on others for their very existence. The biggest difference is that we can readily see one and not the other.

The choice in abortion is whether or not to destroy this human life. To say that abortion is a "matter of choice" says nothing. We have to ask ourselves what is being chosen, and whether, as a humane society, we accept killing as a solution to social problems.

Today many women feel isolated when confronted with an unintended pregnancy. To face pregnancy not knowing how you will feed, shelter, and raise a child can seem overwhelming. It can also be agonizing to wonder if you can handle giving birth to a child you will relinquish to others to raise. So often women are expected — and expect themselves — to face such agonizing situations in a vacuum, as if they lived for and by themselves and not as members of a community.

We need programs that enable women — and men — to make choices that they and their children can live and thrive with, before and after birth. We can and must work together to help those who grapple alone with problems related to pregnancy. If we are a community that cares, we must find ways to help carry the burdens of all.

Abortion is not simply a matter of choice. But it does present a choice: Will ours be a society that values and protects each and every human life, born or unborn, or will it be a society that considers some human lives expendable? That choice is ours to make.

On January 22, 1973, the U.S. Supreme Court issued decisions that legalized abortion throughout pregnancy. Those decisions ushered in an era in which more than twenty million unborn children have been destroyed, and an untold number of women suffer the physical, emotional, and spiritual consequences of abortion.

Confrontation over abortion has escalated because on July 3, 1989, the U.S. Supreme Court's decision in *Webster* v. *Reproductive Health Services* gave states some leeway to regulate abortion. Additional court rulings and increased legislative activity in the states have heightened the public debate even more.

Confrontation is unsettling and may tempt us to step back from the debate. Besides, we think, it doesn't matter what one person more or less does. And so very often we leave it to others to do.

But our faith challenges us to act when faced with human need.

What Can We Do?

- Pray that all human life will be respected and protected. Be ever mindful of the words of Saint Paul: "In him who is the source of my strength, I have strength for everything" (Philippians 4:13).
- Work to provide services for pregnant women and their children so that no woman will ever feel pressured to abort her child (cf. Birthright).
- Follow the public debate; become informed. Communicate your information and concern to others (cf. our pro-life office).
- Encourage legislators and candidates for public office to represent your views. Ask federal, state, and local representatives to support life-affirming legislation and thank them for their support (cf. Missouri Catholic Conference).
- Join parish and community groups that engage in education, service, and public-policy efforts to protect the lives of all, born and unborn.

Myths and Realities

Myth: Abortion must remain legal or many women will die from illegal and unsafe abortions.

Reality: Legality does not make abortion safe. Women continue to die from unsafe abortions, partly because the courts have shielded abortion from safety regulations and informed consent requirements. Those who advocate abortion claim that as many as ten thousand women died each year from illegal abortions prior to 1973. There is no truth to that assertion. Before 1973 fewer than one hundred women died annually from abortion. For women to die from any surgical procedure is unacceptable. It is also unacceptable for 1.6 million unborn children to die each year and for many thousands of women to suffer the physical, emotional, and spiritual consequences of abortion.

Myth: Pro-lifers don't care about the child or his or her mother after birth.

Reality: Nothing could be further from the truth. Today there are thousands of programs — many sponsored by the Catholic Church — to help women and children before and after birth. Pro-life groups continue to work for legislation to provide maternal, family, and childcare help and were instrumental in urging Congress to adopt the Civil Rights Restoration Act. The Catholic Church operates almost nine hundred health facilities, and in 1989 those facilities cared for more than three million of our nation's poor. By comparison, what do abortion rights groups offer a woman but the freedom to destroy her child?

Myth: Most Americans believe abortion should be legal.

Reality: Public opinion polls show consistently that most Americans do not want abortion legal as it is now. According to a July 1989 Gallup poll, twenty-nine percent of Americans want to keep abortion legal in all circumstances; seventeen percent would make abortion illegal for all reasons; fifty-one percent would restrict abortion to very limited circumstances. Thus, sixty-eight percent of Americans want to see the law on abortion as articulated by the Supreme Court in 1973 changed.

"Know the truth and the truth shall set you free" (John 8:32).

(St. Louis, September 28, 1990)

The Consistent Ethic of Life

If this column were a television program, I would begin it with three 15-second segments:

- a teenager talking to her high-school counselor. She's pregnant, scared, and wondering about getting an abortion.
- a forty-three-year-old man standing at the hospital bedside of his comatose father. His dad has had three heart attacks. "What do you want us to do if he has another?" the doctor asked.
- a jury sits in a courtroom at the conclusion of a murder trial. They must decide whether to recommend the death penalty.

The three scenes seem quite different and they are: but they have one thing in common. Each of them has its focus on human life. Two of the questions being asked are as old as western history (Aristotle talked about abortion: Capital punishment is older than the Bible). Only our advancing technology, however, allows us to initiate or maintain a life-support system for the terminally ill.

There has been a growing feeling in recent years that all three issues are linked. In an address he gave at Fordham in 1983, Cardinal Bernardin spoke of a "consistent ethic" of life. All human life, from conception to death, he said, is a seamless garment. Allow one part of it to unravel and we endanger the whole. A consistent ethic of life sees all human life as deserving protection because it is sacred. It demands that we defend the right to life of the weak and the powerless.

In 1984 the bishops of Tennessee published a joint pastoral letter rejecting the use of capital punishment. It was the eve of Tennessee's first execution in twenty-four years. "Let us not attempt to meet violence with violence," they said.

We Americans live in what is arguably the most violent nation on earth; our murder rate is many times that of other "civilized" nations. Chicago's Mayor Daley described his city as another Beirut; citizens were outraged, and newspaper editors clucked their tongues at his "slip." The fact is that the sheer volume of violence in America would appall a terrorist. The mayhem that fills our television screens is a dim reflection of the everyday reality that fills our streets. And St. Louis is gaining on Chicago.

The irony of all this is that Gallup polls tell us we are the most religious of all people. Since we are mostly Christian, the implication is that we are the most Christian of people! Yet Jesus was nonviolent in word and deed. All the days of his life.

(St. Louis, January 17, 1992)

- 15 -
WOMEN

In creating the human race male and female, God gives man and woman an equal personal dignity, endowing them with the inalienable rights and responsibilities proper to the human person....With due respect to the different vocations of men and women, the Church must in her own life promote as far as possible their equality of rights and dignity."

(Pope John Paul II, *Familiaris Consortio*, #22f)

Beautiful Women

Now that may seem a somewhat unusual title for this staid column, but I think it most appropriate. I would like to say a word about our Sisters.

All of us in our diocese are so very fortunate in having a grand total of two hundred eighty-six Sisters serving here in South Alabama. Some are Alabamians themselves, but most come from all across our country and across the sea. They have been coming here for one hundred fifty years now. And I wonder whether we sometimes take them all a bit for granted.

What would we do without these beautiful women? Some are young, some are senior citizens. Some teach our children, others care for our sick and aged; still others administer our social-service programs; there are Sisters working in government programs, and some are praying and doing penance for all of us in cloisters in Mobile and Marbury. Almost everywhere you go in this diocese, you will find Sisters working, working, working.

Some are widely known all over their community. Others are living their vocation in relative obscurity. They are typical of one of the most amazing group of women America has produced in its history, which we recall in this bicentennial year.

As we Americans look back over those two centuries and we Catholics of South Alabama look back even over this past school year, I believe we must say that no women in America can equal the record of solid service established by Catholic Sisters.

Now and then there are words of criticism about Sisters as they struggle in their individual communities with the changes of these difficult days. But I believe that a moment's serious reflection will convince us that we are truly blessed by these remarkable women. We need to tell them that now and then. They don't live for that kind of praise, of course, but it wouldn't hurt them or us if we said it more often.

(Mobile, May 30, 1975)

ERA?

In this preliminary period of the Reagan administration, there seems to be great silence about the proposed Equal Rights Amendment. It might be a good time to say a few words quietly.

Because I am *for* women's equality, I have serious questions about ERA. If ratified, it is sure to disappoint the hopes of those who believe it will end discrimination against women. It could well endanger numerous legal protections women now enjoy, based on their longer life span and the choice of many women to be nonwage-earning homemakers, wives, and mothers. Most important, I believe ERA in practice may violate the sacred order of creation established by God when he made us male and female.

There can be no question whether discrimination against women should be eliminated where it still exists. Of course, it should. The only question is whether ERA will do the job. I really doubt that it will. Here are a few reasons for my uncertainty.

The most frequent complaint of ERA backers, and the most justified, is that women are discriminated against in hiring and pay. If ERA would really guarantee equal pay for equal work, the case for ratifying it would be greatly strengthened. Discrimination against women in public employment is *already* forbidden, however, by statute law. The real problem is in the *private* sector. And here the wording of ERA may even add to the problem.

What does ERA really mean? A good question! Professor Kenneth Karst of UCLA Law School, an ardent ERA supporter, describes its wording as "magnificent opacity." That is legalese for "wonderfully unclear." Professor Jules Gerard of Washington University Law School, an ERA opponent, has told the Missouri State Legislature: "No one knows exactly, or even approximately, what those words mean."

Given this vagueness, the one certain consequence of ERA is years, probably decades, of court cases to determine what it *does* mean. Is it wise to entrust to the courts power to decide questions about the relations between the sexes that affect family life and thus touch the lives of all of us? Under our Constitution, the courts are the branch of government least responsible to the public will and whose actions are hardest to correct when wrong. Just *how wrong* even the U.S. Supreme Court can be is shown by its 1973 abortion decision that has been attacked by leading legal scholars as the worst judicial decision in our country's history. Experts in constitutional law who oppose ERA because of the legal tangles it would create include Paul Freund (Harvard), Herbert Wechsler (Columbia), Philip Kurland (Chicago), Erwin Griswold (former dean of Harvard Law School and former U.S. solicitor general), and Professor Gerard (already mentioned).

In view of the vagueness of ERA, it is important to examine the aims and methods of its leading supporters. Most of them favor abortion on demand. Some constitutional lawyers of national reputation state that ERA would make laws restricting abortion difficult to enact because such laws would obviously relate to a specific sex. So say Professor Joseph Witherspoon of the University of Texas Law School, Professor Charles Rice of Notre Dame, and even Professor Thomas Emerson of Yale University Law School, who argues this point as a reason for ERA. So does Betty Friedan, who said in March 1978 that "ERA has become both symbol and substance for the whole of the modern woman's movement. I am convinced that if we lose this struggle for ERA, we will have little hope in our lifetime of saving our right to abortion."

Equality? When it became clear in 1978 that ERA would not be ratified by the necessary number of states in the seven-year period originally set by Congress, ERA backers said the rules must be changed in the middle of the game: "more time" was needed to counter a "fog of propaganda." It turned out that the only states that were permitted "more time" were those willing to change their No to Yes. States that had ratified hastily and then changed their minds (as four have actually done) were told they could not do this. Senator Danforth, who supports ERA, told the Senate on October 3, 1978, that this amounted to telling ERA opponents: "You should have read the fine print." He called the tactics of his fellow ERA backers "practices which any one of us would roundly condemn if they were applied to the sale of pots and pans by door-to-door salesmen."

The most determined support for ERA comes from those who want to create a "unisex" society in which those who make and enforce our laws would be forbidden to make distinctions between the sexes. All laws would be sex-neutral. This position denies the Christian doctrine of creation, which holds that sexual differences are God-given treasures to be preserved, not obstacles to be overcome.

To the demand that women be given equal access to jobs with men and equal pay for equal work, we say Yes. Simple justice demands that. When we find people working for a society, however, in which women who do not choose to enter the labor force are typed as unprogressive or unproductive, we say No. We hold the demanding career of homemaker and mother to be supremely productive. To women alone, the Creator has given the privilege — and the burden — of childbearing. Laws that ignore the sacred order of creation, in this or any other matter, do not enhance human happiness and freedom. They diminish them.

The truth is that God has made people *different.* Men are different from women, the nationalities and races are different, artists are different from engineers. These differences contribute to the variety and beauty of human life. They reflect, each one of them, the infinite perfection of God, our Creator. As Christians and Catholics, therefore, we say Yes to equality. But when equality is interpreted to impose identity, we say No.

(St. Louis, February 20, 1981)

— ◆ —

Women and Jesus

On Good Friday, as Jesus carried his cross through the streets of Jerusalem, the city seems to have been divided into two camps, one masculine and one feminine. The masculine said it had a law that decreed Jesus must die. The feminine said it had another law, the law of love, and this law said that he should live.

In their home or shopping conversation, the women of Jerusalem would say, "Have you heard or seen the prophet from Galilee? His miracles are wondrous, but his kindness is more wonderful." Our Lord's heavy cross did not make him unsympathetic or unmindful of the real, if lesser, sorrows of others. He stopped on his way to Calvary to speak to the same women of Jerusalem, to greet his sorrowful mother by his glance, to reward the heroic Veronica by leaving her his image.

Reading the gospels, we do not recall one episode in which a woman was a cause of distress or scandal to Christ. We see men, however, including even the apostles, behaving badly at times. His male disciples were slow to understand his mission; they were jealous about place and prominence in his kingdom; they abandoned him in his last hours; one of them finally betrayed him to his enemies, those who falsely accused Jesus and brought him to the cross on Calvary. All these episodes involved men.

But each of the four accounts of the Passion tells us that at the cross "there were some women watching from a distance. Among them were Mary Magdalene, Mary who was the mother of the younger James and of Joses, and Salome. These women used to follow him and look after him when he was in Galilee" (Mark 15:40-41). From Mary at Nazareth to the converted Magdalene at Golgotha; Elizabeth, who sensed a divine Presence within the body of Mary at the visitation; Anna, with the infant in the Temple; the Samaritan woman who gave water and received wisdom; the Syro-phoenician woman who begged the crumb of a cure from the Master's healing table; the trapped woman, made a public convert by him who cautioned others about throwing stones; Veronica, who offered Jesus comfort on the road to Calvary — all are placed close to the heart of Christ.

Sadly, men got lost trying to approach truth in the mind and word of Christ. Women, it seems, grasped this truth better.

At the eighth station of the cross, Jesus, bludgeoned and bloodied, tried to comfort the women: "Do not weep for me, but rather weep for yourselves and for your children" (Luke 23:28).

Although this scene is called the one in which Jesus comforts the women of Jerusalem, it is strange that the comfort is reduced to a warning of future suffering. But even a warning can be a comfort. It serves to prepare us for unsuspected adversity. God himself revealed that any gold of good we possess must be tried by the fire of trial.

Each of us sooner or later will be invited to join the suffering Christ, to recognize him in the challenges of our own lives. The cup of suffering offered us will be bitter, but we must drink it, and it will make us better or bitter, according to the way we accept it.

But it was not only in his suffering that Jesus found women leading. He chose a woman on Easter Sunday to be the first herald of the good news of his Resurrection. Ever since, women have done the same in homes, schools, hospitals, missions — everywhere.

"Jesus said to her, 'Mary!' Turning, she said to him, 'Rabbouni' [Master] ...Mary Magdala came and announced to the disciples, 'I have seen the Lord, and these things he said to me' " (John 20:17,18).

(St. Louis, April 8, 1982)

— ◆ —

Q What about this new inclusive-language *Lectionary* with the National Council of Churches nonsexist translation of the Bible readings? Are we Catholics going to be using it at Sunday Mass?

A No. The Word of God was revealed in a specific time and place with social mores far different from our own with regard to the role of women. Preachers and teachers must always situate the books of the Bible in their proper context and show how social patterns have changed since. But altering the words of the Bible to suit today's various movements in the Churches is to falsify history. These translators meant well, but they changed not just literary style but doctrinal substance. Accordingly, I am sure that this translation will never be approved for use in our Catholic liturgy.

(St. Louis, November 4, 1983)

— ◆ —

Jesus and Women

The local media just recently focused on the role of women in the Catholic Church. It might be helpful to spend a little time on that subject today. As in everything in the Church, it really begins with Jesus.

Jesus was a Jew, devoted to the law and tradition of Israel. While Jewish women were generally treated better than their sisters in the pagan cultures surrounding them, women in Israel were still considered inferior to men. Jesus clearly rebelled against that tradition among his people.

In his teaching on divorce, our Lord referred back to the passage of Genesis: "God created man in his own image; in the divine image he created him; male and female he created them" (Genesis 1:27). Jesus indicated in his treatment of women that he believed they were equal with men, with no less dignity than men. He shows that belief in his teaching on marriage and divorce and also in his association with women all through the gospels.

Jesus the Feminist: Saint Luke sums it up this way:

> After this, he journeyed through towns and villages preaching and proclaiming the Good News of the kingdom of God. The Twelve accompanied him, and also some women who had been cured of evil spirits and maladies: Mary called the Magdalene, from whom seven devils had gone out; Johanna, the wife of Herod's steward Chuza; Susanna; and many others who were assisting them out of their means.
>
> (Luke 8:1-3)

This may not seem remarkable to us, but it was amazing behavior for a Jewish teacher to associate women in his company and even in his ministry.

Martha and Mary were close, good friends of Jesus. He taught them the Torah (Luke 10:39-42). But more unusual was his approach to the Samaritan woman at Jacob's well. He shocked his disciples by speaking to her alone and in public, but he revealed not just the Torah to her but his own gospel, which she carried to her people (John 4:4-30). Jesus broke the rules again.

Jesus constantly showed special, respectful concern for women. Remember the poor widow of Naim, the embarrassed bride of Cana, the grieving sisters of Lazarus, the sinful woman at Simon's banquet, the woman with the hemorrhage, the crippled woman cured on the Sabbath against the rules? And who can forget our Lord's sensitive handling of the issue of "the woman taken in adultery"? He treated her with compassion, forgiveness, and healing.

There are many more striking scenes in the gospels of the courage of Jesus in his respect and regard for women, but none more amazing than his entrusting to women the Good News of his Resurrection. Mary Magdalene is the first to be sent as his witness: "Go to my brothers and tell them," said the risen Lord (John 20:17). Above all, of course, there is the reverence of Jesus for his mother and his care for her.

His Church: Through the years, the Catholic Church has not always been fully faithful to Jesus in following his example with regard to women. The Church has not always been in the lead for the status and rights of women. But today the Catholic Church is striving earnestly to be true both to Jesus and to women. In doing so, the Church will agree with the feminist movement sometimes, but at other times she will disagree with some feminists. In our judgment, they often undermine the true role of women and the family in our society, even though we may sympathize with their motivation. This will be the case, for example, in some feminist positions on marriage, children, abortion, divorce, homosexuality, and so forth.

Before we preach to our society though, we should put our own house in order in the Catholic Church. There has always been a remarkable record of women's leadership and accomplishment in the world of religious Sisters in the areas of education, healthcare, and social service in our country. Just look around St. Louis and see the remarkable institutions founded and operated by these women. Where do you see anything comparable in American society? Where do you see American women in such positions of leadership in such numbers? It would seem high time then that we associate such talent of all our Catholic women more fully in decision-making in the Church — in the various councils and commissions on every level.

In the liturgy, women have finally been authorized to fill many roles — as readers, song leaders, musicians, eucharistic ministers, commentators, ushers, and so forth, but still there are some parishes where women are not allowed to share these ministries. Sometimes it is the reluctance of the clergy and often the resistance of the congregation. (I can show you some of the letters I receive!) But we must do better.

Ordination? What does all this say about women priests? The Catholic Church again looks back to Jesus. Despite his above-mentioned concern for women, there is no evidence that Jesus called any woman to priestly leadership in his Church as he did for his apostles. Jesus was not limited by the conventions of his time or ignorant of what future developments would bring. His apostles continued to call priests as he did and so did their successors century after century, even though there were priestesses in other religions and in heretical Christian groups from the beginning. There is no proof of women ever ordained to the priesthood. The Orthodox Churches of the East also continued in that tradition, even after their separation from Rome. Accordingly, the Catholic Church today does not believe she is free to change what Jesus did and what his Church has done ever since.

In Catholic doctrine this is not considered a matter of equal rights in the Church. The issue is the example of Jesus, that of his Church, and the role of the priest who acts in the person of Christ in serving his Spouse, the Church. While women and men are equal, because the priest acts in the person of Christ, and Christ was a male, it is therefore the ordained male who presides over the Christian assembly and celebrates the eucharistic sacrifice (Congregation for the Doctrine of the Faith, Rome, October 15, 1976, approved by Pope Paul VI). The issue is theological, not one of equal rights. There is no human right to priesthood. The Church alone calls to priesthood. That is the clear teaching and position of the Catholic Church.

(St. Louis, November 1, 1985)

– ◆ –

Women in the Church

Recently, the report on women in the Church in St. Louis commissioned by the archdiocesan pastoral council was published in printed form.

Surely, one of the most controversial topics before American Catholics today is the place of women in society and in the Church. On one hand, the advocates of women's ordination demand: "Either ordain women or stop baptizing them" and "Equal rites for women." Some of their opponents, on the other hand, contend that much of the modern feminist movement is a sinister conspiracy to undermine the Catholic faith.

It is easy enough to dismiss the arguments of extremists. But are the feminists completely wrong? Isn't it true that women often *have* been treated like second-class citizens — in the Church as well as in society at large? What would Jesus say about this controversy?

The world in which Jesus lived was a man's world. A male child was considered more valuable than a female (Leviticus 27:6). A mother's period of ritual impurity after childbirth was twice as long following the birth of a girl as after the birth of a boy (Leviticus 12:1-5).

When a girl married, she passed from the control of her father to that of her husband. If he died before her, his brother, or some other male relative, assumed power over her (Genesis 38:8). Divorce was available only on the initiative of a husband, never of his wife (Deuteronomy 24:1-4). From childhood to old age, the Hebrew woman belonged to the men of her family.

Jesus broke with this tradition of male domination. Take, for example, his encounter with the Samaritan woman at the well (John 4). She was astonished when Jesus asked her for a drink. The reason was not merely Jewish national prejudice but the fact that Samaritans did not keep the Jewish dietary laws. Drinking from a Samaritan cup could make a Jew ritually unclean.

In speaking to the woman, Jesus was also violating the taboo that forbade a rabbi to speak to an unattached woman. In the society of that day, this was making improper advances. Jesus was less interested in what was considered proper than in the woman's mixed-up life. She had five husbands and was living with a sixth. By engaging her in conversation, Jesus gradually lifted her to a higher, spiritual level. When his disciples returned, they "were astonished to find him talking with a woman" (John 4:27). Yet none of them ventured to question him. They had come to recognize that Jesus went his own way.

An even clearer example of Jesus' openness to women is his visit to Mary and Martha (Luke 10:38-42). Instead of supporting Martha's complaint about her sister refusing to help in the kitchen, Jesus said that Mary had chosen "the best part, which shall not be taken from her." To us, that seems unfair. What upset people then, however, was something quite different. Only men sat listening to a religious teacher. Women were supposed to wait on the men. Jesus repudiated this subordinate role for women.

The most striking example of Jesus rejecting the subordination of women, however, came after his Resurrection. He appeared first to women and sent them as witnesses to his male disciples. This was really turning things upside down! The legal system of Jesus' day viewed the testimony of women something the way our courts view the testimony of small children. Yet Jesus deliberately chose women to be the first witnesses of his Resurrection. (Note the new mosaic of the Resurrection in our cathedral.)

Jesus' refusal to accept a subordinate role for women makes their exclusion from the Last Supper all the more striking. Not even Jesus' mother was present as he instituted the Eucharist by saying to his apostles and to them alone: "Do this in memory of me" (Luke 22:19). Pope John Paul II comments on the significance of Jesus' action as follows:

> The fact that at that decisive moment Christ acted in this way is a sufficient indication and one that binds us in conscience. The Church abides by that without any intention of belittling woman. The fact that she alone can be a mother, and not man, is not a sign of inequality between them either. It is in the order of nature.
>
> (Andre Froissard, *Be Not Afraid!*
> [Doubleday Image Books, Garden City, NY, 1985], page 121)

The Holy Father adds, however:

> There is absolutely nothing in the Church's position to suggest any sort of inequality, which would be quite alien to the gospel and to tradition. ...Although it may be true that it is the successors of the apostles, and hence men, who govern the Church from the hierarchical point of view, there can be no doubt that in the charismatic sense the influence of women is no smaller; perhaps it is even greater. I beg you to think often of Mary, the Mother of Christ (*op. cit.* 119f).

Those who reject this position usually confuse two things that need to be kept separate: equality and sameness. With Jesus Christ, we affirm and defend the *equality* of the sexes. With him, however, we respect the *difference* between man and woman given to us by God in creation. This is not, as many people today suppose, an obstacle to be overcome. It is a treasure to be cherished.

Does the Church perfectly reflect Jesus' treatment of women? Of course not. The Second Vatican Council recognized "how great a distance lies between the message [the Church] offers and the human failings of those to whom the gospel is entrusted" (*Church in the Modern World,* #43). Paul said the same when he wrote that God entrusts the treasure of his truth to the "clay vessels" of our sinful humanity (2 Corinthians 4:7).

It is true that through the centuries the Church worked to improve the status of women in the Roman world and then especially in the "barbarian" nations as they were converted to Christianity. She did so especially in holding fast to the teaching of Jesus on marriage and in devotion to his Mother, Mary, as Mother of us all. Here in the U.S.A., Catholic women and especially religious Sisters have been the leaders in Church and society in education, healthcare, and social service. Under the encouragement of the Church, their record of accomplishment for women and all of society has been unique.

Nevertheless, we need the help of the Holy Spirit, but also of women, in narrowing the distance between our message and our conduct. The Church, to quote Vatican II again, is "at once holy and always in need of purification" (*Constitution on the Church,* #8). We pray that the coming Synod on the Laity in Rome next year and the tenth Synod of the Church of St. Louis, which we are preparing to hold in 1989, will contribute to this continual purification that the Church always needs.

(St. Louis, July 18, 1986)

– ◆ –

Unpreached Homily

Recently, sixteen hundred Sisters of St. Joseph came to their roots, Carandolet and our Old Cathedral, to celebrate one hundred fifty years of service to our Lord and his Church. I had prepared to preach at the sesquicentennial liturgy, but then the plans were changed — I gave just a brief homily at the Mass in the Old Cathedral.

Here is the full homily I had prepared.

Joy: "Each Sister of St. Joseph," the complementary document to your constitution tells you, "gives public witness to the gospel by the joyful quality of her life" (page 7). Joy is the theme of this celebration. We rejoice as we commemorate one hundred fifty years of God's blessing on your congregation. We do so by celebrating together the Eucharist, which your constitution calls "the source of our union with the Lord, with one another, and with all others," in which, therefore, "we are most deeply community" (#15).

Perhaps, however, there are Sisters here today who find it difficult to rejoice as fully as they would like.

- You may regret the passing of the style of religious life that drew you to the convent years or decades ago, when everything seemed ordered, peaceful, secure.
- Or maybe what clouds your joy is the slow pace of change due

to the inability of many to affirm the renewed vision of the Church and your place in it that is expressed in your constitution approved by the Holy See less than two years ago.

- And surely for more than one Sister here today, joyful gratitude for past blessings is clouded by fears for the future in a day when recruits are few and the average age of the Sisters is steadily rising.

It would be dishonest, and cowardly as well, to pretend that these concerns did not exist, or that they were unimportant. Let me address each of them in turn.

Change? The concern of those who look back with regret at the passing of the old order in religious life was well expressed by the Sister who asked some fifteen years ago when things were far more chaotic than they are today: "Are the vows I made still binding when the congregation to which I made them no longer exists?" It is a fair question, and one that more than one Sister here today has asked — if not verbally, at least in her heart and conscience.

Married people often ask a similar question. "How can marriage vows still bind," many are asking today, "which I pronounced years or even decades ago, to a spouse who has changed beyond recognition and when I have found someone else with whom I could be happier than with the partner I now have?" We all know the answer to that question. Marriage vows are unconditional, they have no strings attached. On their wedding day, husband and wife promise to be true to each other "in good times and in bad, in sickness and in health...until death do us part." Do we who have pronounced religious vows really want to claim that they are less binding than those of our married sisters and brothers?

The outward forms of religious life that drew you to the convent long ago have changed almost beyond recognition. The One to whom you pronounced your vows, however, and in reliance on whom you made those vows, and have renewed them on the Feast of Saint Joseph every year since then, has not changed. The disappearance of so many things in religious life is the Lord's challenge to you to move closer to him. No one asks you to affirm every change. Of course, there has been loss as well as gain. The Lord does ask every one of us, however, to view the changes we have seen in the Church in the last twenty years as opportunities to grow. No one has said it better than John Henry Newman: "To live is to change, and to be perfect is to have changed often."

Renewal? Perhaps, however, you are one of those whose joy at this celebration is diminished by the slowness of change. Despite all the attempts at renewal in recent years, the past still lays its burdens on you, and its baggage. This is the concern of many in the Church today, not only of religious Sisters. Bishops have similar thoughts, I assure you.

Wouldn't it be wonderful, we think, if we had a totally renewed Church? One in which every member, from top to bottom, was filled with zeal for the Lord and sincere love for others? In which there was no polarization, no factions or cliques, no political infighting, no scramble for power, position, and influence? How beautiful such a Church would be! Yes, and how wonderful your congregation would be if it truly modeled that for all the rest of us.

If those thoughts are yours, let me suggest a further question. If the Church, and your congregation, were as totally renewed and as spiritually pure as we would all like them to be, are we really sure there would be room in them for us? The Church is not only the Church of saints. It is also and always the Church of sinners. That alone makes it Catholic, which, as you know, means "universal": the fact that it stubbornly insists on making room for people who are weak in faith, people with high ideals and mediocre performances — people, in short, like you and me. And what is true of the Church is true of every group within the Church, your own congregation included.

Future? Finally, what about our fears for the future? More than one Sister here today is asking anxiously whether your congregation will receive the vocations necessary to continue the splendid record of achievement for which we thank God in this celebration. None of us knows the answer to that question. The Lord who has promised that the gates of hell shall not prevail against his Church (Matthew 16:18) has not guaranteed permanence for any particular part of his Church. Once flourishing religious orders have disappeared, just as formerly thriving local churches have died, leaving no trace beyond the title of some auxiliary bishop who must consult an atlas to discover the location of the diocese named in his letter of appointment.

The Lord *does* promise, however, that he will be with us always, to the end of time (Matthew 28:20). Let me conclude, then, with some words of

Saint Francis de Sales, whose spirit you invoke in the beautiful Consensus Statement to your constitution. I quoted them in your local celebration on April 6. They are a restatement of Jesus' words in the gospel assuring us of God's providential care.

"Do not fear what may happen tomorrow," Saint Francis de Sales wrote. "The same loving Father who cares for you today will care for you tomorrow and every day. Either he will shield you from suffering or he will give you unfailing strength to bear it. Be at peace, then, and put aside all anxious thoughts and imaginings."

To which I would like to add Saint Paul's words at the beginning of his Letter to the Philippians and make them my own:

> I thank God whenever I think of you. And when I pray for you all my prayers are always joyful, because of the part you have taken in the work of the gospel from the first day until now. Of one thing I am certain: the One who started the good work in you will bring it to completion by the day of Jesus Christ (1:3-5).

(St. Louis, August 8, 1986)

A Modern Mother

On this Mother's Day, we all have our memories. But over and beyond our precious personal thoughts, we priests remember very specially the mothers of our own congregations in our Masses and prayers. I will do the same for all our mothers, living and dead, today.

1990s Mother: She gets up at 5:15 to be sure she's safely in and out of the shower before her three teenagers begin pounding on the door. She can hear her husband coming up the stairs; he's just getting in from his night's work. He'll be asleep in a few minutes, just as she and the kids are hurrying through last-minute preparations for school and work.

This is her second marriage, his too; and they're still working through the thousand complications of blending families, personalities, and lives. Money's a problem, even with two incomes. Still, she managed a pledge to help build the new parish church. Mass has come to mean a lot to her again; for a long time, it hadn't. Now she's strangely moved when she kneels there with the kids; she wishes her husband would come more often; he's not

Catholic. She's applied for an annulment of her former marriage; it's "being processed," and she's waiting and praying. Her husband's first wife died.

There are times when she feels frightfully inadequate to the task of raising three teenagers; it might be easier if her husband would open up more. Like so many American males, he's the strong, silent type. She'll be glad when spring comes and one of the kids gets her driver's license. The after-school marathon of volleyball, basketball, cheerleading, grocery shopping, and teacher conferences will be a bit easier to handle with two drivers, providing, of course, that their second car, an old clunker, will start when it's supposed to.

What impresses me about the mother I have been describing is her instinctive Christianity. What worries me about her is that she doesn't see it. Life has not been easy for this lady, nor is it now. She might well be an angry, bitter, self-centered person. She feels that way at times; and feels guilty about it as well. There is no denying the feelings. But that is not who she is. She's a thoughtful, caring, gracious human being; I wish that she were more aware of it. For I'm convinced that it's God work as well as hers.

Without him, she might easily have shattered under the pressures she's faced, the problems she's encountered. The mothers of the nineties face challenges that would have sent Donna Reed screaming into the night. I hope that, like the young woman I've been describing, they develop a growing sense of faith. For at the center of their being, there is a God who delights in who they are and what they are becoming, a brighter reflection of their Creator.

(St. Louis, May 11, 1990)

– ♦ –

Sexism

The Catholic Bishops of the U.S.A. have been working on a pastoral letter about the role of women in Church and society for about seven years now. It was to have been voted up and down finally at the NCCB meeting this month. As you know, the Holy See has recognized the probable ramifications of this proposed document and has suggested wider world consultation with other episcopal conferences before a final decision. You will recall that the same process was followed before the final vote on the NCCB pastoral on peace in 1983. So the pastoral on women will be further delayed. But it has not been jettisoned.

Meanwhile, I believe that we should not delay our own efforts for greater sensitivity and fairness to women in the Church of St. Louis. Accordingly, I would second the following suggestions of a brother bishop in this regard:

- Promote the equality of the sexes in preaching, teaching, and Church practice.
- Sensitize our priests and other leaders to women's unique needs, gifts, and charisms, and make an ability to work well with women an essential qualification for ministry within our diocese.
- Open to women all ministries not requiring ordination.
- Adopt inclusive language wherever it is appropriate.
- Work for affordable day-care centers, shelters for the victims of domestic violence, and guaranteed alimony payments for a woman and her children when a marriage has failed.
- Mobilize to condemn pornography and the exploitation of women in the media.
- Do more to provide alternatives to abortion, post-abortion counseling, and support groups for the separated, divorced, and widowed.
- Work more closely with women religious and continue our superb commitment to support retired nuns.
- All of those thrusts are possible and indeed encouraged within the framework of present Church teaching and discipline.

(Notanda, November 23, 1990)

Recently, there has been an outpouring of comment on the history of Catholic nuns and their influence on the education of untold numbers of successful Catholics. Most of it seems to have started with the story of Judge Clarence Thomas, the recent nominee of President Bush for the place of retired Thurgood Marshall of the U.S. Supreme Court.

Thomas has expressed his undying gratitude for the influence of Sisters in his early education as a Protestant black boy in segregated south Georgia. The Sisters welcomed him into their school, gave him a fine basic education, and inspired him to have vision for his life from then on. He continued in

Catholic schools for much of his education (some of it in Missouri) on the secondary and university level, and he has eloquently praised the treasure he received from Catholic schools.

Widespread: Pretty much the same story was told by a number of other celebrities in the cover story of the July 18 *USA Today.* Of all people, Phil Donahue pays tribute to the role of Sisters in his education and his overall life in his recent syndicated column:

"I think the nuns suffer from extraordinarily bad and misleading press," Donahue says. "I object to the grotesque stereotype of nuns in plays and other media as two-dimensional people — either whacking kids with rulers or playing softball."

Yes, the nuns were strict. And that's the way his parents wanted it.

Sure, he admits, "we had an occasional Sister Mary Cranky. We've got that in talk-show hosts."

He calls himself the "fortunate recipient" of sixteen years of Catholic education, including college at Notre Dame in Cleveland. In all his years, he received corporal punishment only once. It came from a religious Brother, not a Sister. And he probably deserved it more often. "I was not in every instance an altar boy. I was no doubt a challenging male student. I have no doubt that I tried the patience of more than one nun."

The sizzling Madonna says the same thing, for whatever it may be worth. In a recent *Rolling Stone* interview, she says that as a child, she wanted to be a nun. "I saw nuns as superstars. When I was growing up, I went to Catholic school and the nuns, to me, were these superhuman, beautiful, fantastic people.

"To me, that was as close as I was going to get to celebrities. I thought they were really elegant. They wore these long gowns, they seemed to glide on the floor, and everyone said that they were married to Jesus. I thought they were superhuman and fabulous."

The comments in *USA Today* continue. Genuflecting in unison to the sound of the clicker. Standing up to answer questions. Forming perfectly straight lines in the hallway. Having knuckles rapped with a ruler. Getting skirts measured to the fraction of an inch.

Discipline. Discipline. Discipline.

The results? Possibly an excellent education. And memories that bond you with other Catholic-school kids for life.

Some look back with reverence: "It's a powerful, enduring experience," says writer Gay Talese, who attended Catholic grade school for eight years and has just finished a book that delves into Catholicism, *Unto the Son,* due out from Knopf in February.

A Catholic education "is not always pleasurable, but it's something that teaches discipline," he says.

USA Today also quotes Dr. Valerie Lee, an assistant professor of education at the University of Michigan, Ann Arbor, who studied Catholic schools for ten years and just finished a book, *Renewing the Common School: Some Catholic Lessons,* to be published by Harvard University Press. Here is some of her analysis.

Times have indeed changed. In 1964, about five million kids attended Catholic elementary and secondary schools; today, about two and a half million do. Once ninety percent of teachers in Catholic schools were religious Brothers and Sisters; now it's ten to fifteen percent.

But a rigorous education is still the rule. Catholic curriculum focuses on academics, Lee says. "There is not a lot of fluff." The students, especially high-school students, take a lot more math and science than do kids in public high schools.

One payoff: Catholic-school students nationwide score substantially higher than public-school students on reading, mathematics, and science tests sponsored by the U.S. Department of Education.

And, Lee points out, minority and disadvantaged students score higher on standardized achievement tests if they've gone to Catholic schools.

Summary: Recently, Monsignor George Higgins, in his Catholic News Service column, put it this way:

The *Washington Post* ran a background piece on these dedicated women religious, some of whom are still living and were interviewed by a *Post* reporter. They modestly stated pride in the fact that one of their pupils had come so far in public life, despite poverty and discrimination, but have made the readers of the *Post* feel a little better about the world that morning.

Most of the nuns who taught Judge Thomas labored all their lives in obscurity. Those still living must be happy to learn in their old age that their work was not in vain.

It was good for the public to learn this, too. I have no doubt that many Americans who never benefited from the ministry of teaching nuns will now, perhaps for the first time, begin to understand and appreciate their selfless contribution to society.

Personally: I believe all of this is long overdue. This metropolitan community of St. Louis owes a tremendous debt to Catholic Sisters for what they have accomplished here over many generations in education, healthcare, and social service. That is why some years back I thought it was in the worst possible taste for this community to ridicule and caricature the work of Sisters in the cheap, little play, *Sister Mary Ignatius Explains It All to You.* I said it then and repeat it now. *[See page 227.]*

(St. Louis, July 26, 1991)

- 16 -
JUSTICE
AND PEACE

Action on behalf of justice and participation in the transformation of the world fully appear to us as a constitutive dimension of the preaching of the gospel, or in other words, of the Church's mission for the redemption of the human race and its liberation from every oppressive situation.

(1971 Bishops' Synod, Introduction)

Just the other day, I heard something very disturbing. A housewife in one of our parishes mentioned that on her street there were many of her neighbors who prided themselves in tithing generously to their churches. And yet these same women had agreed among themselves not to pay their maids more than six dollars a day — lest these working women start to ask for more. This same housewife mentioned hearing many a sermon about tithing, but never one about a living wage for maids or other domestics.

All of this sounded a bit incredible, but the alleged hypocrisy she described recalled to my mind the biting words of the Old Testament Book of Sirach in Chapter 34. The Word of God there is this:

The sacrifice of an offering unjustly acquired is a mockery;
the gifts of impious men are unacceptable....

Offering sacrifice from the property of the poor
   is as bad as slaughtering a son before his father's very eyes.
A meager diet is the very life of the poor,
   he who withholds it is a man of blood.
A man murders his neighbor if he robs him of his livelihood,
   sheds blood if he withholds an employee's wages.

Just recently, our diocesan Social Justice Commission asked for a review of our employment policies in our homes and in our diocesan institutions. Certainly, defrauding a laborer of his wages is a sin that cries to heaven for justice — and even more so when it is done ostensibly for the cause of Christ.

(Mobile, July 31, 1970)

Everywhere these days we hear of the agony of our public schools. Parents are torn in one direction or another by calls for school boycotts in September, marching children to the school of one's choice no matter what or simply abandoning the public schools completely in favor of so-called "academies."

We even heard a black man in Mobile calling for a segregated school system just recently. His reason? "Integration has never worked and never will work," he said. All of which brought to mind what a British Catholic author once said to a man who claimed that Christianity had been tried and found wanting. Chesterton answered, "Christianity has been found hard and just never tried."

Sometimes Catholics can give the impression that we stand aloof from the school issue in smug satisfaction, since our children attend our own Catholic schools. Such should never be the case. The public schools are also our schools, supported by our taxes and attended by many of our children.

We Catholics should, therefore, have a great concern with all people of goodwill for our public schools — and especially now. Catholic schools must never be used to undercut the public schools in their strenuous efforts to implement the law of the land requiring full racial integration and equal education opportunity for all children. We must not use our status as private, church-owned schools as a subterfuge to evade the purpose and meaning of the law of this nation. We must do all we can to help our public schools.

Therefore, the Mobile Diocese adopted a very clear policy last spring after the most recent school integration court rulings. Our Catholic schools will not accept transfers from public schools at this time. The only exceptions will be in favor of people moving in from out of town. Our schools must not be used as havens from integration; nor do we intend to use the public-school crisis to boost our school enrollment.

Furthermore, we should take a good look at our own house right now to see that it is in order. Obviously, there are vast differences in our Catholic school system as compared to the public system. Our schools are supported by tuition and parish subsidies, most of our pupils are Catholics, a regretfully small percentage of black people are Catholic, each parish maintains its own school for its own people, and so forth. Nevertheless, we must make every effort to follow the spirit of the law of our country in striving for truly meaningful racial integration in our schools in both faculty and students. We believe in American law and order in the original sense of that phrase, and we must practice what we preach. We believe in quality education, and we must continue to make every sacrifice to give it to our children in fidelity to our Catholic faith and to American principles.

Our faith tells us that God is Father of all and that in Christ there is no distinction between Jew or Greek, slave or free, black or white.

Our country tells us that all men are created equal and are endowed by their Creator with certain inalienable rights.

This is what our schools must teach — and not just in theory but also in practice.

(Mobile, August 3, 1970)

— ◆ —

I am begging for a big collection for self-help programs for the poor around us.

I can just imagine the reactions out there in the pews: "Not another handout!" "I work hard for my money; why can't these people do the same?" "Aren't we paying enough taxes for all these people on welfare without giving to them in church, too?" "Besides, most people in this country who are poor just do not want to work, and most of them are Black."

Suppose we just look at the record. According to official figures

- forty percent of poor people are under eighteen.
- twenty percent of the poor are over sixty-five.
- thirty percent of the poor belong to families headed by a father or mother who works throughout the year.
- sixty-five percent of the poor are white.

So most of our fellow citizens officially classified below the poverty level are white, and while many of them work full time, their families are still trapped in poverty.

Many of the people in our diocese, urban and rural, black and white, are truly poor. Jesus had great love for the poor. The gospels constantly remind us that his followers must have this same love. We are sacrificing more and more for Catholic schools, which are ironically becoming too expensive for the poor. We could become a Church identified with the middle class and the rich. If so, how could we be the true Church of Christ?

This national collection is not to give handouts. It is for human development, to stimulate self-help projects under Catholic auspices. Someone has said, "If you give a man a fish, you feed him for a day. If you teach him how to fish, he can feed himself for life."

The idea is to help people help themselves. The Church cannot do everything, but it can do much — in tutoring, job training, health, hygiene, money management, housing, cooperatives, credit unions, and so forth.

We hope to develop such self-help programs in our parishes and charity agencies that could qualify for seed money from this national collection.

For years, we have cooperated in government programs such as Head Start, adult literacy, and neighborhood youth corps. But there are many services we could provide not funded by the government. One rural pastor has already proposed a laundromat for his poor people, most of whom have no running water whatever. Cleanliness can be next to godliness.

I am more and more convinced we must be more identified with our many, many poor as I get around this diocese. These people need interest, direction, and hope from us. That we can give.

Please do not say that the government is doing enough. On the national level, the Senate Finance Committee rejected the Nixon welfare reform proposal that would have pushed people to work their way up from poverty. We saw the same backlash trend in local politics — especially before the recent election. Meanwhile, the latest figures show more and more unemployment. In most of this country, Catholics were poor and despised not too many generations ago. The Church worked mightily for the poor and laboring man in those days. Some of us have come a long way since then. Have we forgotten the poor? If so, as a Church we have forgotten Christ. He said, "Whatever you do to them, you do to me."

(Mobile, November 9, 1970)

— ◆ —

The following column, on the My Lai massacre in Vietnam, caused a furor in Alabama.

"Never pass off light for darkness, nor darkness for light; never call evil good or good evil." This was the charge given me before God in the ceremony when I was made a bishop. And that is the reason I speak about William Calley.

I have read how so many in Alabama feel about this sad case. I don't care to dispute people publicly, but in my position, I think I must speak.

Lieutenant Calley committed a terrible crime. How guilty he was in his heart that tragic day at My Lai only God knows. No one may judge. Very possibly, he acted under considerable emotional strain. But what he did that day must be condemned. He committed a crime against the law of God, the law of all civilized men, and the honor of his country. What he did denies the stated reason for the American presence in Vietnam — the protection of life and liberty for helpless people.

It may be that President Nixon will reduce or commute Calley's sentence. That is the President's right and responsibility. But neither the president nor any man may dare defend what this man did.

The attempted whitewashing by so many Americans of Lieutenant Calley's conduct is frightening. Such talk should make us all ask what is happening to the soul of this nation. What has this terrible war done to us?

Some say Calley was just following orders. (His superior officer denies that allegation and will stand trial on the charge.) In any case, no man can morally follow such an order. The Army Code and God's law forbid it. Calley was in charge at My Lai. He ordered and carried out the killing. Other soldiers refused to have any part in it. They had the same training as their Lieutenant, but they refused to kill helpless old men, women, and little children weeping and pleading for their lives. By his own admission, Calley killed them, dozens and dozens of them!

Others say the Lieutenant is a scapegoat — that our leaders are more responsible, that we all bear some of the burden of My Lai. This raises the basic moral question of whether we should be in Vietnam at all (an issue many of today's loudest protesters have refused to face); but that terrible day it was Calley who was there, and he was in charge.

And others blame the Army, the system that teaches killing. But the Army has always forbidden Calley's kind of killing at My Lai. The recent court-marshal vindicated some of the tarnished honor of the Army, which had tried to cover up their buddy and his sorry story. Surely, his fellow officers would like to have exonerated Calley. They would have preferred to forget the whole thing. But they had to declare what he did a crime. They finally did what was right.

Every thoughtful person must have great pity for Lieutenant Calley. But no American, certainly no Christian, can ever defend what he did. To do so, would be to deny our faith, to debase our nation's honor.

Is it not strange to see so many people who have been so loud in demanding more law and order, with stern courts and stiffer penalties suddenly trying to sweep a ghastly crime under the rug? On this Good Friday, each of us must search his own conscience. We have all sinned in shedding innocent blood — the precious blood of Jesus Christ. Have we done so by condoning the bloody horrors of My Lai? Jesus said, "What you do to the least of my brothers, you do to me."

(Mobile, April 9, 1971)

— ◆ —

"The degree of civilization in any society can be measured by how it treats its weak and helpless members."

I don't recall who said that, but I've been thinking of it more often. Here's why.

- *Abortions:* There is a growing voice in our state to liberalize our law so that we can dispose of weak and helpless unborn children who might somehow be a problem for us.
- *Dependent Children and the Disabled:* This past month, Alabama cut its welfare payment to these weak and helpless people even lower. (State and local funds give them twenty-five percent; the federal government seventy-five percent. Our state is the second lowest in the nation in this regard.) The average monthly grant to a permanently and totally disabled person below sixty-five years of age is $52.64.
- *The Elderly:* There is a pressing need for low- and moderate-cost housing for the elderly, as in the new Crichton buildings, and for

more facilities for old people no longer able to live on their own. (The Little Sisters of the Poor want to do more, and they hope for communitywide support, since their present institution has been classified obsolete by the state.)

- *The Sick:* Some time back, the Mobile area voters turned down continued financing of medical care for the indigent at Mobile General Hospital. Sick people were turned away if they had no money until finally a group of private citizens decided something had to be done. They formed "Conscience Mobile" to raise emergency funds by begging from individuals to provide some help. But no governmental action has been taken, and there is no solution foreseeable.

There was also the food-stamp hassle of some months ago. Another symptom of the continued tendency of state and local government in Alabama to trim the budget by cutting aid to poor people. The citizens suffering in all this are the weak and helpless, those unable to speak for themselves, the unorganized.

The state legislature is reportedly considering these matters now and will set budgets for the next two years. During the recent visit of the President, one of our senators informed President Nixon that in our state, people still believed in God and practiced true patriotism.

Does it not seem that Alabama's treatment of its poor and helpless citizens would be a fair yardstick of our boasted love of God and country? What are the Christians of Alabama doing about this issue? Is it enough for us Catholics to make that annual pledge to Catholic Charities for our social-service program? Should we be speaking up with our Christian and Jewish brothers in our state administration that says so often that it is so concerned for the little man? What do you think?

(Mobile, June 18, 1971)

– ♦ –

Several people have called recently asking about a column published two weeks ago in one of the community weeklies in this diocese. The editor had resurrected that tired old canard that the late Cardinal Spellman somehow got us into the Vietnam War "in order to have the Roman Catholic Church the strongest physical and political power in South Vietnam."

Such an accusation against a dead man (no proof whatever is presented) would normally deserve no recognition here. But it is coincidental that the recently published *Pentagon Papers* have shot this particular bit of gossip full of holes.

From these documents, we now know that President Diem (a Catholic whose government, according to the Buddhists, was controlled by the Church) was extremely reluctant to accept growing American participation in the war, and so informed our leaders. Shortly thereafter, Diem was assassinated with the subsequent waning of Catholic political influence in Vietnam. The way was clear for the United States to move into the war all the way, and we did.

This whole American experience in Vietnam is so complicated, so riddled with uncertainty, so frustrating, that it is understandable that some Americans are looking for scapegoats to blame for the whole sorry mess. Some religious leaders have denounced the entire American involvement in the war as "grossly immoral from beginning to end." The Catholic Bishops have been constantly asked to do the same.

What are we to think? What especially is a young man facing the draft to think as he tries to follow his conscience according to his religious beliefs?

It is clear that the Communist government of Hanoi continually violated the 1954 Geneva agreement protecting the freedom and independence of South Vietnam. Infiltration and guerrilla warfare against the South grew in intensity after hundreds of thousands fled from North and South. Our leaders, rightly or wrongly, apparently felt that the people of South Vietnam would lose their freedom and perhaps so would the neighboring nations of Indochina if the United States did not help. American intervention had worked in Korea; why not here?

It just didn't work. Through the years, there has been terrible loss of life for everyone, widespread destruction of a whole nation, incredible waste and corruption in Vietnam and in America. There no longer seems to be any proportion whatever between the good we hoped to accomplish and the ghastly suffering involved in our use of war to achieve it. The whole sad story is a graphic picture of the futility of war in this day and age. Tragically, that fact is so much clearer by hindsight.

War is worse than ever. So as Vatican Council II has taught us, we Catholics must work harder than ever for peace. The Pope has shown that in all his words and works.

Without judging any man's guilt for the tragedy of Vietnam, it seems more and more clear that now we are morally bound to stop the hopeless fighting and get out of there as fast as we can.

(Mobile, July 23, 1971)

— ◆ —

Justice for All: Talking about the true heritage of our country usually involves the basic truth of the dignity of every man in this nation. Most often we think of our black people and their long struggle for civil rights in this connection.

In this part of the country, we seldom think of another minority — one, by the way, constituting at least twenty percent of the Catholic population of the United States. In the Southwest, especially, our Spanish-speaking people have been some of the most oppressed people in American history. But these people are now making heroic efforts toward full participation in the rights and benefits of our great nation.

This is most graphically true in two intensive struggles going on right now. One is in Texas, the other in California.

As I have written previously, thousands of Mexican-American predominantly women workers are trying to achieve the right to organize and bargain collectively with the Farah Company, a nationally known manufacturer of slacks in El Paso, Texas. Their struggle has been dragging on for months and there is still no agreement in sight. The Catholic Bishops of Texas and many other leaders have asked the cooperation of all of us in supporting these workers by not buying Farah products.

In California, the situation is almost unbelievable. The farmworkers there, often migratory people, finally were able to organize for their welfare in recent years with the help of Americans across the country who backed them up in the grape and lettuce boycotts. Now when their contracts were up for renewal, the growers called in the Teamsters Union and arranged "sweetheart contracts" with them to exclude the local United Farm Workers. George Meany, president of the AFL-CIO, has himself condemned this disgraceful interference of the massive Teamsters Union in the efforts of these people to run their own affairs. Once again, these people see Anglo owners and union officers working together to block the efforts of Spanish-speaking people.

All this sounds complicated, but these are poor people who need the support of all of us as they struggle for their "dignidad."

How can you help? When you do your shopping for table grapes and lettuce, buy only produce marked with the "black eagle" UFW label. Ask for it in the stores of our community. The message will get to California very quickly as it did three years ago. I am convinced that this is one of the great struggles for social justice, which have become milestones in the history of the American laboring man. The victory of these California farmworkers will help make this truly a country with liberty and justice for all.

(Mobile, July 13, 1973)

– ♦ –

Just before the recent national meeting of the Catholic Bishops in Washington, Mr. William Buckley instructed them unto justice. His syndicated column appears in a number of daily papers in our diocese. Although I had seen it, a number of folks sent me copies just to make sure.

A debonair Easterner who also publishes the *National Review,* Mr. Buckley proceeded to tell Bishop Metzger of El Paso what the Mexican workers in the Farah Company plants in that area really think. Several thousand of them have been striking against Farah for the right to collective bargaining. Their bishop for over thirty years now, Bishop Metzger has listened to both sides, and he has endorsed the cause of the workers.

For that, he has incurred the wrath of Mr. Buckley, who felt obliged to warn the rest of the nation's bishops not to believe their brother from El Paso. Last week, all the bishops heard a report, first of all from the Farah Company, who also sent their public-relations man to the meeting. (Curiously enough, he was registered in the press section representing Buckley's *National Review.*)

Then the bishops listened to a report from Bishop Metzger, after which he received the week's most enthusiastic and prolonged ovation. His brother bishops saluted him as a good shepherd who has spent most of his priesthood serving these poor Mexican people of the southwest. They were convinced that he knows this issue inside out. They were satisfied that his position was for basic justice for thousands of people who have no one else to speak for them.

Above all, they know that Bishop Metzger was not butting into politics or economics. He was standing up for a moral principle, as all the popes have done throughout this century in their defense of the rights of the workingman.

Perhaps they recalled, too, that the same Mr. Buckley's *National Review* referred to Pope Paul's encyclical on social justice some years back as "a venture in triviality."

In any case, I have considered carefully what Mr. Buckley and Mr. Farah have to say. And I have considered what Bishop Metzger has to say. I am more than ever convinced that these thousands of workers (over eighty-five percent women) have a just cause and deserve our support. These Spanish-speaking people of the southwest in the fields and factories are asking for the same rights and security won by other workers many years ago in other areas of this country. In accordance with the papal encyclicals, their pastors spoke up then for the rights of laboring people in the face of Buckley-type ridicule. I am proud to see them doing so again in Texas. In doing so, they follow in an old tradition stretching all the way back to the Old Testament prophets — Amos, Isaiah, and Jeremiah — who also got into trouble for taking a stand on such subjects. As the Bible says, there is nothing new under the sun.

(Mobile, November 23, 1973)

— ◆ —

"We Hold These Truths..."

We hold these Truths to be self-evident, that all Men are created equal, that they are endowed by their Creator with certain unalienable Rights, that among these are Life, Liberty, and the Pursuit of Happiness....That to secure these Rights, Governments are instituted among Men, deriving their just Powers from the Consent of the Governed, that whenever any Form of Government becomes destructive of these Ends, it is the Right of the People to alter or to abolish it, and to institute new Government, laying its Foundation on such Principles, and organizing its Powers in such Form, as to them shall seem most likely to effect their Safety and Happiness.

Recently, twenty-three hundred federal employees in Washington were shown that quotation and asked to sign it — without being told it was from the Declaration of Independence.

Only thirty-two percent would sign; sixty-eight refused. Some considered the statement anarchy and claimed they had read it before — in the *Communist Manifesto*. Others said they couldn't sign because they work for the government, which does not accept such principles.

Return to '76: This experiment was staged by the People's Bicentennial Commission, which has asked church, labor, and civic groups to circulate the Declaration of Independence widely this year. They ask us all to ponder and sign this document in our name as did the Founding Fathers two centuries ago.

Back to Basics: It would be well indeed for all Americans this year to return to their roots, to read our early American documents. The Mayflower compact begins, "In the name of God, Amen!" The same belief in God as the source of our liberty is emphasized in the Declaration and the Constitution. Even our currency made it clear that "In God We Trust." Somehow we do not hear that kind of belief in governmental documents today.

Quo Vadis, America? Where are you going, America? That is the question so many thoughtful people are asking in this bicentennial year, in this time of Watergate, escalating crime, and epidemic immorality.

We are a nation of immigrants. The faith of our own fathers in a new land brought them to this nation. They also brought the same faith in God that our Founding Fathers wrote into this country. On this Independence Day, we beg the Holy Spirit of God that we might see in 1976 a rebirth of the faith of 1776. It may well be our last real hope.

> *Our fathers' God, to Thee*
> *Author of liberty,*
> *To Thee we sing;*
> *Long may our land be bright*
> *With freedom's holy light'*
> *Protect us by Thy might,*
> *Great God, our King.*

(Mobile, July 4, 1975)

— ◆ —

Will We Overcome Some Day?

Did you see those three episodes on the NBC-TV special on Martin Luther King last week? One father of a large family told me that on Ash Wednesday the television set in his house is disconnected and a big purple ribbon is tied across the screen until Easter Sunday. He said the whole family has agreed on this Lenten penance, and it has done wonders for their family life each Lent. If you have not yet done that, I hope that all your family watched "King" last week. Most of the action in that historical recreation occurred right here in Alabama.

I am sure it is hard for many teenagers today to believe the kind of racial discrimination that existed all through our society just twenty years ago. And it was not just tolerated but accepted and even defended by most white people and by many Christian churches then. Martin Luther King forced us all to face that monstrous sin in our hearts. It seems incredible today that we could have been so insensitive to the suffering of black people in the discriminatory laws and humiliating practices of racial segregation back then. We need to be reminded of the evil that good people were responsible for by doing nothing.

The Present: How will we look twenty years from now — to our grand-children? What about our clubs and societies and even some churches in which a black person, no matter how qualified, is never invited or accepted under any circumstances just because of a darker skin color? Despite the sins of our past, many of us still belong and cling to such groups and teach that to our children today in 1978. And despite much recent progress, so many jobs and positions in the public and private sector are still subtly maneuvered away from black people again and again.

What about those schools (many advertising nondiscriminatory policy because of federal law) that very effectively still keep their enrollment ultrawhite and teach their pupils by action if not in word that racial segregation is still the way to live in 1978 America? That it is really not the thing for "the better families" to mix with "those other people." And these schools are ostentatiously patriotic and American! And many of them are called Christian schools — often organized hastily by churches a few years ago to flee racial integration in our public schools. And there are Catholics who send their children to such schools and teach them that it is Christian and American to stay away from and look down on all these other children. What do we say to the minds and hearts of our white children — and our black children?

The Future: What will people in this country be saying of us in A.D. 2000 as they look back on what we are doing in 1978? Will they shake their heads in disbelief as we did this past week recalling what went on in the 1950s? Will our society still be split by mistrust and animosity, the fruits of the seeds planted in the minds and hearts of children today?

Or will we have overcome our past and, as Christians and Americans in an area where thirty-five percent of the people are black, finally come to live and learn and work and pray together? Some black people today in reaction have become just as separatist, just as prejudiced as some white people. We all need to search our hearts in this time of Lent. Jesus has told us that a house divided against itself cannot stand. Blessed are the peacemakers, he said. How do we measure up? What are we teaching our children by word and example? When will we have in our communities one people under God, with liberty and justice for all?

(Mobile, February 24, 1978)

– ♦ –

Thoughts While Driving

Just the other day while driving along the railroad yards beside the Mobile State Docks, I saw a line of heavy battle tanks ready for shipment. Stenciled on the turret of one was the apparent trade name "Barbarian."

I began wondering where those war machines were going — to Bolivia, Jordan, Angola, Bangladesh? Would they be used by a repressive government of a developing country to suppress the just demands of their own people? Would they be used against a weaker neighboring nation endangering the peace of an entire area of the world?

Two Facts: There are two facts that should come to mind as we see these fearsome machines of war leaving our docks for worldwide destinations. First, our country has become the "number one" arms merchant of the world.

Second, so many of these countries around the world are spending huge amounts on arms while their people suffer in tragic need for the economic development of their impoverished nation. Pope Paul VI told all the nations of the world, "Disarm in order to develop....When so many people are hungry, when so many families suffer from destitution, every armaments race becomes an intolerable scandal."

Just Think:

- The $400 billion that the world will spend on weapons this year equals all the income of the people of Africa and Latin America combined.
- We spend sixty times more equipping and supplying each soldier than we do for each teacher.
- The United States can destroy every Soviet city over one hundred thousand at least forty times over. The U.S.S.R. can destroy every American city at least seventeen times over.
- Our country now has thirty thousand nuclear weapons in our stockpile (and we produce three new nuclear bombs each day).
- We Americans spend per capita $32 on education, $35 on food and nutrition, and $418 on defense.
- To arm and train one soldier in much of the world today costs as much as it does to educate eighty children.
- The cost of building one modern bomber could wipe out smallpox in many African countries for ten years.
- One nuclear submarine costs as much as four hundred fifty thousand modest family homes in many areas of the world.

In summary, the nations of the world are all trapped in this spiral of the arms race. Meanwhile, people all over the world pray for peace every day and they pay for war with their taxes each day. Where will this mad race end?

What About Me? A few years ago our present Holy Father published a book of poetry while Archbishop of Crakow. One poem portrays the thoughts of a worker in an armaments factory. He says:

> I cannot influence the fate of the globe.
> Do I start wars? How can I know
> whether I'm for or against?
> No, I don't sin...
> I only turn screws, weld together
> parts of destruction,
> never grasping the whole,
> or the human lot...
> Though what I create is all wrong,
> the world's evil is none of my doing.
> But is that enough?

Every Christian has the same problem as that poor worker. We know clearly the Catholic teaching on marriage, on abortion, on the holy Eucharist. The doctrine of the Church on the arms race has been set forward just as definitively by our Holy Father. You may be sure it will ring loud and clear once again when Pope John Paul comes to the United Nations in October.

Here is what he has already said: "We all know well that the areas of misery and hunger on our globe could have been made fertile in a short time if the gigantic investments for armaments at the service of war and destruction had been changed into investments for food at the service of life.

"The Church, which has no weapons at her disposal apart from those of the Spirit, of the Word, and of love, does not cease to beg all men in the name of God and in the name of man: Do not kill! Do not prepare destruction and extermination for mankind."

Let us pray. Let us form our own minds on this issue. Let us form public opinion insofar as we can. Let us be Catholic Christians.

(Mobile, August 3, 1979)

— ◆ —

Q What is the policy of our Catholic schools in view of the court order for desegregation of the St. Louis public schools?

A Here is our position as promulgated by our archdiocesan Catholic school office. Needless to say, I approve fully of this statement and stand behind its full implementation.

Policy: Public-school students from public-school districts directly affected by any court order for integration may not be accepted into Catholic schools (adopted June 1974).

Additional information: (1) This policy applies to *all* students. Catholic or non-Catholic, Black, White, Oriental, and so forth.

(2) This policy is based on *FACT.* If the fact is that a student was enrolled in a city public school this past school year, no transfer is permitted into a Catholic school. This includes city public-school students who were on waiting lists for city Catholic schools.

(3) The policy *follows* the student. If a student, for example, was enrolled in the city of St. Louis public schools for 1979-80, that student cannot transfer into a Catholic school in St. Louis County.

(4) Only in a specific case may an exception to this policy be made.

(5) Public-school students may be accepted at normal entrance points: first and ninth grades. (Where applicable after public junior high school.) Moral certitude is always necessary that application made by a student is not for unacceptable or unethical reasons.

Obviously, this position has been adopted so that our schools will not be used to undercut the public-school desegregation program. Furthermore, our Catholic schools will also make renewed efforts to achieve meaningful racial integration and multicultural education in their own programs. All of us in our metropolitan area, city and county, public schools and parochial, need to work together at this crucial time for the common good of our entire community.

(St. Louis, July 18, 1980)

Bad News

St. Louis has one of the highest per capita murder rates among the major cities in our country. Last week a local police official mentioned that more and more people here are buying handguns, not just because of the recent crime picture but because such weapons are a "good investment." Such a mentality is really bad news.

According to recent figures from the FBI, there were 21,456 murders in the U.S.A. last year, and about half were committed with a handgun. In the city of St. Louis, the figures were two hundred thirty-one and fifty-four percent respectively. In the entire *country* of Canada last year, there were sixty murders by handguns. There is strong regulation of handguns in Canada. Our statistics are even more tragic, since fifty-two percent of the murder victims in the U.S.A. were acquainted with their assailants and over twenty percent were actually related to their murderers. Over half of the handgun murders were committed by otherwise law-abiding citizens who simply happened to have a gun available when they got into an argument — often after a few drinks. How many more are killed by accident (so often children) because a gun is around the house?

The victims of growing handgun violence are often at both ends of the gun barrel. An ounce of prevention is worth a pound of cure. There will always be sins of anger and violence in our society, but cannot we help our people avoid the terrible tragedy of thoughtless murders committed in a moment of passion? One way to do so is to have much stronger regulations of handgun possession as they do in Canada and in most other countries of the Free World.

You will hear that it is more effective to punish handgun attacks with more sure and severe punishment. That was the approach in California. It has not reduced the murder rate there, even though their prisons are now more crowded. But there is no reason why such efforts cannot continue *along with* handgun regulation.

Then you will hear that free and easy handgun possession is a Second Amendment right and that gun regulation is somehow un-American. That amendment to our Federal Constitution and similar provisions in many state constitutions do not guarantee easy private-citizen access to handguns according to every federal court decision in this issue. Careful regulations of handgun possession is clearly constitutional.

We need to ask ourselves if we are going to tolerate the growing violence in our society or if we are ready to use all lawful means to stop it. As Christians, we need to take a stand as Jesus did. He warned us that those who trust in the sword will die by the sword. So what about the handgun?

More Bad News

Did you read the pathetic story last week about the eight available jobs advertised by a local factory with about three thousand applicants lining up? Some came during the night and most waited for hours to fill out an application. Most were young and Black, the people who are so often accused of preferring welfare to work. And now there are plans in Washington for considerable cutting back on unemployment insurance. Will that shorten those unemployment lines in St. Louis?

(St. Louis, June 26, 1981)

— ◆ —

It is a hard time to be president. Despite his striking election victory and his continuing standing in the popularity polls, President Reagan is under growing criticism for many of his policies as he continues forcefully to implement his programs. It may seem puzzling sometimes that some of that questioning has come from Catholic Bishops here in our country.

The Church always stands for respect for lawfully constituted authority. We must pray for our president always and for his administration, which means so much not just for our country but for people all over the world. We must encourage and support the man who has the awesome burden of the presidency. Catholics have always been noted for their patriotism and their disproportionate numbers in the armed services of our country. And bishops know something of the complexity of leadership today.

But there are things that worry us in Washington today. The tone of heightened belligerency, the increased commitment to arming not just ourselves but ever more of the world, the barely discernible efforts for bilateral disarmament — all this is ominous. We live in dangerous times indeed, and the American people have elected a man who said he would build a strong defense. So he probably has the majority with him. But we also hear the voice of the Pope and many thoughtful people all over the world calling for some brake on the arms race, which is cheating people everywhere of what hope they have for a decent life.

These are enormously complicated issues. But there are some facts we need to remember.

- With our stockpile of nuclear weapons, the United States can already destroy every major Soviet city forty times over. The Russians in turn can destroy every major American city seventeen times over.
- As Einstein said, "The splitting of the atom has changed everything save our modes of thinking, and thus we drift toward unparalleled catastrophe." He said those words years ago, but our thinking in the arms race does not seem to have changed.
- The neutron bomb is being pushed as a clean, tactical nuclear weapon. The idea of a limited winnable nuclear war is now being sold as a further refinement beyond increasingly horrendous conventional weapons.

It is often said that these weapons are now so unthinkable in their consequences that no country will ever dare to use them. Their destructive potential and continuing development have made modern war incredible and so we need no longer fear a global conflict.

In thinking about our President, the Soviet leaders, and the rulers of the other nuclear armament nations, we might recall this quotation:

The tremendous powers which modern science has given to weapons of destruction, the tremendous powers which lie in the hollow of the hand of a few powerful men, must make them pause. They feel that the power of destruction which lies at the mercy of one word from them is so tremendous, the responsibility which it imposes is so large, that I am not sure that the securities of peace are not more sensibly increased than they would be if we reverted to the old time when the weapons of war were weak and war was a pastime which could be easily and cheaply undertaken.

Does that sound encouraging? It was proclaimed by the marquis of Salisbury in 1887.

(St. Louis, October 16, 1981)

– ◆ –

A Good Land

Thanksgiving Day has become our American holy day. People do not have to go to work, and they do not have to go to church on Thanksgiving — as on a holy day of obligation. But in most of our churches there is always a big crowd at Mass.

And the liturgy on Thanksgiving Day is very American. It talks about our immigrant ancestors as passing through a desert to arrive finally at a promised land. Truly, we do live in a land flowing with milk and honey — and even in this time of recession and inflation. As you look across the face of the earth, we know that we live in a good land. That is why we come to church to thank the Lord on Thanksgiving Day — as the pilgrims did.

Tough Talk: We all like to feel good about America. I know that sometimes Catholics are a bit disturbed to hear Church criticism of our president or our country. We are a patriotic people. There have been critical articles in past months in the Catholic press about the Reagan administration — about civil rights, cutbacks on social programs, Central American policy, and mostly about the arms race.

Especially has Catholic criticism deplored the rhetoric of our president, the secretary of state, and other administration spokesmen. They used such ominous phrases — "first strike capability" and "limited nuclear warfare." They spoke of winnable nuclear war, one restricted to the European theater, demonstration of a nuclear strike, and so forth. There is proposed development of B-1 bombers, MX missiles, and the neutron bomb. Until this administration, the defensive aspect of nuclear weapons was usually stressed, retaliation only as deterrence from a nuclear holocaust, which the Soviets hopefully considered as unthinkable as we did. But in recent months, the belligerency level has kept pace with the proposals for escalation of the arms race. Such talk has scared our European friends into the streets as never before and shaken the NATO governments. We can only guess what effect it has had on Moscow. Our tough-talk approach has been criticized in the Catholic press across the world as diametrically opposed to the position of the Pope in his repeated pleas for reduction in threats and arms.

Thank God: So on November 18, just before Thanksgiving Day, it was beautiful to hear our President make us proud once again. The Catholic press should praise and encourage President Reagan now as it criticized him before. His proposal for nuclear arms reduction was eloquent and courageous. It is exhilarating to see our President leading the way to the coming Geneva talks on arms limitation. The world reaction was enthusiastic in seeing America speak out for sanity in the arms race. The Russian reaction was typical, but they are clearly on the spot. Our president has clearly taken the initiative from them.

Obviously, all this shows that our government can be influenced by world opinion and the constructive criticism of its own people. That is the beauty of America. Our leaders do depend on the votes and opinions of our people. The President, we hope, has charted a brave, new course, and he will need our support. We pledge it to him and pray that he will be strong and brave enough to stick to the path he chose last week.

Our country is still the hope of people all over this earth for a new world of peace. At Thanksgiving time, we pray for our President and this country. We thank God for this good land.

* * *

"Senator," said an army officer testifying before a congressional committee, "I have observed that those who say they are ready to shed their last drop of blood are always quite careful about that first drop."

(St. Louis, November 27, 1981)

— ◆ —

Politics?

At their last meeting in November 1981, the Catholic Bishops of this country reviewed the work of their ad hoc committee on war and peace. This committee is working on a positive theology of peace with specific reference to the morality of modern war and the nuclear arms race. Since then, various columns and letters in local papers have accused the bishops of playing politics. It might be well to review some facts.

For the last thirty-five years, there have been political efforts to control the scope and pace of the arms race. Such leaders as Albert Einstein and Dwight Eisenhower warned the world of the horrendous danger of continuing proliferation of nuclear weapons. First the United Nations efforts to control nuclear weapons failed. In 1963, the Nonproliferation Treaty was signed. In 1972, SALT I was signed by Russia and the United States to limit the number of nuclear weapons. Then in 1980 SALT II was worked out to limit new kinds of nuclear weapons, but it has never been implemented. Hopes for limitation now seem bleak.

The 1980s look ominous in the superpower arms race. According to the 1981 Department of Defense annual report, Soviet weapons in some categories outnumber ours, and our greater accuracy and numbers in other categories outstrip them. They lead us in total intercontinental ballistic missiles and submarine launched missiles. We lead them in bombers and total nuclear warheads. Both superpowers are now moving toward possession of ten thousand warheads, which would annihilate at least two hundred million people in an all-out United States-Soviet exchange, not to mention the radiation consequences, and so forth.

In this arms race, we can probably stockpile more weapons because of our greater wealth, but the cost is increasingly straining our economy. The Soviet economy is staggering under its growing weapons cost. The domestic welfare of both countries is being bled white by the cost of the arms race. The rest of the world is being sucked into the same pit by the spreading nuclear capability in nation after nation and the galloping sales of conventional military hardware, even in the Third World.

Now in the face of all that, should the Catholic Church in its responsibility to speak to the whole world for Jesus Christ have nothing to say? What has it said?

- After World War II, Pope Pius XII warned of the growing horror of modern war in view of these new weapons.
- John XXIII stated that the threat of nuclear war is a new moral challenge to the conscience of all men, so he begged for the banning of nuclear weapons.
- Vatican Council II termed the "total war" concept of nuclear weapons as "a crime against God and man, which merits unequivocal condemnation." So it called for "a real beginning of disarmament, not unilaterally indeed but at an equal rate on all sides, on the basis of agreements and backed up by genuine and effective guarantees."
- Paul VI spoke to all nations at the United Nations and said the arms race "must be condemned unreservedly as a danger, an injustice, a theft from the poor, and a folly."
- Pope John Paul II has done the same. Last year at Hiroshima, he said, "In the past, it was possible to destroy a village, a town, a region, even a country. Now it is the whole planet that is threatened. This fact should finally compel everyone to face a basic moral consideration: From now on, it is only through a conscious choice and through a deliberate policy that humanity can survive."

Last month, the Pope sent a team of scientists to Washington, Moscow, Paris, London, and the United Nations to deliver a scientific study on the world consequences of a nuclear conflagration and he said, "I am deeply convinced that, in light of the effects scientifically foreseen as sure in a nuclear war, the only morally and humanly valid choice is represented by a reduction in nuclear arms, in anticipation of their future total elimination, simultaneously implemented by all sides, through explicit accords and with the commitment to accept effective controls."

Here in the U.S.A., should the Catholic Bishops have nothing to say to our own country on this issue? What have they said? (I have yet to read a local writer who cited the text of the Bishops' report.)

- The National Conference of Catholic Bishops has not called for unilateral disarmament by our country.
- They do not deny our right of self-defense or lecture the Pentagon or Congress on defense strategy.

- They do not say that we should trust Russia to be influenced by moral judgments.
- They do say that this country must stand before the world in its commitment to bilateral nuclear arms reduction and a reversal of the arms race and its readiness to take every feasible step in that direction. The U.S.A. can be the symbol of hope to the whole world in this issue.
- We must state our trust not in nuclear threats but in the conviction that the Soviet people's own self-interest also demands a halt to the arms race. We must never speak as if our consideration of arms limitation is a favor we grant to Russia.

This is the position of the Pope (who knows something about the strategy of world communism) and the Catholic Bishops in this country. The survival of the world is primarily a moral concern, and the teachers of faith and morals cannot be silent. Jesus told his apostles, "He who takes the sword will perish by the sword." And he told them, "You shall be witnesses for me." If this is politics, so be it.

(St. Louis, January 29, 1982)

— ◆ —

Contradiction

Our times are filled with contradiction. A glaring example of this fact occurred this past week in Rome.

Last Saturday a happy group of people attended a bar mitzvah in the old synagogue in the center of the city. As they left, grenade and machine gunfire killed a little boy and wounded more than thirty others.

The next day across the Tiber, about a mile away in the Basilica of Saint Peter, Maximilian Kolbe was declared a saint. Pope John Paul dramatically contrasted the significance of these two events in the center of Rome — one of vicious anti-Semitic hatred, the other of heroic Christian love.

Saint Maximilian Kolbe died a martyr to the same hatred that killed so many Jews and Christians in the Nazi extermination camps. He was in Auschwitz because he was a Catholic priest, and he was condemned to slow death by starvation in place of a fellow prisoner because he identified himself as a priest willing to die for a man who pleaded to be spared for the sake of his family.

You have read the story, and I hope you have seen the television feature on Saint Maximilian. He is surely a saint for our time. He is the living model for the words of Jesus, "Greater love than this no one has, that one lay down his life for his friends" (John 15:13).

Threat: Since Israel's invasion of Lebanon, signs of anti-Semitism are appearing everywhere once again. No matter how it may be camouflaged, this virulent hatred is the same old shame of Christians that led to Auschwitz. Even though the Nazi doctrine in Germany was so clearly denounced by Pope Pius XI in his famous encyclical in March 1937, many Catholics and other Christians did not heed the Pope. They did not see that the racist and hateful Nazi propaganda posed a threat not just to Jews but to Christians as well. Jews died by the millions in Hitler's extermination camps. Many Christians did too, but far more were forever dishonored by not recognizing anti-Semitism as a horrendous crime against the Lord and his people. Once again Christians need to recognize this same threat in the spreading anti-Semitism of our time.

We need to heed and practice the teaching of Vatican Council II in which the Catholic Church officially said, "Remembering, then, her common heritage with the Jews and moved not by any political consideration but solely by the religious motivation of Christian charity, she [the Catholic Church] deplores all hatreds, persecutions, displays of anti-Semitism leveled at any time or from any source against the Jews" *(Nostra Aetate,* #4).

Never Again: Since the Holocaust, there can be no more excuse for us. We need to root out every shred of prejudice against our Jewish brothers and sisters, everything that may have come down to us from a less enlightened age burdened with centuries of ignorance and cruelty. The canonization of Saint Maximilian Kolbe calls us to that. Otherwise we do not learn the lesson of his life and the meaning of his death. Otherwise his death and the death of millions of innocent people in the Holocaust will mean nothing to us. And that for us would be a lingering loss, a terrible tragedy.

(St. Louis, October 15, 1982)

— ◆ —

On Death Row

Just recently here in Missouri, four prisoners on death row have apparently exhausted the possibility of further appeals from the death sentence. Unless there is extraordinary federal or state intervention, they are scheduled to be executed soon.

That will be just the beginning. Since the mid sixties, executions have been extremely rare in this country. In many states, capital punishment was outlawed. But the voters have been outraged by rising crime in the last few years and have demanded the return of the death penalty in state after state. In southern states such as Florida and Texas, there are already well over a hundred prisoners waiting out the appeals process that inevitably will end in a flood of executions in the not too distant future. In lesser numbers, the same will happen here in Missouri.

Several times in recent years, the National Conference of Catholic Bishops has deplored this return to the death penalty and has taken a clear stand against capital punishment in our penal system. So has our Missouri Catholic Conference led by the bishops of our state. We believe this position is consistent with our pro-life stance in reverence for every human life — no matter what.

Over a year ago, the Missouri bishops spent a full afternoon on death row in the state prison in Jefferson City. We wanted to have firsthand contact with the warden and his staff and with each of the prisoners under sentence of death. We heard of the growing problems of the prison staff in the increasingly dangerous conditions in which they work. We heard of the heinous murders in society and in prison for which these death-row men were condemned. We learned, too, in reviewing their cases and then visiting with each of them that most of them had been "losers" from childhood on. Still, we know that other such "losers" did not commit such horrendous crimes. Finally, we came away convinced that the return to capital punishment is a tragic step backward in our state and in our nation. We take that stand as teachers of the gospel of Jesus Christ.

At the same time, we know that there are sincere Christians who disagree and feel that the state must have the right to execute certain criminals who are given every legal opportunity and finally are judged a grave threat to the common good or deserving of this ultimate retribution that justice be done. This discussion goes on and on among people in good faith on both sides. Recently, I saw it highlighted as follows in a Florida Catholic paper:

The death penalty is or is not a deterrent to murder: Both sides will present studies and arguments for their position. But is that the issue among Christians?

The Bible says "Thou shalt not kill" (Deuteronomy 5:17): But other Scripture passages seem to uphold the death sentence by a responsible government acting to defend its people. Both sides invariably argue from individual Scripture quotes usually taken out of context.

Jesus never forbade the death penalty: Not in so many words, of course, but he certainly never gave any sign of approving it, either. And he was the ultimate example of the horror of capital punishment under false and mistaken evidence.

The death penalty saves taxpayers' money: If this is a primary ethical consideration, we should admire Russia's work-'em-to-death camps as the best penal system. Under our own laws, prisoners could certainly be made to earn the cost of their incarceration.

Families of victims have their rights, too: Yes, they have the constitutional rights to testify against the accused and to do everything to see that justice is achieved under our system. But the Constitution and the Bible do not confer the right of revenge.

So the argument goes on among people of goodwill on both sides. In their hearts, many of these people, I suspect, are uncertain of their stand. On one hand, they hear of habitual criminals killing innocent victims and terrorizing our communities and they want to take a strong stand against such outrages. On the other hand, they cannot face the death throes in the gas chamber, the burning stench of the electric chair, the casting out of a fellow human being as a piece of refuse, the preponderant numbers of the disadvantaged on death row, and the always possible execution of an innocent person. Surely, we all shrink from the bloodbath of executions about to pour down upon this country in our time already so scarred with violence.

We all have to listen to both sides, ponder what the Lord would have us do in this difficult problem, and face our consciences honestly in the light of all the facts and the clear position taken by our Church's teachers. This is another pressing human-life decision we need to face as committed Catholic Christians and responsible citizens of our beloved country. Before God, what would he have us do?

(St. Louis, December 2, 1983)

Thieves in the Night

Jesus describes sudden death as a "thief in the night." In the early hours of Thursday, November 16, the dreadful news from San Salvador brought his words into our hearts once again.

Six Jesuit priests, their cook, and her fifteen-year-old daughter were murdered in their residence near the Central American University in San Salvador where the priests taught. Among them was the president of the university, Father Ignatius Ellacuria.

Immediately, I issued this brief comment in the name of our archdiocese:

> Surely, I speak for all our people in deploring the savage murders of six Jesuit priests in San Salvador today. We express our full sympathy for all their Jesuit confreres here in St. Louis. The victims all served the Central American University in San Salvador, and one was a 1966 alumnus of St. Louis University. Just recently, I recommended the movie *Romero* to help us understand what is really happening in El Salvador. The murders of Archbishop Romero, our four American religious women, and now these six Jesuit priests must force us to see what is happening to the poor Salvadorian people. With Archbishop Rivera Damas of San Salvador, we demand an end to the killing and we ask our U.S. government for peace and justice in El Salvador.

Subsequently, people everywhere expressed shock and revulsion in Rome, Washington, and across the Free World about this latest abominable atrocity in the tragedy that is El Salvador.

Little by little the facts are coming out. The priests lived at the university in the area of the city totally controlled by government troops under an absolute overnight curfew. The priests had been threatened for the past year by army thugs. Recently, these threats had esclated. Thirty uniformed, fully armed men broke in and killed the Jesuits in cold blood, and then ran away leaving a crude message implicating the rebels.

For more than ten years, and especially this past week, El Salvador has been torn apart by civil war with thousands of innocent civilians the primary victims. From the beginning, the Jesuits and the bishops have pleaded that no armaments be sent into the country. They have argued for cease-fire only by negotiations.

All through the years, the rebels have received guns from Cuba, Nicaragua, the black market, and so forth, and the government directly from the U.S.A. We have sent our planes and guns, so the rebels have never won but they have not been stopped either. They continue to say they fight for the poor. The government meanwhile continues to attack, saying they must protect the helpless poor. And both sides continue killing the poor.

Now in the final obscenity, the Salvadoran attorney general blames the bishops for it all as they bury their priests and people. Once again the bishops and Jesuits repeat what they have said over the years. Stop the killing. Send no more munitions to either side from any outside nation. Come to a negotiated settlement.

For saying that, the words of Jesus, the words of the gospel, six more priests were killed this week.

(St. Louis, November 24, 1989)

– ♦ –

Desert Storm

Pope John Paul and the bishops of the U.S.A. spoke together. For those months before January 15, we pleaded for some other approach to solve the Persian Gulf crisis — something other than war. War must always be the last possible choice. President Bush and our allies made the decision — and so did Saddam Hussein. War has begun, but when and how it will end is unknown. As we prayed and fasted to prevent this war, we must continue now for a swift and just peace for all that troubled area and its poor people. In God we trust.

Thus far one fact stands out. The technology, the power of the United States military forces, are truly awesome. We remain the only superpower left in today's world. And what an awful responsibility in world affairs goes with that fact. More than ever, we are called to lead in justice and peace. All that might calls for greatness indeed. To whom so much has been given, of them so much will be expected. Before the whole world, before the just Judge of all the world, we shall have to render an account. God help us.

(St. Louis, January 25, 1991)

– ♦ –

Responding on March 29, 1991, to President Bush's request for a National Day of Thanksgiving for victory in the Persian Gulf War, the Archbishop wrote:

I believe that we should all observe President Bush's request for this observance. Accordingly, I ask that the regular intercessory prayers in our liturgy be so directed and that our bells be rung and our flags flown.

I do so not, of course, to gloat in national victory but in humble thanks and sorrow too for our country's part in Desert Storm. We are grateful that we suffered so few casualties, but we deplore that there were perhaps one hundred thousand people who died in Kuwait and Iraq — and many continue to suffer and die. War is terrible and tragic always. Jesus warned us, "They who take the sword shall perish by the sword." We need a national examination of conscience about our part in the world arms race. Pope John Paul has called for that.

President Bush, however, follows in our national heritage of national prayer, and we must respect that and honor it in our churches. I believe it is right and just that we do. But I also believe we must always remember the words of President Lincoln when he was assured that God was on our side. He mentioned ignorance about that but great concern that the U.S.A. be on God's side.

(St. Louis, March 29, 1991)

- 17 -
"NO LASTING CITY"

I am but a wayfarer before you, a pilgrim like all my fathers.

(Psalm 39:13)

Here we have no lasting city; we are seeking one which is to come.

(Hebrews 13:14)

This concluding chapter gathers personal material, including the Archbishop's reflections on noteworthy experiences and milestones in his own life and those of others.

We begin with May's report about the death on December 4, 1976, of his predecessor at Mobile, Archbishop Thomas J. Toolen. Bishop of the See since 1927, he received the personal title of archbishop in 1954 and resigned in October 1969.

Since you are all members of the far-flung family in Christ called the Diocese of Mobile, I know you would like to know about the final hours of a man who was father to us all — Archbishop Toolen. I speak to you as members of his family, since I know he always felt that way about all of us.

Last Saturday morning the Archbishop began his day as usual. After breakfast, he reviewed his mail and sealed a few more Christmas cards. (He had finished and mailed all the rest the day before.) Then he joined Monsignor Oscar Lipscomb[1] in concelebrating Mass at 11:30 a.m. in his chapel down the hall from his sitting room, with Sister Gonzaga assisting. After Mass, he said he wasn't very hungry and after a few bites of lunch, he received a phone call from his family in Birmingham. Then his doctor dropped in for a quick check (the Archbishop was recovering from chest congestion) and he prepared for his siesta. Sister Gonzaga, his nurse, asked Monsignor William Friend[2] to help the Archbishop negotiate the short walk to his bedroom, and he began his nap.

Shortly after 4 p.m., Sister Gonzaga decided it was time for the Archbishop to get back into action. She found he had passed away in his sleep. Sister called upstairs; I came down, and after giving him a final blessing, we both shed a few tears and thanked the Lord for calling the Archbishop so beautifully as we marveled at his completely peaceful appearance. Obviously, he had breathed his last within the hour.

He was active and happy right to the end — just the way he always was. I am sure he left us just as he prayed he would — quietly, with no fuss.

Since his retirement seven years ago, Archbishop Toolen has been the inspiration of the clergy and the staff of the cathedral rectory. There was a time before his resignation when predictions were made that he could never make the adjustment from his vigorous life of administration to the quiet of retirement. He confounded the prophets, as usual. His years have been full, peaceful, happy ones. His interests have been as keen as ever, and his prayers and penances continued to serve all of us as all his years of work had done for so long. So did his constant sense of humor.

The Archbishop was blessed in so many ways, and in these retirement years, he was especially blessed in the beautiful people who helped him live and die so happily. First, of course, was Sister Mary Gonzaga, R.S.M., a registered nurse from the Archbishop's hometown of Baltimore, who cared for him twenty-four hours a day since 1970. No one could have done more, and I cannot say enough for her loving care for Archbishop Toolen — only the Lord knows the full story of her total service and we know he never forgets.

Among our clergy was Monsignor Oscar Lipscomb, the Archbishop's strong right arm for so many years now, the one priest who was with him

---

1 Since 1980 Archbishop of Mobile.
2 Later Bishop of Shreveport-Alexandria, Louisiana.

almost every day. Monsignor Thomas M. Cullen, his oldest friend, heard the Archbishop's confession the day before he died, as he did week after week.

After listing many others who had ministered to and helped the Archbishop in his retirement — priests, doctors, and many women — May concluded:

He always had a way with our ladies, and they could never do enough for him.

I know it has been foolish of me to try to list people near and dear to the Archbishop, and I know I have overlooked some because there were so many. Please excuse my forgetfulness at this time. But I just wanted to give you this brief report of these final beautiful days of Archbishop Toolen and the people who helped make them so. He was always so grateful. I am sure he would want me to say these few words....

Eternal rest grant unto him, O Lord.

(Mobile, December 10, 1976)

Bereavement

During the fifteen years that Pope Paul filled the Chair of Peter, it was my privilege to meet him on four occasions. We exchanged just a few words each time. So I cannot say that I really knew him personally.

Still last Sunday afternoon when I heard so suddenly of his death, I felt a deep personal loss — much as when my father died. He was the Holy Father to so many millions, and yet he seemed somehow near and dear to me.

Very probably many people felt that way, some who never saw him except on television. Somehow we identified with him. He had such a hard time to be pope — fifteen years of change from one era to another in the life of the Church, in the life of our contemporary world. We saw him work so hard and suffer so much for the family of faith — much as we recall in the lives of our own fathers.

As everyone knows, Pope Paul suffered considerable and constant abuse and even ridicule from people both within the Church and from many who hate the Church. It seemed at times as if the frustrations of every group fell upon him. He was blamed by some for being "soft" on Communism, an easy tool of wild liberals. Others said he had no prophetic vision and was inflexibly conservative.

It was the old story. As a friend of mine recently wrote, children criticize their fathers for being "old-fashioned" until the day when they have children of their own. Employees gripe about their boss until they take over management. And how many times have we met the permissive liberal who overnight becomes a tyrant in a position of authority.

Pope Paul once said in visiting a poor parish in Bogota, Colombia, "Who am I? I am a man just like you, a simple and needy person — in need of the mercy of God and of your prayers because I have been given charge, without merit or choice on my part, of representing the Lord Jesus."

We have answered his plea for prayers in every Mass these past fifteen years. Let us do so in all gratitude now and especially next Sunday, August 13. I have asked that on this day following Pope Paul's funeral in Rome, every Mass in this diocese be a memorial liturgy for him. In the cathedral, I will offer a solemn pontifical Mass for our late Holy Father at 10:30 a.m. The ancient Latin Gregorian chant will be used together with the vernacular liturgy that the Pope gave us. We shall come together as one flock and praise God in all our churches this Sunday for a courageous teacher, a loving father, a pastor who was truly faithful unto death. He was in every way these past fifteen years "the servant of the servants of God."

May his soul and the souls of all the faithful departed, through the mercy of God, rest in peace. Amen.

(Mobile, August 11, 1978)

— ♦ —

"We Hardly Knew You"

Some years back, after the sudden and unexpected death of President John Kennedy, a popular book appeared that was later made into a touching television documentary. It was titled, *Johnny, We Hardly Knew Ye.*

That title came to my mind in the wee hours of last Friday morning when a telephone call informed me of the sudden, unexpected death of Pope John Paul. In more formal language we can truly say, "John Paul, we hardly knew you!"

But what we did come to know of our new Pope was so beautiful. Suddenly, he came smiling and shy from relative obscurity to the center of the world's stage. His performance there has been superb.

Who will forget the first line of his first talk to the assembled cardinals who had just elected him to the papacy — "May the Lord forgive you for what you have done!" Who will forget his quick smile and self-conscious little waves to the crowds from the balcony on his election day? He seemed so amazed to be there, but he came back again a few minutes later to greet the latecomers, and he still seemed so overwhelmed by it all.

But very shortly in succeeding days as he received delegations from all over the world and gave an amazing number of talks, he seemed completely and easily in charge of his new responsibility. How simply and beautifully he dealt with the crowds at his general audiences. His explanations of Catholic doctrine were clear and yet remarkably thoughtful — much like the book he published some years ago, *Catechism Crumbs*. Several times he delighted his audience by interviewing a child from the crowd to bring out a doctrinal point. Thanks to the massive media coverage he received, John Paul had become a warm and engaging world figure over night. He seemed like the best possible man for his awesome job.

And then just as unexpectedly as he appeared in the limelight, Pope John Paul quietly and without a word of farewell faded into the wings and left the world stage forever. Truth is surely stranger than fiction.

John Paul's ministry as pope was brief but significant to the Church, especially in his emphasis on the simplification of some traditional procedure in the Vatican. But we must recognize that our late Holy Father never had the opportunity to make the major decisions that now await his successor. The honeymoon of the new pope would have come to an end and he would have to face the painful issues that so troubled Pope Paul VI. John Paul was spared all that and if there could be a shred of envy remaining in heaven, I am afraid it would be in the heart of Paul VI as he welcomed his successor this week to the joy of the Lord.

John Paul, we hardly knew you — there was just not enough time. But we loved you from the first and we thank the Lord for you. We thank the Lord for giving us such a beautiful example of the Good Shepherd.

May flights of angels lead you on your way
To paradise and heaven's eternal day;
May martyrs greet you after death's dark night

And bid you enter into Zion's light.
May choirs of angels sing you to your rest
With once poor Lazarus, now forever blest (Roman Liturgy).

(Mobile, October 6, 1978)

— ◆ —

The manuscript for the following column, published in the Mobile
Catholic Week *for September 21, 1979, shows clear evidence of the hur-*
ricane it reports. Unlike the other columns, which were typed on modern
electric machines, this one bears the mark of the older manual typewriter
from which it issued.

— ◆ —

What a Week!

For the first time in many, many years you did not receive your *Catholic*
Week. And for the first time in fifty-three years, Mobile suffered a direct hit
by a hurricane. Along with so many other things, our last issue was knocked
out by Hurricane Frederick.

Here is a report of these past days as I saw them from our Catholic Center.
Like so many other Mobilians, I could not really believe what I saw the day
after the hurricane. The devastation was staggering, but we were all grateful
for the minimal loss of life and bodily injury. It was truly amazing. The local
disaster preparedness program had paid off.

The next couple of days I tried to check on all our parishes and institutions. Most of the telephones, including our incoming lines, were out. With
the help of Bishop-elect Friend and Monsignors Sullivan and Lipscomb, I
finally visited or contacted personally just about every Catholic entity in
Mobile and Baldwin Counties.

What I learned was most impressive. Each pastor and administrator was
busy caring for people and securing property. Invariably, I found them on
the job in every place and doing all they could. Our hundreds of geriatric
residents were secure and comfortable at the Little Sisters of the Poor, the
Allen Home, Villa Mercy, and Cathedral Place. The same was true of the
children at Saint Mary's Home. Our schools were cleaning up and plans
were coordinated by Sister Margaret Alice, C.S.J., our superintendent,
for the overall resumption of all school programs. The regular schedule

of Masses (except during the curfew hours) was observed in all Catholic churches, with the single exception of inaccessible Dauphin Island.

Meanwhile, Providence Hospital gave a beautiful witness of service to all suffering people. Our Service Center on Dauphin Street distributed its entire emergency food stock, and Father Weise, our Vicar for Charities, and the Catholic Social Services staff made plans for the overall program of follow-up aid in the weeks ahead.

Meanwhile, messages were coming in from all over the country. The Dioceses of Louisiana, under the leadership of Archbishop Hannan of New Orleans, took up a collection at all Sunday Masses to help us. Trucks of food and supplies came from New Orleans, a check from the Catholic high-school students of Birmingham, and so forth. I remembered the line from Scripture, "Bear one another's burdens and so you will fulfill the law of Christ." This was Catholic faith in action, and it was beautiful.

For years now, we have been under a protected self-insurance program. Our local diocesan representative, Mr. Edward Behm, began checking every single property loss with the help of adjustors from our service company, Gallagher-Bassett. All seems well in hand.

So there is a brief report. There will be pictures and forthcoming information as it develops. But it seems that our diocese has weathered a major disaster and is still alive and well. Thanks be to God!

Exactly ten years later the Archbishop would add a footnote to the report above in his column in the St. Louis Review *for September 29, 1989.*

From the current *Catholic Digest:*

"Gone With the Wind"

For forty years, Mobile's Bishop T.J. Toolen somehow bribed heaven to protect the city from the ravages of a major hurricane. He was succeeded by Bishop John L. May. During May's time as bishop here, Hurricane Frederick came to Alabama's coast and did extensive damage to Mobile. The following year, Bishop May was transferred to St. Louis, Missouri.

On leaving, he was heard telling his successor, Archbishop Oscar Lipscomb, "Remember, Oscar, one hurricane and you're gone!"

Big News!

This was a big news week around the Catholic Center. Here is the inside story.

Surprise! Early on Monday morning, January 21, the phone rang. It was the apostolic delegate, Archbishop Jean Jadot, calling from Washington. He informed me that the Holy Father wished to transfer me to St. Louis if I would agree. Once I could speak, I told him that whatever Pope John Paul wanted was all right with me. Archbishop Jadot said he would send a formal letter later with the definite date of publication. Meanwhile, there was to be complete secrecy. He added that he would pray for me. I spent much of that day in a daze.

The next morning when I woke up, I was not sure whether it had all been a dream, but then the phone rang again. This time it was John Cardinal Carberry, the recently retired Archbishop of St. Louis. He had just received official notification and was calling to welcome me with open arms. He gave me a brief report on the archdiocese and said I would find the clergy, religious, and laity beautiful to serve. He was most reassuring. He also said he would pray for me.

The days passed until Tuesday, January 29, when the news from Rome broke at 7 a.m. as the apostolic delegate had promised. Since then, I have been busy answering questions from Mobile and St. Louis. The following information may answer some of your questions.

- As yet I do not know the date when I will leave Mobile and be installed in St. Louis. It will all depend on the arrangements in St. Louis when I visit there in the next few days and on the apostolic delegate's calendar. Five or six weeks from now is my guess.
- Actually, I know as much about the Archdiocese of St. Louis as I did about the Diocese of Mobile when I came here just over ten years ago. It has been years since I visited St. Louis. The cardinal and the three auxiliary bishops are good friends, of course, but I know very few of the clergy and even fewer religious and laypeople — except for my niece and nephew who are attending St. Louis University.
- As you might imagine, I have been reading a certain section of

The Official Catholic Directory rather closely this past week. (This is the annual publication with all the facts and figures on every diocese in the United States.) The St. Louis section of this book indicates that I should have enough to do in the years ahead. But there should be considerably less driving — even though it may be through ice and snow at times. (I thought I had left all that.)

- I have no idea who will succeed me as the new Bishop of Mobile, and I do not know how soon the appointment will be announced. It would be nice if it could come before my departure, but I doubt that very much.
- It will be hard to leave south Alabama — especially with the future looking so promising here. There will be many a day, I am sure, when I will look back wistfully to the Heart of Dixie — and it will not always be in the middle of winter, either. But I am sure the Lord's finger is in all this, and so we all need to say together at this time in Mobile and St. Louis, "In God we trust."

(Mobile, February 1, 1980)

Transition

Questions: This is a strange time in the life of a diocese — when the bishop has been named to another diocese, but he is still around for a while.

Who's in Charge? Until I am installed in St. Louis on March 25, I remain the Bishop of Mobile with responsibility for this diocese and no other. So the work of the diocese continues, and I am trying to tie up as many loose ends as possible before my departure.

After March 25, the Clergy Senate in their role as diocesan consultors will elect a priest of our diocese as administrator, who will be in charge until the new bishop takes over.

Who? Who will the new Bishop of Mobile be? I can say in all honesty that I do not know. The apostolic delegate has been sent a complete list of our diocesan pastoral council members for possible consultation. A diocesan pastoral council committee will also compile a profile of the needs of our diocese at this time and the qualities accordingly needed in the new bishop.

Our priests are invited also to submit names for consideration by Rome. Once this process of consultation is completed, the apostolic delegate in Washington, Archbishop Jean Jadot, will compare this input with what he has received from bishops in the New Orleans Province and from around the country. A list of possible appointees will then be sent to Rome, with the final appointment to be made by Pope John Paul. This is the process, and it will probably take several months.

Meanwhile: I have been to St. Louis for two days to make plans. Everyone there has given me a wonderful, warm welcome — except for the weatherman. It was seven degrees above zero and snowing during my visit. I thought of those words in the gospel, "Pray that your flight not be in the winter." I was on a radio call-in program for one hour with questions from all over the area. Later, there were two TV half-hours with questions again. Since I know so little about St. Louis as yet, most of my replies were based on what has been done in south Alabama. And we got some free publicity in the newspapers, also.

Meanwhile Back Home: Here in our Diocese of Mobile, I have been having lots of farewells. This Saturday, February 23, I will have a final gathering with all the sisters and brothers. There will be the regular meetings, confirmations, and so forth. And I will also be making my retreat next week and getting some rest.

Then on Saint Joseph's Day, March 19, in the beautiful cathedral of Mobile, I will offer a final Pontifical Mass at 5:30 p.m. for all the people of our diocese, followed by a reception for all in the Mobile Municipal Auditorium. A few days later, on March 23, I will leave for St. Louis. I will truly be leaving a very happy home here in south Alabama. But enough of this. It is not yet time to say good-bye.

(Mobile, February 22, 1980)

— ◆ —

This Is It!

Here it is — my last column. It is hard for me to believe that there have been more than five hundred of these weekly pieces since I began writing them in December 1969 when I came as your new bishop.

I have found it a real joy to write to you each week. This column has been a great opportunity not just to expand my work of preaching and teaching here in our diocese, but I believe it has given you a chance to get to know me a little better. It has always been gratifying to find folks in my visits to our parishes eager to discuss some subject from a recent column. Sometimes it was just to suggest a better joke than my last gem, but it was always good to see how many of you were reading and pondering these weekly thoughts.

But the columns were just one enjoyable aspect of my years here. There were so many more. All my years in the priesthood have been happy ones — nine as an assistant pastor, three as a hospital chaplain, nine on the staff of the Catholic Church Extension Society, and one as a parish pastor before coming to Mobile. But I believe I can say that my ten years here have been the happiest of my life. I came to a new part of our country knowing practically no one, and now I am really leaving my happy home.

One of our teenagers said, "I have never heard of anyone retiring to the north before." I guess he figured that at my advanced age my moving to St. Louis was just to round out my twilight years. Once again, I am going to a new locale with new people. I will have to start learning names and faces all over again. But that helps to keep life interesting, I know. Each new priestly assignment has convinced me more and more of the striking basic unity of our Catholic Church. There is truly one Lord, one faith, and one beautiful Catholic people. Everywhere I go, I find that same love of the same Lord reflected in the lives of his people. I look forward to seeing it ever the same but with new highlights in St. Louis.

My final words to you are thanks, apology, and a request. Thank you for so much during these years — your friendship, your cooperation, your loyalty, your love. Please accept my apology for anything I may have done at any time that inadvertently hurt any one of you or for what I did not do when it would have helped you. And may I ask for a final favor — your prayers for me in the days ahead. I will also keep you in my Masses and breviary always.

And don't forget, if you ever find yourself under that big Arch on the banks of the mighty Mississippi, give me a call. Let's remember that golden oldie, "Meet me in Saint Louie...."

* * *

He who makes no mistakes never makes anything.

(Mobile, March 21, 1980)

"Be It Done to Me According to Your Word"

(Homily at the Mass of Installation as Archbishop of St. Louis, March 25, 1980.)

The last time I preached my own installation homily, a little boy came to me at the reception following. He looked up at me very solemnly and said, "Bishop, y'all talk funny." I hope I can do better this time.

Today I came to you as a stranger and you took me in. You took me in with open arms. I have been heartened and overjoyed by your letters, your assurances of prayer, your warm welcomes, your loving devotion, and this magnificent liturgy. All of this, I recognize, is not just typical Midwestern friendliness; this, I know, is an act of faith. You have shown your faith in the Church of Jesus Christ and your loyal affection for our Holy Father, Pope John Paul, who has sent me to you, whose representative has graciously come here to present me to you. Let us now, shepherd and flock, in our first act together as the Church of St. Louis, renew our loyalty to our Holy Father, successor of Peter, as we pray in this Mass that the Lord may indeed preserve him, give him life, and make him blessed in all the earth.

As our beloved apostolic delegate led me a few minutes ago to the bishop's chair here, I realized that the mantle of DuBourg, the mantle of Rosati, was falling upon me; Joseph Rosati, who in 1822 was appointed Bishop for the Territory of Alabama but asked instead to remain in St. Louis, where he became the first bishop in 1827. Shortly thereafter his first episcopal consecration here was that of Michael Portier, first bishop of Mobile.

I came to the chair of Kenrick and Kane and took the very crosier so firmly gripped by Glennon, Ritter, and Carberry. I came as the first native son of Chicago, which has received five prelates from St. Louis, including its present Cardinal-Archbishop, who ordained me to the episcopacy. I came in esteem and reverence for Cardinal Carberry, who, twelve years ago to this very day, was installed the sixth shepherd of St. Louis and who has served so wisely and faithfully. Mindful of all my revered predecessors in this historic See, I am indeed conscious today of my personal limitations. My brother bishops, family, and friends, to whom I owe so much and whose presence here means so much to me today, know that I come not as a scholar, an orator, or an administrator. They know that, in the words of Saint Paul, "I come to you not with any gift of eloquence or philosophy but simply to tell you what God has guaranteed. During my time among you, the only knowledge I can claim is about Jesus, the crucified Christ" (1 Corinthians 2:1). I come to live among you the words of Vatican Council II, "A father and pastor, the bishop stands in the midst of his people as one who serves." This is why I have come.

Now, what does all this mean — this noble rhetoric? What does it mean to the young couple raising children in the face of today's pagan pressures; to the aging couple trying to get by on a fixed income? It means that in all the clamor, confusion, and clash of contradiction all around us today, we need more than anything else, the Good News of Jesus Christ.

- We need to hear again that there is neither Jew nor Greek; there is neither slave nor free man; there is neither male nor female. We are all one in Christ Jesus, and we must not be hearers only of that Word but doers.
- We need to hear that he came especially for those at the side of the road in our society, left there wounded and stripped. As we go down from this magnificent temple of Saint Louis of France, we need to remember the patron of our cathedral and our city in his love for those at the side of the road. We dare not pass by.
- We need to hear again how blessed are the peacemakers, especially at this time in our country.
- We need to hear again how much we need one another, all of us who share our rich Jewish and Christian heritage. I therefore pledge to work closely with all the representatives of all the churches and synagogues who honor us so much today, that more and more we all may be one.
- We need to hear again the gospel word of Jesus, who came not to condemn the world, as we promise to work with our civic leaders and all men of goodwill in this community, that ALL our people may have life and have it more abundantly.

Beneath all these needs of our time, we know it is not by bread alone that man lives. Whether ancient man stood on the earth gazing in wonder at the moon or modern man stands on the moon looking back at our good earth, the backdrop is the same blackness of space with the same perennial questions about the meaning of life and death. And we believe that there is the one Light in all this darkness — the risen Jesus with his Good News. And so I pray that the words of our responsorial psalm today will be true in me, "Here am I, Lord, I come to do your will…to announce your justice in the vast assembly and not to restrain my lips, as you, Lord, know…Your faithfulness and your salvation I have spoken; I have made no secret of your kindness and your truth in the vast assembly. Here am I, Lord; I come to do your will."

It is not always easy to be people of the gospel. So we need one another. Especially do I need you, my brothers — bishops, priests, and deacons of St. Louis. As the Second Vatican Council says, "Bishops should recognize priests as necessary helpers and counselors…the bishop must regard his priests as his brothers and friends." So I was happy yesterday to join all our religious and diocesan clergy in my first meeting in St. Louis. I look forward to working closely with you in brotherhood the rest of my life.

Speaking now for all our clergy and for myself, I say to you brothers and sisters of this archdiocese how much we need you. St. Louis has been rich, indeed, in vocations to the religious life. Just reading the list of religious communities of men and women here and your glorious service to our people has encouraged me tremendously. As you can see, I have spent some time with the *Catholic Directory,* and I look forward to Saturday with all the brothers and sisters of our archdiocese.

I have also read Father Faherty's *Dream by the River* and other historical literature of the Church of St. Louis. Again and again, I have been struck by the vision and the leadership of the laymen and women of this archdiocese, and that spirit seems to be alive today as I read your expectations and your assurance of cooperation in all your beautiful letters. And so I recall what Vatican Council II tells us clergy about all of you, "Priests should listen to them willingly, consider their wishes in a fraternal spirit, and recognize their experience and competence in the different areas of human activity, so that together they will be able to read the signs of the times." I will do my best to do that always, since I need your help so much.

Now as we close our service shortly and prepare to come together as one family around the Lord's eucharistic table for the first time, all of this sounds fine. But is it not still so much noble rhetoric? What will it mean in the years to come?

We must admit today that really we do not know — any more than our Lady did on the first Annunciation day, as we just heard in today's holy gospel. The Lord called her by his angel to a new time in her life, an unexpected, overwhelming work. She did not know what it would require, where it would all lead. In all reverence, with no desire for dramatics on this Annunciation day, I must ask as she did, "How can this be...?" And I know that the answer is the same, "The Holy Spirit will come upon you and the power of the Most High will overshadow you...."

Along with Mary, the woman of faith, I know that God, our Father, can use human weakness so that his Son, Jesus, may come again among the men and women of our time.

And so I know, too, that my response must be the same as her beautiful words on this Annunciation day — "Behold the servant of the Lord. Be it done to me according to your word."

This month I will be marking my third anniversary here in St. Louis. In coming here, I knew practically no one. I was a stranger and you took me in, and now I feel very much at home. My most important ministry here will always be to my fellow clergy, and you have also been my greatest support and joy here. I believe we have a superb brotherhood of clergy, diocesan and religious, and I am honored and grateful to be one of you. Let us pray for one another.

(*Notanda*, March 4, 1983)

Free Lunch

Right in the middle of Holy Week, Wednesday before Holy Thursday, President Reagan invited a group from our Catholic Bishops' Conference to lunch. I thought you might like to hear some human interest details.

Last October, I was with twelve bishops invited to dinner with Pope John Paul in the Vatican during our regular five-year report. The Pope welcomed us that evening at his apartment door and showed us to his chapel for a visit and then to his dining room. There was only his secretary, Monsignor Diwisz, with him at the table. It was a Friday, so we had fish in a rather small dining room. It was a very intimate and pleasant setting for our free and easy conversation mostly about the Church in the U.S.A. for an hour that evening.

Last week at the White House, there was a very thorough preliminary security screening before our reception by the President in the Oval Office. We were presented individually, and then after we had a quick look around, he led us over to the family area of the White House by a covered walk through a magnificent flower-banked garden. (It was a beautiful day in Washington and the spring blossoms were glorious.)

At regular intervals along the way, there were secret-service men on duty. On arrival at the Old Family Dining Room, we were served sherry, white wine, or fruit juice in a brief reception before lunch. The President stood near the fireplace. (In both his office and the dining room, there was a wood fire going, even though it was a warm day.) He was most affable reviewing experiences at Notre Dame during his famous movie days there and since. (The Marine quartet in the corner quietly played "The Bells of Saint Mary's.")

Lunch began with a prayer by Cardinal Krol, and the President told how Mrs. Reagan had restored the room, which was decorated in yellow and white. He told us quite a bit of homey detail about the White House. Then the more serious conversation began. Joining us for lunch were Assistants to the President Edwin Meese, James Baker, and Michael Deaver; Security Council Director Robert McFarlane; and Public Liaison Director Faith Whittlesey. Bishop Malone, president of the Bishops' Conference, thanked the President for his invitation and for his leadership in the pro-life cause, his advocacy of aid to private schools, and his restoration of diplomatic relations with the Vatican. The President responded, and then we all got into the ensuing conversation on such diverse topics as the problems of our low-income people, our cities and schools, family life, Central America, the arms race, family planning in foreign aid and domestic programs, and so forth.

The food and service were magnificent, and I noticed there were secret-service men at the doors of the room at all times. The President was relaxed and yet closely involved in the conversation as his aides and all of us joined in. Besides the active Cardinals Krol of Philadelphia and Bernardin of Chicago (Manning of Los Angeles could not make it), the Bishops' Conference Executive Committee, Archbishops Kelly of Louisville, Law of Boston, Szoka of Detroit, Bishop Malone of Youngstown, and me, together with Archbishop O'Connor of New York and Monsignor Hoye, conference secretary, made up our representation. It was a free and frank exchange, and after nearly ninety minutes, the President's assistants indicated that he was late for his next appointment. After a pleasant farewell and best wishes for his coming trip to China, we were led to the old Executive Office Building for ninety minutes of briefings by administration representatives.

What was my impression? The President could not have been more affable. He seemed in fine health and ate a good lunch (I noticed he did not pass up a thing.) On almost every subject, he took a definite part in the conversation and seemed informed. The time passed very quickly and the President seemed reluctant to leave. In fact, he lingered awhile despite the impatience of several of his aides. He walked with us part of the way to our briefing session. All in all, it was a most enjoyable experience for me and most thought-provoking. To break bread with the Pope and the President in such an intimate setting helps one to have a great compassion for them in their tremendous responsibilities. Through it all, they are men with human limitations. We need to pray for them.

(St. Louis, April 27, 1984)

Reunion

The Class of 1947 of St. Mary of the Lake Seminary near Chicago had a reunion last week on our ordination anniversary. Six of our original class of 1934 are now with the Lord. Several others are serving in far-off dioceses and in Rome, and four more could not come for various reasons. But there were nineteen of us survivors there. It was a great day.

Our seminary alma mater was affectionately known as "The Rock." Discipline was strict and, like the West Pointers of those days, we led a Spartan existence. A seminarian went through the halls ringing a bell at 5:30 a.m. Bells regulated our entire day — chapel, classes, refectory, and recreation — and we were supposed to be on our way immediately. The rector wanted to be sure we had enough sleep, so the lights went out at 9:45 each night.

The seminary course lasted seven years, three for philosophy and allied sciences; four for moral and dogmatic theology and canon law. Most of the classes were conducted in Latin, and the students answered the professors' questions in Latin. All of our Jesuit teachers were erudite men who knew their subjects well, but the give-and-take of today's classroom was largely absent.

There were no Christmas or Easter vacations. We had a break in January after the examinations. In retrospect, Christmas at the seminary was a day of deep spiritual happiness. The strong bond of fraternity among the seminarians helped to make up for the separation from our families. Most of us after the seminary days would remain close friends for life. Priests speak the same language and can share their common hopes and disappointments more easily with those who have had a like experience.

When we entered the seminary and sat in the pews at the rear of the chapel, the pews occupied by the deacons near the high altar seemed far away. But the seminary years passed quickly.

Then came the big day in May 1947 when Samuel Cardinal Stritch asked us if we knew and were willing to accept the obligations of the priesthood. Happily, but humbly, we took the decisive step into the unknown future, confident that the Lord would sustain us. We did not enter the ministry as conquering heroes but with an earnest prayer that we might become good priests.

At last week's reunion, we all reminisced about those seminary days and the times we tried to put something over on the rector or our teachers. The faculty had the better batting average. Despite the strict regime and our grousing about the rules and the food, St. Mary's gave us a sound spiritual formation and the intellectual training we needed. The discipline helped us to develop the stability that would see us through rough situations later on. We owe a real debt to our alma mater and the priests, Sisters, and laypeople who made it possible.

During the dinner, there were many references to our age. "If a young priest came in now, he'd say we're a bunch of old men," one said, then added, "but none of us feel like that." We agreed that there was still some salt of our youth in us. Old age, after all, is always fifteen years older than you are. We looked around at one another and felt that the Lord had been good to us through the long years. I hope he will spare us for many more gatherings before the Class of 1947 meets for its final reunion in the world to come.

Many of our clergy are having reunions and anniversaries here in our archdiocese these days also, and I have been privileged to attend some of them. Every priest feels at home in any such gathering. That is the spirit of all Catholic clergy everywhere. I cannot think of a more fulfilling, meaningful life. May many of our young men in the years ahead come to know the same joy.

(St. Louis, May 11, 1984)

Clergy Dinners

As you know, I have been hosting dinner for our clergy in groups often this year. There have been about two hundred guests thus far, and I hope we can move right ahead now, going down the list of diocesan priests and religious serving in parishes first of all. Those invited are not informed of their fellow guests until they arrive at 4510 Lindell, but the group is always varied by seniority. Accordingly, the conversation has always been broadly based and open to all. I have enjoyed these evenings very much, and I am grateful to my fellow hosts, Bern Sandheinrich and John Gaydos,[1] for handling the practical details so well. If you have not yet been invited, I assure you that you have not been overlooked. I look forward to an evening with you before long.

(Notanda, September 6, 1985)

A Visit to Russia and Baltic Christians

As mentioned previously here, I was appointed last March to the National Conference of Catholic Bishops' new committee for the Church in Eastern Europe. Pope John Paul II has challenged the Church in the West to respond to the needs of the emerging Church behind the Iron Curtain. The Catholic Bishops of the United States decided to respond promptly to the call of our Holy Father.

Accordingly, this summer three delegations of bishops went to Eastern Europe with staff people to see the Church situation there for themselves. The first group, led by Archbishop Roger Mahony of Los Angeles, visited

---

1 Monsignors Bernard H. Sandheinrich and John R. Gaydos, archdiocesan director of the Propagation of the Faith Office and chancellor respectively, were living at Archbishop's House, 4510 Lindell.

Hungary, Romania, and Bulgaria and finally met in Vienna with the major European-based Catholic aid organization. The second delegation visited Poland, Czechoslovakia, and Yugoslavia, under the leadership of Archbishop Theodore McCarrick of Newark. I was privileged to lead the third group, which also included for several days Joseph Cardinal Bernardin of Chicago in our visit to the Soviet Union.

Fast Start: On Saturday, August 25, we left New York for the overnight flight to Milan in northern Italy. We arrived on Sunday morning just in time to join in the solemn Mass in the ancient and magnificent Cathedral of Milan. After some rest in the afternoon we met for two hours with Carlo Cardinal Martini, president of the Federation of the European Bishops' Conferences. He summarized the impressions of his brother bishops as they have surveyed the emerging situation of the East European Church and what they plan to do. The next morning we had a breakfast meeting with Dr. Gerhard Meier, president of Caritas International, who came up from his Rome office to brief us on the plans of this world Catholic aid organization. We then flew to Moscow, arriving there in a cold, driving rain about 6 p.m. We were met by the chaplain of the American Embassy who took us to our Intourist hotel, promptly labeled "the Gulag" since there was no heat, hot water, and so forth. It was to be our happy home for three nights.

On Tuesday we had Mass in the chapel near the Embassy and visited the parish church nearby dedicated to St. Louis of France. We continued on to a tour of the Kremlin churches, Red Square, and so forth. Then to the American Embassy for a briefing by the chargé d'affaires. It was a sunny but cool and windy day in Moscow. On Wednesday, August 29, we met Cardinal Bernardin, who had just arrived, and conferred with him in planning our visit with the newly elected Russian Orthodox Patriarch, Alexy. The Patriarch received us very formally in his impressive head-quarters at the Danilov Monastery for a ninety-minute discussion that was quite candid and positive as to ecumenical cooperation with Catholics in the Soviet Union. After a quick visit to a couple of typical Moscow department stores (pretty grim), we went on to a conference with the Soviet chairman for religious affairs in his government ministry. It was a long conversation in which we were assured of an official change of policy by the supreme Soviet. Henceforth, all citizens would have full freedom of conscience in practicing the religion of their choice, and all churches were to be recognized by the Soviet State. Our efforts to assist the Catholic

Church in the Soviet Union were welcomed. With some amazed skepticism, we thanked the chairman and moved on. The next morning we had our first experience with Aeroflot as we went through several hours of delay before flying from Moscow to Vilnius in Lithuania.

The Baltics: An exuberant crowd welcomed us with flowers, speeches, native dress, and so forth, at the Vilnius Airport. Most of this was intended for Cardinal Bernardin and his party from Chicago who had come specifically to visit Lithuania, but it was nice to be included. We were taken to the Curia of Archbishop Steponavicius, tall and erect despite his more than seventy years, much of it spent as a Soviet prisoner because of his loyalty to the Holy See. After conferring with him and other clergy and laity, we were taken to a number of churches that had been used since the Stalin days as warehouses, museums, factories, and so forth. They have now been returned to the Catholic Church and need extensive renovation. After a concelebrated Mass in a packed church with people weeping with joy, we conferred with an American Jesuit doing a research sabbatical on the emerging religious situation in the various Soviet republics. The following morning it was on to Kaunas for another tumultuous welcome and a grand concelebrated Mass with Cardinal Skladevicius and the rest of the Lithuanian Bishops, most of whom were also former Soviet prisoners of conscience. A simple lunch followed in the national seminary, packed with two hundred students, and then a full conversation for the afternoon with all the bishops who presented their plans and needs. We visited Caritas, the Kaunas Catholic Charities, and took our bus back to Vilnius for the night, where we said good-bye to Cardinal Bernardin and the Chicagoans. Catholics in Lithuania are most impressive and hopeful as they push their efforts for independence from the Soviet Union.

The next morning we left for a six-hour drive in a Volkswagen van to Riga in Latvia. We arrived at the newly reopened seminary and met the remarkable Bishop Nukss. The seminarians live in the most primitive circumstances, but they gave us their best in dinner and showed us around before we went on to the bishop's Curia for our usual conference with the clergy to learn their plans and needs. Catholics in Latvia are a small and struggling minority unlike their majority neighbors in Lithuania. They are even fewer in Estonia, which we were unable to visit. Baltic Catholics overall seem hopeful and progressive in every way.

Early the next day we moved on to Bylorussia where we were received

335

by the dynamic Bishop Thadeus Andruskiewicz in Grodno. The new papal delegate to Russia, Archbishop Colussuanno, was also visiting there for the reopening of the seminary, another brave beginning in incredibly poor conditions with over one hundred new students. We met with the bishop and then I was privileged to lead the concelebrated Mass and preach at 7 p.m. on Sunday evening. The cathedral was jammed and the people were overwhelmed that we American Bishops had come. The churches returned by the state in recent months are in shambles, but they are working to restore them throughout Bylorussia.

Monday, September 3, was a horror, with a grueling drive from 10 a.m. to 9 p.m. from Grodno to Lwow in the Ukraine. It did, however, give us a good impression of the Russian countryside.

The Ukraine: All along we had visited with Latin rite Catholics, but in the Ukraine there are over five million Eastern rite Catholics. One of our group was Bishop Basil Losten of the Ukrainian rite, Eparchy of Stamford, Connecticut, so I was happy to have him take over. We began with a concelebrated Old Slavonic liturgy in Lwow's St. George Cathedral, which was recently repossessed by Catholics after a bitter struggle with the Russian Orthodox Church to which Stalin gave the cathedral when he suppressed the Catholic Church in the Ukraine in 1946. We then conferred at length with Archbishop Sterniuk in his one-room apartment where he has lived for more than thirty years. We went on to the newly reconstituted seminary meeting in a restored church, the only place available. The nearly two hundred students live wherever they can. Visits followed to some underground Sisters and the archdiocesan youth group, which is planning an outdoor rally for the young people of Lwow now that it is legal to hold such a gathering. We also went to a clinic that had been appropriated from the Church. The needs everywhere are staggering in this Soviet republic, which is seething with nationalism. It is also the scene of Chernobyl, the terrible nuclear accident situation. But the Catholic Church in Ukraine is full of new life.

Back Home: The next day, Wednesday, September 5, featured another Aeroflot experience as we flew back from Lwow to Moscow and reentered "the Gulag" for the last night. They even had hot water this time. We spent the evening riding the Moscow subway and went to the Moscow circus. It was wonderful. Thursday we flew back on Pan Am to God-blessed America.

On September 12, we gave our report to the bishops at their administrative committee meeting in Washington. We await their decisions for our committee's work ahead. It promises to be interesting.

(St. Louis, September 14, 1990)

— ♦ —

"Thanks for the memories" — remember that closing theme from Bob Hope's weekly TV program? For many of us, it might very well be our theme this Sunday, Father's Day.

We all have our memories of our dads. Mine go back a long time indeed. My dad would be ninety-seven years old this year, but he died in October 1969. He was a tired man of seventy-five, worn out by hard work from his fourteenth year when he left school to labor side by side with his father in the family greenhouses and truck farm. I don't remember that he ever had a vacation until I finally prevailed on him and my mother to go with me about 1960 to see the sights of Washington and New York. He thought that trip was also "a waste of money," since he had passed through New York when he was shipped out from there with the infantry on his way to the battlefields of France in World War I. Today I have beautiful memories of my father who lived and died faithful to his family, his country, and to the Lord. How much he gave; how little he took in return. Thanks today for the memories.

(St. Louis, June 14, 1991)

— ♦ —

"I am proud to be your archbishop." It seems that I have been saying that on quite a few occasions. Some captious clerics smirk a bit when they hear it, but on Sunday, July 7, I felt it more deeply than ever, even though I never said it. I was really too choked up.

It all began in that brilliant Bolivian sunshine that morning as we marched in procession by the hundreds down the streets of LaPaz following the waving banners and singing those glorious Spanish hymns. Finally, the Church of Cristo Rey (Christ the King) lay before us as we poured through its open doors into the standing-room-only crowd. Psalm 96 came to mind:

337

Sing a new song to the Lord!
Sing to the Lord, all the world!
Sing to the Lord, and praise him!
Proclaim every day the good news
  that he has saved us.
Proclaim his glory to the nations,
  his mighty deeds to all peoples.

And I was so moved I could hardly begin the liturgy when the people finished singing.

What struck me at that moment was the realization that this all began thirty-five years ago in St. Louis when Cardinal Ritter made the decision to send our own priests and Sisters to the poor people of Bolivia. And now look how gloriously grateful they are to the Lord and to our archdiocese. You can be proud indeed.

There are now thriving parishes not just in LaPaz but in nearby Altiplano villages. There are priests ordained and seminarians in formation. There are a school, clinics, orphan care, the only place in all that area for homeless and chemically dependent people, a radio station beamed to the poor of the countryside, and so forth. Over the years, there have been nearly eighty of our priests, Sisters of the Precious Blood from O'Fallon, and lay volunteers from this archdiocese serving the poor people of Bolivia. And all of you have helped to make it possible by your prayers and contributions year after year.

No wonder the people came in droves to celebrate in the glorious liturgy they had prepared, concelebrated by the papal nuncio and the local bishops and priests. Eighty percent of the Bolivian people are of Aymara-Indian stock, and they contributed their colorful music, chant, and dancing to the universal Catholic liturgy and to the spirited fiesta in the churchyard for hours after Mass. (Incidentally, as we mark five hundred years since Columbus discovered the new world, so many of our country deplore Spanish colonization of Latin America. Looking at all those burnished bronze-colored folks, I compared their situation to what has befallen the Indians of North America. At the very least, the native peoples are still in the majority in Bolivia.) I finally told them all about you, your love for them, your unity with them. And I was prouder than ever to be your archbishop.

(St. Louis, July 19, 1991)

— ◆ —

Fateful Choices
(Thoughts on Retreat)

The bookstores are filled with peoples' stories, the biographies and autobiographies of the rich and famous: Bo Jackson, Nancy Reagan, Winston Churchill, Shirley MacLaine. The list is endless. We seem to have an insatiable interest in the words and works of others, especially the rich or the powerful. And I suppose most of us have given at least a fleeting thought to our own autobiography.

If we were to write our own personal stories, we would find ourselves walking across a landscape full of happenings, a great many of them apparently disconnected. Nevertheless, certain decisions would emerge that give meaning and pattern to the whole. Once made, these critical choices set a large part of our lives beyond our control. We choose to become a lawyer or an electrician; and a course is set that we will follow for much of our lives. We marry and bind ourselves to another person "until death do us part." We buy a home and so commit a major part of our lives and resources to a village or a neighborhood. The awesome thing about these decisions is that we make them with limited wisdom; yet they set a pattern for much of our history.

As we stand at the edge of a new year, we may seek some assurance that the decisions we have made are the right ones or that the wrong ones we have made can be corrected. In fact, God has given us just this sort of reassurance. Through the sacraments, he works to ensure that the major events of our lives will be meaningful and gracious, that they will serve him and others, too. Birth, growth, sexuality, illness, guilt, our relationships, and finally death itself are all accompanied by his sacramental presence.

Baptism introduces us into God's family and surrounds us with the love the heavenly Father has for his children. As we approach maturity, confirmation brings the gifts of wisdom, understanding, counsel, fortitude. The sacrament of the sick brings his comforting, healing presence. Matrimony and holy orders are sacred dedications to others. Reconciliation deals with the guilt of our flawed choices; and in the Eucharist we find Christ calling us to intimate union with himself and our brothers and sisters in a bond of peace and love.

The journey we have been on is one that we have made with our God. Like the Israelites in the desert, we see that he marches with us, feeding us when we are hungry, shielding us when we are threatened, setting us free when we seemed trapped by the happenings of our history. He is Emmanuel — God with us — as the story of our life unfolds.

(St. Louis, January 10, 1992)

— ◆ —

Everyman

"Remember that you are dust and unto dust you shall return." Those first words of Lent last Wednesday were a bit rough, weren't they?

During the Middle Ages there was more.

"Morality plays" were a favorite form of entertainment then. Townspeople gathered in the cathedral square to watch wandering troops of actors perform their favorite plays; one of the favorites was entitled *Everyman* — a pretty good meditation these first days of Lent.

The play opened to find the lead character (his name was "Everyman") walking home at day's end. Lost in this thoughts of dinner, family, and fireside, he nearly bumped into a tall, dark figure standing directly in his path. Startled, he asked the stranger's name.

"My name is Death," he replied, "and I have come to take you with me." Everyman was horrified. "There must be some mistake," he pleaded, "I've never felt better in my life." Death shook his head, "There is no mistake. You must come with me."

Desperate, Everyman pleaded, "At least let me bring a friend with me. I don't want to go alone." Death smiled, "If you can find a friend who will go with you, he may come. I will give you one hour; then meet me here."

Everyman hurried back toward town to the house of a friend he knew well, knocked on the door, and poured out his story to his friend. The man looked at him with mingled sadness and terror. "I cannot come, my friend," he said at last. "It's impossible." The friend's name was "Riches." Not yet discouraged, Everyman hurried off to the house of a second friend, then a third. In each case, the answer was a frightened, "I'm sorry. I cannot come." Their names were "Fame" and "Pleasure."

Slowly, Everyman turned back down the path to his rendezvous with Death. As he walked along, he came upon another old friend, one he had not seen lately. Without much hope, he told his story again. To his utter amazement, this last friend replied: "Of course, I'll go with you." His name was "Good Deeds."

Death was a familiar figure during the Middle Ages. Average life expectancy was less than forty; infant mortality was at a frightful level. There were no hospitals or nursing homes. People tended their dying and buried their dead. Death at a great age was rare. We, of course, take it for granted. For whatever reason, Americans tend to insulate themselves from death; and when we must face it, we cosmeticize it. Perhaps it's all a way of avoiding Everyman's questions.

Who will go with me on this final journey?

(St. Louis, March 6, 1992)

Curriculum Vitae
JOHN LAWRENCE MAY

Born: March 31, 1922, Evanston, Illinois

Parents: Peter Michael May and Catherine Veronica (Allare) May
(deceased)

Education: St. Nicholas School, Evanston, Illinois
Quigley Preparatory Seminary, Chicago, Illinois
St. Mary of the Lake Seminary, Mundelein,
   Illinois. Graduated, 1947

Degrees: M.A. (Philosophy): S.T.L. (Theology)

*Priestly
Ordination:* May 3, 1947, St. Mary of the Lake Seminary,
   Mundelein, Illinois,
Samuel Cardinal Stritch, ordaining prelate

Appointments: Assistant Pastor, St. Gregory Church,
   Chicago, Illinois, 1947-1956
Chaplain, Mercy Hospital, Chicago, 1956-1959
Vice President and General Secretary, Catholic
   Church Extension Society, Chicago, 1959-1967
President, Catholic Church Extension Society,
   Chicago, 1967-1969
Pastor, Christ the King Parish,
   Chicago, 1968-1969

*Special
Assignments:* Part-time assignments have included:
Teaching on faculties of St. Gregory
   High School and Loyola University, Chicago;

Lecturer for the Cana Conference, Chicago;
Metropolitan Tribunal, Archdiocese of Chicago:
  Defender of the Bond, 1949-1958,
  Pro-Synodal Judge, 1958-1965;
Chairman, Clergy Personnel Board,
  Archdiocese of Chicago, 1967-1969

Ordination
as Bishop: Appointment as Auxiliary Bishop of Chicago,
                  June 21, 1967
                Ordination, August 24, 1967, Cathedral of
                  the Holy Name, Chicago, Illinois,
                John Cardinal Cody, ordaining prelate

December 10,
1969:   Installed as seventh Bishop of the Diocese
                  of Mobile

March 25,
1980:   Installed as seventh Archbishop of the
                  Archdiocese of St. Louis by the Most
                  Reverend Jean Jadot, Apostolic Delegate
                  in the United States

1986-1989:   President of the National Conference of
                  Catholic Bishops and the United States
                  Catholic Conference

Memberships: National Conference of Catholic Bishops
                  and United States Catholic Conference
                Missouri Christian Leadership Forum
                National Conference of Christians and Jews
                Board of Governors, Catholic Church
                  Extension Society
                Board of Catholic Relief Services